The Road to Eden

The Journey Home

John S. Romain

Full Circle Publications

HĀNA, HAWAI'I

Copyright © 2019 by **John S. Romain**

All rights reserved. No part of this publication may be reproduced, distributed or transmitted in any form or by any means, without prior written permission.

Full Circle Publications
P.O. Box 374
Hāna, Hawai'i 96713
www.RoadtoEdenBook.com

Book Layout by Margot Ott

The Road to Eden/ John S. Romain. -- 1st edition
ISBN 978-1-7337405-2-4

For Sadie, Will and Clark

Contents

Callings

HAWAI'I BOUND 5
LEAVING LONG BEACH 12
SENIOR-YEAR REFLECTIONS 15
HAWAI'I, 1964 18
COLLEGE DAYS 22
CONNECTIONS 27
ELVIS 33
DECISIONS 38
FIRST VISIT 41
CAREER AND FAMILY LIFE: PART ONE 43
CAREER AND FAMILY LIFE: PART TWO 51
SHOWTIME 56
FAMILY FOURSOME 59
WHAT IF? 63
HARD RAIN 66
STORM WARNINGS 75
WIN THE CAR OF RINGO STARR 78
ALL THINGS MUST PASS 81
ON THE REBOUND 84
NEW HORIZONS 89
POT OF GOLD 94
ENDINGS AND BEGINNINGS 98

Letting Go

THE SMITH BROTHERS 105
E I PRODUCTIONS 110
ESSENTIAL INSANITIES 115

THE WAITING GAME 121
WEATHERING THE STORM 126
PROGRESS 131
WEDDING KAZOOS 135
HONEYMOON IN BUFFALO 141
THE PARTY 143
HEAD GAMES 149
SUMMER'S END 153
ADJUSTMENTS 157
FULL CIRCLE 162
CAVE WITH A VIEW 168
THROWING CAUTION TO THE WIND 174
UNFORESEEN EVENTS 180
THE DANCE OF SHIVA 185
WORLDS APART 189
OMENS AND ENDINGS 197
ODDS AND ENDS 202
A ROUND OF FAREWELLS 207

The Journey

PICKING UP THE PIECES 217
HOUSE RAISING 221
SETTLING IN 226
MATTERS OF THE HEART 231
HOME STRETCH 236
FINISHING LINE 240
OLD HAUNTS AND NEW PROSPECTS 245
"WOODPECKER" RISING 249
DRAMATIC CONCLUSIONS 252
A YEAR OF SERVICE 257
MATTERS OF TIME 266

RECKONINGS AND RELIEF	269
RITES OF PASSAGE	274
BUILDING A BUSINESS	282
OLD DOOR, NEW PERCEPTIONS	285
INAUGURAL CRUISE	289
SIDETRACKS	293
GUARDIANS	298
RESTORATIONS	299
REGENERATIONS	304
AUSPICIOUS VISITORS	310
DEEP TARO	315
FILLING THE VOID	319
FIRST HARVEST	323
GOING TO THE HUKILAU	326
REBIRTH	332
CLOSE TO THE EDGE	335
A PLAN AND A PLAN B	337
TURNING POINT	342
HOME	345
THE ROAD TO EDEN REVISITED	353

*The future is up for grabs.
It belongs to any and all who will take
the risk and accept the responsibility
for consciously creating the future they
want.*
—Robert Anton Wilson

Preface

The genesis of *The Road to Eden* is an essay of the same name included in *Sacred Trusts: Essays on Stewardship and Responsibility*, edited by Michael Katakis and published in 1993. The piece, written just a few months after I restored an ancient Hawaiian fishpond, chronicled the year of restoration and alluded to the transcendental nature of much of the process.

Elaborating on the essay from a perspective twenty-five-years hence, *The Road to Eden* recounts the seemingly unrelated events, activities, accomplishments, and adventures that led from a career in advertising and film production in Los Angeles to fish farming and innkeeping in a tiny village on the remote eastern side of the island of Maui. The quest to find a place apart from the ethos of the prevailing world order, touched upon in the essay, is the spine of this story. Heeding a call that has beckoned since childhood, the following is an account of my journey home.

Part One
Callings

"We are kept out of the Garden by our own fear and desire in relation to what we think to be the goods of our life."

—Joseph Campbell

Hawai'i Bound

The dream of making Hawai'i my home began when I set sail for the islands in June 1957. I was aboard the S.S. President Wilson, sailing from the Port of Long Beach, California, to Honolulu, Hawai'i. I was traveling with my parents, Hal and Betsy, and younger sister, Kathy. Dad worked for American President Lines, and the voyage was one of the perks of his job. The S.S. President Wilson and its sister vessel, the S.S. President Cleveland, carried both passengers and freight. Freight was loaded in hulls below deck, bow and stern. First-class passengers resided midship in staterooms on the upper decks, and third-class passengers occupied smaller rooms and dorms on the bottom deck back toward the stern.

The four of us occupied a modest upper-deck stateroom just large enough for two sets of bunk beds, a wardrobe, a petite table and chairs, and a small private bathroom. Air was circulated by a single fan, and cracking the porthole provided ventilation. Other than a built-in radio that was operable only when leaving or approaching shore, everything in the room was functional and basic. The S.S. President Wilson was among the last in the tradition of the grand ocean liners. Although the golden era of ocean voyaging was passing, even a child of eleven was still expected to wear a white dinner jacket to the evening meal.

Kathy and I, like most of the younger passengers, were assigned to the first meal seating; our parents followed at the later seating. We were placed at the captain's table, a special honor, we were told. Walter, our waiter, was rather portly and spoke with a deep voice in an unfamiliar accent. He seemed delighted in helping us select meals to our complete liking—Walter saw nothing wrong with ice cream for breakfast.

After meals we were on our own, and it didn't take long for us to discover the Marco Polo Lounge, a recreational room for the exclusive use of young passengers. It became our special place where we met and mingled with our peers and exchanged shipboard gossip. The lounge was well stocked with books, magazines, and various games for our amusement. It was here where I was first exposed to the subversive wit of Mad Magazine.

The five-day voyage passed quickly, each day filled with activities from engine room and bridge tours to deck-side shuffleboard tournaments. My greatest pleasure was the free time to roam the ship or to lean on the deck rail and gaze out at the vastness of sky and sea. The air temperature and humidity rose slightly but noticeably each day as we approached the tropics. The sea, however, remained a constant hue of blue, deep, dark, and mysterious.

A high-flying seabird appeared in the southwestern sky early on our fourth morning at sea. Later that day, I picked up a Waikiki station on our stateroom radio. The unfamiliar voices and exotic music were like a siren song beckoning us to the Islands. That evening, the adults gathered in the ship's ballroom for a gala that would last well into the night. Kathy and I marked our last evening at sea in our cabin, listening to the radio while writing postcards and letters to friends and family back home. Excited and restless, I took one last stroll around the deck before going to bed. The balmy night sky was cloudless and still, more brilliant than I could ever remember. I sensed a communion with the tropics; it felt good, I was happy. I returned to the cabin and turned in early.

Awakening before dawn, Kathy and I quickly headed to the deck. The ship's crew was at work setting up a topside breakfast buffet, adding some pomp to our morning arrival. The sun was just beginning to rise as Kathy and I found a spot starboard side toward the bow. On the horizon, the distinct shape of an island began to emerge in the growing daylight. The deck soon filled with passengers, everyone slightly giddy at the first sight of land after five days at sea.

We circled south around Diamond Head and followed the coast along Waikiki beach to the Honolulu harbor. A tugboat met us at the entrance and escorted us to our berth next to the landmark Aloha Tower. We were greeted by flower- and grass-clad hula dancers and 'ukulele-strumming musicians, while children swam in the water below, diving for coins tossed from the deck. Soon, the gangplanks rolled into place and the whistle blew. The voyage over, it was time to disembark.

🌺 🌺 🌺

Mr. St. John, a business associate of my father's, met us on the dock with an arm full of flowers. He greeted us with a hearty "Aloha!" as he draped us each with a fragrant lei. Gathering our belongings, we followed our host to his car and headed straight to Waikiki, the sweet smell of plumeria blossoms permeating the air.

Waikiki in the mid-1950s was still relatively undeveloped, with only a handful of hotels scattered along the shoreline. We checked into a two-bedroom garden bungalow at the Halekūlani Hotel. The hotel, in operation since 1917, was known for its manicured grounds and lush landscaping. As a child of nature, I couldn't wait to see what kind of creatures might be lurking in the foliage. That evening, when returning from dinner, I spotted a gecko perched on the wall just under the porch light. Hawai'i, it seems, was definitely my kind of place.

My mother and sister, however, did not share my fondness for garden critters and, after being buzzed by thumb-size flying cockroaches on our lanai, they insisted that we relocate to higher quarters. The next morning, we moved into a suite at the nearby Reef Hotel, the first high-rise in Waikiki. The Reef Hotel was right on the beach, and even though I regretted the move from the bungalow, I had to admit that the view overlooking Waikiki Beach was travel-poster perfect.

I was familiar with beaches, having spent a good amount of my childhood at my great-aunt and godmother Etta's home on Alamitos Bay in Long Beach. Still, nothing prepared me for Waikiki. The shimmering aquamarine water looked unreal, like a gigantic watercolor painting in motion as it gently rolled and crested over the outer coral reef. Even the sand was exceptional, its pure white granular texture sparkling like tiny diamonds beneath the surface. Best of all, the water was warm, so warm I fantasized about growing fins and gills, so I could live in it forever.

I spent every available hour snorkeling on the ocean's surface, completely enchanted with the sea life below on the shallow inner reef. My mask was a window to another world, an aquatic wonderland—alien, exotic, alluring. There was a rhythm to the reef, as if the movement of every fish, crustacean, and even the current itself, were in harmony with a grand, silent score. Although there would be other memorable events and activities during my week in Hawai'i, none would match the impact of seeing the reef and its multitude of dwellers for the first time.

The beach in front of our hotel was, like all beaches in Hawai'i, open to all. Local families mingled with tourists. The atmosphere was warm and inviting, and strangers felt like friends. A small contingent of Hawaiian men known as the Waikiki beach boys typified the spirit of aloha. The beach boys, all skilled watermen, taught surfing and paddled outrigger canoes for tourists. When not in the water, they would be on the beach strumming 'ukulele and singing songs, often well into the night. The beach boy hui was formed early in the twentieth century, the legendary Duke Kahānamoku being among its founders.

On the last day of our visit, Mr. St. John took us on a tour of Pearl Harbor. We shared our small guide boat with a handful of other visitors. The mood was solemn. Other than our guide's reverent narration, not a word was spoken. Sixteen years had passed since the fateful morning of December 7, 1941, yet ghostly remnants of the attack remained. The damaged and destroyed vessels had long since been removed, but some scattered piles of debris still littered the harbor's shores. Our guide told us the details of the attack as we made our way around the harbor. The last stop on the tour was the site of the USS Arizona, resting place for over 1,100 sailors still entombed in the sunken wreckage of the once-mighty battleship. There was no memorial then, only a small platform with a placard commemorating the ship and lost crew. A more fitting and elaborate monument would be built a few years later thanks in part to the generosity of Elvis Presley.

We boarded the S.S. President Cleveland early the next afternoon. The ship had arrived that morning, Honolulu being the last port of call after a six-week cruise to the Orient. Mr. St. John and another business associate and his wife came by to see us off. We greeted them in our tiny stateroom and exchanged parting gifts. As is custom, they adorned us with flower lei. Soon, a ship's officer walked the halls, his chime alerting us that we were about to set sail.

As the last of the visiting guests filed off the ship, passengers gathered on deck jostling for positions on the portside rail. Crew members mingled among passengers, passing out handfuls of colorful streamers. Each streamer was a tightly rolled strip of paper with a small appendage-like tab in the center. The trick was to hold the tab between thumb and forefinger while tossing the streamer to waiting hands on the dock below. After a few failed attempts, Kathy and I got the technique and let fly, launching at least a couple dozen streamers. For a brief moment, we were tethered to the dock with thousands of strands of paper. Then, in an instant, we started to move, and the streamers snapped in unison.

There is a tradition for passengers leaving Hawai'i to toss their lei overboard as the ship rounds Diamond Head. The story holds that if your lei drifts back to shore, then it is assured that you will return to Hawai'i. With this in mind, I hurled my lei out to sea with all the strength I could muster.

I was a changed young man after returning from Hawai'i. I felt different. I saw myself differently. I was different. I was still a kid, played softball in the streets with neighborhood friends and family, and lived in the same house with my parents and siblings, Kathy, Cindy, and Rick, but I felt as if I was living in one world while drawn to another. I had tasted the tropics and was finding my home turf mundane by comparison. Concurrently I was experiencing the onset of puberty. My body was beginning to change and so, too, were my interests and feelings. My identity was in flux: I was outgrowing childhood and irresistibly being driven toward the mysterious stage of adolescence.

Music was a really big thing that summer. The first battery-powered transistor radios were coming onto the market, and like every other kid in the neighborhood, I had to have one. The problem was money. I had none. I tried working on my folks, but even my mom lacked sympathy for my pleas. Eventually, they offered an arrangement whereby they would advance me the cash for a radio in return for my commitment to water the lawn every evening for the duration of the summer.

My late afternoons were spent with a hose in one hand and my transistor radio held to my ear with the other, listening to Art Laboe's live broadcast of song requests and dedications from Scrivner's Drive-In in East Los Angeles. Rock and roll, in its early prime, was moving into top-40 radio, but KPOP, a small independent AM station played the more gritty, cool stuff that was outside mainstream radio. I loved listening to slightly older peers share stories and talk about their favorite records. I couldn't wait to become a teenager.

Then there was Elvis. I had been a fan since the first time I had heard his voice a year earlier. By the summer of 1957, Elvis was everywhere. "*All Shook Up*" and "*Teddy Bear*" were blasting from the radio even in some of the remote places that we visited on Oʻahu, and the release of his second film, *Loving You*, had made him a superstar. There was change in the air, and Elvis' appeal was more than just music. There was something exciting and rebellious, almost forbidding, about him, a wildness just waiting to cut loose. He was like the outcast older cousin luring me to a new freedom, unrestrained by convention. My first hero was an antihero.

I never let go of the dream of living in Hawaiʻi, but by summer's end I was eager to start my sixth and final of my year of grade school, with all the benefits of seniority. My enthusiasm dampened when I found that Etta, my benevolent if sometimes misguided godmother, had enrolled me in after-school ballroom dance classes. I feared it was going to be a long year.

The U.S.S. Arizona memorial was then just a simple plaque on a platform directly over the sunken ship. From left Mr. St. John, author, parents Hal & Betsy, sister Kathy. Pearl Harbor, June 1957.

Leaving Long Beach

The last vestiges of my childhood came to an end in the summer before my junior year of high school. Dad got a promotion, and with it the family would be moving to the San Francisco Bay Area. There was no discussion. My folks had already located a large canyon-side home in Hillsborough on the San Francisco Peninsula, and the family would be moving by summer's end. I took the news with mixed emotions. I was intrigued by the change but also apprehensive about leaving Long Beach. My saving grace was that I was to stay behind to assist my grandmother Elsie sell her nearby house and move in with her sister Etta. Along with the responsibility came the keys to a brand-new Chevrolet Impala SS to assist the transition.

Living with my grandmother was easy, and the reprieve allowed me to spend time with friends and complete the fall semester at Millikan High School, yet it was also a lonely time. I was still in Long Beach, but my home was elsewhere. The toughest part of all was winding down with Ann.

Ann was more than a girlfriend; she was my best friend. We had met in the eighth grade, not long after I returned to school following a three-month medical absence. I had been stricken with a digestive inflammation known then as regional ileitis, a miserable chronic condition that began just after I started junior high school the year before. By summer, I was in near constant pain, could barely eat, and was so weak that the doctor withdrew me from school on opening day. Fortunately, I had a pediatrician who was able to diagnose the somewhat rare disorder and prescribe treatment without resorting to immediate surgery, which then was the standard approach but not always an effective cure.

I responded right away to the medication and spent my medical sabbatical gaining back weight and strength and acquiring a new attitude toward school. The adjustment to middle school was not as easy as I had expected. I was good at math and grasping concepts, but not the best at rote memory. Memorizing all fifty state names and their capitals made no sense to me. Why waste all that mental concentration on something that had no relevance? The more I thought about the contradictions between what I was being forced to learn and what I wanted to learn, the more stressed I became, which may have at least in part contributed to my affliction.

My illness provided me with a welcome break from the mechanistic educational process that I was rebelling against. The school district provided a tutor who came to the house for a couple of hours two or three days a week. It was a one-to-one learning situation where I was able to discuss my assignments rather than just recite facts. I looked forward to the visits, finding home tutoring much more engaging and inspiring than classroom-style education.

Besides being a respite from institutional education, my illness provided an opportunity to engage in studies apart from the classroom curriculum. My parents, who initially feared my undiagnosed condition to be life-threatening, were lavish in their support of my interest in saltwater aquariums. The hobby was in its infancy, with a single supplier of fish and equipment in Long Beach and only a scattering of others throughout the Los Angeles area. We set up a twenty-gallon tank for tropical species imported from Florida, and a second tank for cooler-water tide pool fish that we collected locally. My greatest joy was a small octopus that I captured in a nearby tide pool. The creature was extremely intelligent and even responsive to my presence. Contrary to the literature at the time that said octopuses seldom survived more than a month in captivity, my cephalopod thrived for several months before succumbing to an ill-fated escape attempt.

The three-month break from school broadened my view of education. I came to see the learning process as twofold: the first being mandatory classroom schooling, where I would have to adapt and conform, and the second being elective self-education, where I could indulge in the unrestrained pursuit of my interests. Having resolved my conflict and feeling recovered and fit, I was ready to return to school.

Unexpectedly, I found that I was also ready for my first affair of the heart. I can't recall the exact moment and place Ann and I met, only that we were quickly drawn to each other and became almost inseparable. As the months progressed, so did our passions. We stayed with each other into high school even though we knew that by graduation we would have to part. Ann was from a devout Mormon family, and her future with the church was preordained. The only way I could fit into the picture would be to become a member of her faith. I respected the Mormon sense of community, but I had too much religious uncertainty to pledge myself to any church.

Nonetheless, we were caught by complete surprise finding that we would be parting prematurely for an entirely unexpected reason. Though we had a few months before our impending separation, just knowing the date seemed to create distance between us. By the end of the semester, after working through the laughter and tears, we were both ready to say goodbye.

The time had come. I packed up the Chevy and headed north.

Senior-Year Reflections

The three semesters I spent at Burlingame High School were academically more challenging than anything I had experienced in Long Beach. The school was small, just over 1,200 students in ninth through twelfth grade. The classes were more intimate, with personal attention paid to each student. My English literature class had two instructors and a reading list more extensive than anything I would face in college. History was taught with a textbook used at Stanford, and calculus, unlike prior math classes, did not come easy. I mostly kept to myself that semester. My homework assignments left little time for extracurricular activities.

By my senior year I had adapted to my new environment but remained somewhat an outsider. Classmates, for the most part, were friendly and engaging, but there exists a difference between friends who share a long history and a newcomer with a different life story. Eventually my newness wore off and, as my face became familiar, I gradually found a place within the Burlingame High social stratum.

The event that bonded my class in a way that none of us will ever forget happened on the morning of November 22, 1963. I had just left my English class when suddenly the halls erupted with screams that the president had been shot. I hurried to my economics class to find our teacher, Mr. Hinds, hooking up an old tabletop radio, frantically tuning the dial in search of a reliable news source. Soon the room filled with dazed and anxious classmates, some outwardly weeping, others in stunned silence. Mr. Hinds remained cool, his assuring manner calming the room and focusing our attention on the radio news. Early reports confirmed that President Kennedy and Texas governor John Connally had been shot and rushed to the hospital, but an official report on the president's condition had not yet been issued. After what seemed like an eternity, news broke confirming our worst fears: The president was dead. A short time later, classes were canceled, and we were dismissed for the day. Cutting through the chaos and confusion, I found my sister Kathy and we drove home in silent disbelief.

Although the scars of that fateful day would remain, by spring our class had functionally recovered, and we were enjoying the rituals of graduating seniors. College acceptances and rejections brought joy and tears as our future lives came into focus. In my instance, I was rejected by the University of Southern California, my first choice of college. The reason given was that I did not have the requisite minimum grade-point average. By my calculations this was not correct. My school guidance counselor concurred, and it was arranged that I would fly down to Los Angeles to present my case to the USC dean of admissions.

The meeting was short and direct. The dean opened our discussion by paraphrasing the letter that I had not been accepted because of an insufficient grade-point average. I responded by presenting him with a letter from my counselor verifying that my GPA was more than sufficient. I also presented him with my transcripts dating back to ninth grade. The dean requested an assistant to join us and, for several rather awkward minutes, the three of us recalculated my grade average. When it was determined that my GPA was satisfactory, the dean, moving beyond the miscalculation, inquired why I had taken so many woodshop classes as electives. I earnestly asked him if it was offered at the university. A couple of weeks later, I received another letter from the admissions office—I had been accepted.

As graduation day approached, I felt at liberty to ditch a day of school. It was a rather spontaneous act. Having toed the line during my time at Burlingame High, I figured I had nothing to lose. It started innocently enough. It was a bright sunny day in late May and, as usual, I left for school with Kathy. On this particular morning, I gave a lift to Francine, a junior that I had been dating. Francine, also known as Jinx, commented that it was a shame to have to go to class on such a gorgeous day, adding that she would much rather spend the day at the beach. Kathy encouraged the idea and I started thinking through a plan. My sister agreed to cover for me by stopping by the attendance office to inform them that I was home ill, anticipating that this would head off the usual inquiring call. Francine's parents both worked, so we figured she'd be OK as well. We dropped Kathy off a short distance from school and headed toward the coast, the nearest beach being Half Moon Bay.

The surf was big and rough and too cold for swimming. Undaunted, we discarded all but our essential clothing and basked in the sun. Later, we drove up the coast and had lunch at a little seaside diner, then back to the beach before heading home late in the afternoon. Upon arriving home, I was met by two stern-faced parents, who were not amused. It seems our plan had unraveled. Kathy had done her best, but in the end, it didn't matter. The one thing that Francine and I had neglected to consider was sunscreen. Our day at the beach was written all over me.

Finally, the big day arrived. After the official ceremony in the school auditorium, our class reconvened at the nearby Mills Country Club for our graduation party. Our class had boycotted the entertainment roster proposed by the PTA, choosing instead the Dartells, a funk-rock-blues band whose then-current hit, "Hot Pastrami," was much more to our liking. The band set up around midnight and, sans coats, ties, shoes, and socks, we boogied the night away. As dawn broke, the doors were unlocked, and Burlingame's graduating class of 1964 took flight.

Post graduation. Author with Francine Nelson, Gary Lindstrom and D'Arcy Bracamonte. June 1964.

Hawai'i, 1964

Two days after graduation I packed my car and drove south to Long Beach to house-sit for Etta and my grandmother, who were touring through Europe. I was returning to my summer job at the Disneyland Hotel for the third straight year, this time as swimming pool captain and lifeguard. It couldn't have been a better way to spend the summer: a place of my own near the shore and a job that required sitting in the sun with occasional dips in the pool (of course as I write this now, I'm paying for my reign as sun king with regular visits to the dermatologist).

When not working, I'd often hang out with my coworkers and their friends at the beach. The beaches of Orange County were different from those in Long Beach. Unrestrained by a breakwater, the waves were bigger and more challenging, and the white granular sand glimmered in the aquatinted shoreline in hues more akin to Hawai'i's than California's. After-hours beach parties were a common event, and I would frequently reroute the drive from Anaheim back to Long Beach by way of Newport Beach just to cruise the coast. In late August, I took leave of my employment in the Magic Kingdom, bid adieu to my new friends and acquaintances, and headed home for the summer finale. As a graduation gift, my parents and the parents of my friend Gary Lindstrom had booked passage for us to sail to Hawai'i.

The evening before our departure, mutual friends of Gary's and mine hosted a bon voyage party that continued onto the next day, when several friends and family members accompanied us to the dock on San Francisco Bay. Again, I was entrusting my passage to the captain and crew of the stately *S.S. President Wilson*. It didn't take long, however, to discover that all was not as it once was. The "stateroom"

that I would be sharing with Gary was barely large enough to contain a set of bunk beds, a dresser, and a broom-closet-size bathroom-shower. Most disappointing of all, it lacked a porthole and the comforting sight of the gently rolling horizon of sky and sea. Still, we had a place to sleep and store our belongings. We shared a parting toast with our friends gathered in the hallway outside our cramped quarters, then ambled up to the deck with our entourage of well-wishers. We set sail a short time later, crossing under the Golden Gate Bridge and out to sea.

Although the ship seemed not to have changed during my seven-year absence, the formality factor had clearly dropped a notch or two. Dinner jackets were no longer required at the evening meal and on-deck attire was more relaxed and casual. I also sensed a change in the atmosphere, a less restrictive feeling. At the same time, I felt that I didn't quite fit. I had outgrown the Marco Polo Lounge but didn't identify with the older, mostly married crowd that made up the majority of the passenger list.

Our social situation changed the second day out, when we chanced upon a passageway leading to an unlocked door that opened into the third-class compartment. To our surprise, we had stumbled upon a small crowd of college students hanging out in a canteen-like common area. There was a food counter on one side of the room and a fairly good-size bar on the other. We went right to the bar. It was as basic and bare as the upper-deck lounge was opulent and well stocked. We felt right at home; San Miguel beer was thirty-five cents a bottle, the company was more to our own age and temperament, and drinking at eighteen was allowable on the high seas.

The early-morning arrival in Honolulu was less dramatic the second time around, but no less exciting. Seeing Diamond Head after five days at sea is a thrill no matter how many times one experiences it. As we rounded the crater, however, the skyline had changed. Waikiki Beach had noticeably expanded in height and breadth. The Reef Hotel, sole high-rise at the time of my previous visit, was now but one of several modern megaliths populating the shoreline. The distinctly pink Royal Hawaiian Hotel was barely identifiable in the shadows of its imposing neighbors. Waikiki was still a beautiful sight, its waters still shimmering in luminescent shades of aqua, greens, and blues, but I'm grateful to have the memory of a time when it was less congested.

The graduation gift included lodging at a residential hotel inland from the beach. Unlike our tight quarters at sea, we had a spacious apartment with a living room, dining area, and kitchen. The location lacked the elegance of the beachfront resorts, but our spread had a kind of funky tropical feel that had a certain charm of its own. We soon found that we had friendly female neighbors next door.

Once settled in we immediately headed to the beach. Other than being a bit more populated with tourists, the biggest change was the diminished presence of the famed Waikiki beach boys. The few that remained kept the tradition alive, but as a group they no longer held sway over beach activities. We rented snorkel gear from a local vendor and took to the surf. Gary, already a good swimmer, easily adapted to fins and mask and soon became as enamored with the reef and its occupants as I was. Early- and late-day snorkels became a daily routine.

The better part of the next day was spent exploring Waikiki from one end to the other. We canvassed Kalamata Avenue, wandering in and out of shops and hotel lobbies, then took a jaunty jog along the beach and followed the shoreline all the way out to Diamond Head. The extinct crater when viewed from below was even more impressive than when seen from afar. As we were marveling at the sheer cliff fronting the ocean, we saw what looked to be a rugged trail leading to the summit 760 feet above us. The idea hit us both at the same time. We were too tired and hot from the midafternoon sun to consider it then, but climbing to the top of the crater became a must-do objective.

We did eventually make it to the top of Diamond Head, a task much more difficult than we had envisioned, perhaps because we went up the steep overgrown front side rather than the gently sloping well-maintained path behind the crater. The high point of the week, however, was the side trip to the island of Kauai. While checking our airline tickets for our return flight, we discovered that we could purchase inter-island tickets for about fifteen dollars round-trip. We caught the island-hopper the next morning.

The Garden Isle is that indeed. Much smaller than Oʻahu, Kauai feels more condensed, like everything is within reach. We had no trouble hitching rides and obtaining local advice. The pace was slow, the people friendly, and the landscape primordial in its beauty. We worked our way up the coast to Hānalei Bay, then backtracked down the road a few miles and checked into the famous Coco Palms Resort. With torch-lit lagoons (setting for the climactic wedding scene in Elvis' film *Blue Hawaiʻi*) meandering throughout the grounds, and rooms featuring clam-shell bathroom sinks, it was the epitome of Polynesian tiki culture and the inspiration for architectural renderings I would produce on my own later in life. The next day we worked our way around to the other side of Kauaʻi before catching a late-afternoon flight back to Oʻahu.

The five-hour flight back to San Francisco felt like cheating compared to five days at sea, but the world was moving faster, and speed was trumping tradition. I'm fortunate to have experienced ocean travel when I did. Two days after returning home, I packed up and headed south to begin my studies at the University of Southern California.

College Days

Stepping onto the campus of a major university for the first time is an inspiring moment for any incoming freshman. At the University of Southern California, in the shadow of Hollywood, the experience has an added element of theater. In the center of campus, emblematic of the ethos of the student body, is an enormous bronze statue, Tommy Trojan, warrior of Troy. Sword and shield at the ready, every muscle flexed, Tommy Trojan towers over the ebb and flow of students and faculty members conversing on the steps of his shrine. Inscribed on his pedestal are the defining attributes of the ideal Trojan: "Faithful, Scholarly, Skillful, Courageous and Ambitious." Tommy Trojan is a revered symbol of school pride.

USC, founded in 1880, had long been regarded as an athletic powerhouse with many national championships in a variety of sports. At the time of my attendance, it was also beginning to receive notice as an academic contender, some of its schools considered among the best in the nation. Like many other freshmen, I had only a vague idea of what I wanted to major in, let alone what I wanted to do with the rest of my life. By default, I selected prelaw. It wasn't that I had a desire to be a lawyer, but it was assumed by my education benefactors that I would continue my studies through law school. I was uneasy with that presumption, but without a clear alternative I just went with the plan.

Most classes were four credits, and a full-time student was expected to carry a load of sixteen credits per semester. Some classes were mandatory for all students, some were required as part of a major, and some were electives just for the credit count. My first-semester elective was the film critic and historian Arthur Knight's Introduction to Cinema, a class that had no bearing on my major, but one that would have a major bearing on my life. Learning to see cinema as "the art form of the twentieth century" opened up a myriad of future possibilities. By comparison, my prelaw studies seemed dull and uninspiring.

I spent the first semester residing in Marks Tower, an on-campus dorm, while at the same time pledging a fraternity. I'd been forewarned to hold off for a semester before committing to a fraternity, as the obligations of pledging can be an excessive burden for someone still just trying to find his way around campus. Still, it was hard to resist the lavish parties and events particular to "rush season." Of the various houses I visited, I kept coming back to one that seemed to have a greater diversity of individuals, and the brothers didn't seem to take themselves too seriously. I liked that and saw no reason to look any further.

While attending a late rush-season party, I was approached by a tall and dapper upperclassman named Bob. In his official capacity as rush chairman, he invited me to pledge the fraternity that I had already decided to join if given the opportunity. I accepted, figuring it best to get the pledging over with. It was already a humbling experience to be a first-semester freshman, might as well be a pledge to boot.

Initiation week, or hell week, as it is commonly known, was just that. Although some of the hazing excesses of earlier times had become tamer, it was still an unpleasant way to spend the break between semesters. Nevertheless, I survived the ordeal and started the next semester as an initiated member of the Alpha Upsilon chapter of the Sigma Chi fraternity. One of my first acts as a member was to nominate my childhood friend Doug Hadnot to be invited to join the next pledge class.

Doug and I met quite unexpectedly one day when I was living in the dorm. Despite having gone our own ways since grade school, it took no time at all to renew our friendship. Doug was readily accepted by the Sigma Chi brothers and joined the spring-semester pledge class. The following semester, we became roommates and remained so until graduation. Surprisingly, Doug wasn't my only childhood friend to become a fraternal brother. During a casual conversation, brother Corky Severson and I discovered that our friendship began while attending Robin Hood pre-school in Long Beach when we were four or five years old.

After completing my freshman year, I returned home to take on a "real" job for the summer. Not that my stint at the Disneyland Hotel wasn't gainful employment, but sitting around the pool all day is hardly a high point on one's résumé. I went to work for a San Francisco-based freight-forwarding company that had an auxiliary trailer office at the airport. Other than the occasional pickup or delivery trip to the city, I spent most of my time at the trailer. The job was mixed: I typed out shipping manifests and customs documents, ran errands around the airport, and sorted and processed freight for the Philippine Airlines flight that arrived and departed twice a week. The job certainly lacked the perks of my previous position, but the pay was good, and the work had its moments.

The trailer was parked in an isolated area on the airport apron. The nearest building was a federal quarantine station for animals being imported for medical research. One morning I had just opened up the office and was sitting at my desk looking out the open door when a monkey came strolling by. Startled but delighted, I raced to the door to see where the wandering primate was heading. Then, another monkey passed by, this one at full romp, with a uniformed attendant, net in hand, in hot pursuit. The monkeys, as if planned, split off in two directions, leaving the perplexed pursuer no choice but to chase one while the other took flight. I later found out they had broken free of their cages during the night and slipped out of their confinement the moment the unsuspecting attendant opened up the facilities. The monkey business that morning is my fondest memory from an otherwise uneventful summer job. Sometimes the best moments in life are the most unexpected.

I had planned to end the summer attending a Beatles concert at the Cow Palace. I had applied for mail-order tickets the day they went on sale in early June and was pleasantly surprised when two tickets arrived in the mail the following week. Shortly thereafter, my parents announced plans to take the whole family to Hawai'i in late August. There was nowhere I more wanted to be than Hawai'i, and no one I more wanted to see than the Beatles. I naively presumed that there would be another Beatles opportunity. Hawai'i was calling, the Beatles could wait.

🌲🌲🌲

Waikiki hadn't changed much in the year that I'd been away, but some things were different. The most noticeable was the abundance of well-cropped young men crowding the beaches and boulevards. The escalation of the Vietnam conflict had begun in earnest, and Hawai'i was a major pre-deployment staging area for the troops. I remember my dad, a veteran himself, commenting on how they all tried to look so brave, but inside most of them were scared to death. My feelings were a mixture of guilt and respect. A year and a half earlier when registering for the draft, I listed my chronic gastrointestinal condition as a physical ailment that might deem me unsuitable for service. After a follow-up letter from my doctor, the draft board determined that I was medically unfit for service. To this day, I have conflicting feelings of gratitude and chagrin about the twist of fate that may have saved me from the fields of battle.

Our family stayed in a large garden bungalow at the Halekūlani Hotel, the place where we began our visit in 1957. The lush grounds remained the same, but it was now my younger brother, Rick, who was beating the bushes for bugs. Rick, the same age I was when first visiting Hawai'i, shared my passion for the inhabitants of the natural world. He seemed to find Hawai'i as astonishing as I did. Kathy, my former steadfast companion, now had sister Cindy to chum around with, so apart from the sporadic family events, I was left to my own devices.

I was a year shy of twenty, the legal drinking age in Hawai'i. My false ID, however, stated that I was twenty-two. While having a beer at a beach-side café, I met an older woman named Shirley who was traveling with her friend Robin. Shirley, in her early twenties, didn't buy the idea that I was her age, but she seemed to like my attitude and played along with the ploy. Robin, who was being courted by a sailor, suggested that we all get together and go dancing later that night.

The four of us rendezvoused again two nights later on the eve of the girls' return to the Mainland. This time, we went to see Don Ho at the Duke Kahānamoku supper club in the International Marketplace. Don Ho, the biggest attraction in town, was masterful in conjuring up the romantic allure of Waikiki.

Afterward, the four of us wandered along the moonlit beach and found a couple of unoccupied palm trees on the secluded end of Waikiki near the lagoon. Pairing off, we settled in for some late-evening stargazing and romance. The balmy night air was still and quiet, the only sounds being the gently rolling surf and occasional sighs and giggles.

Two days later, my family and I headed home. It was the last family outing we all shared together.

Connections

Some of the most consequential events of my college career occurred during my sophomore year. Prior to the fall-term registration, I met with my counselor, who, when learning of my lack of enthusiasm for prelaw, suggested majoring in business as an alternative. It would still provide a good foundation for a law degree, but it did not require four semesters of a foreign language. Dropping language in favor of four more electives was a no-brainer. I changed majors on the spot. It was a business decision.

Fraternity life is anything but private. It is accepted protocol to roam the halls at night in search of a reason not to study. Barging in on a brother at work on a paper or reading a text is allowable, as long as the interruption is for a worthy reason—like going out for a beer or catching a late movie on Hollywood Boulevard. I learned early on that the best time to get my studying done was in the afternoon. My classes were in the morning, so while most of the brothers were in class or otherwise preoccupied, I managed to keep current with my assignments.

One afternoon, my concentration was broken by the voice of a brother hollering from the pay phone at the end of the hall, "Anyone want to work in a movie tomorrow?" Intrigued, I put down my book and raced down the hall to investigate. I was handed the phone, and the voice on the other end asked me to confirm that I was blue-eyed and blond. After I stretched a little and answered affirmatively (my hair was light brown) she offered details. She was casting for Nazi soldiers for a World War II comedy, *What Did You Do in the War, Daddy?* and because the call exceeded the number of Screen Extras Guild members available, they were hiring nonmembers as "waivers," but at union scale. I said yes.

Early the next morning, I, along with a couple of my fraternity brothers, reported to the appointed studio. We were checked in and directed to wardrobe. After being fitted in heavy, scratchy wool uniforms—complete with ill-fitting boots—we were bused off to the set at Lake Sherwood in the Santa Monica Mountains. Had it been other than a first-time experience, the day could have been described as boring. Most of the time was spent waiting for something to happen. When we did work, it amounted to little more than standing still and looking stern as German soldiers guarding an occupied Italian town. During the extended breaks between takes, the actual SEG members confidently sat around the set playing cards, reading books, and chatting in small groups. Some even catnapped. Conversely, we tended to wander around, uncertain of what was expected of us and feeling slightly uncomfortable as outsiders. When a wrap was called in late afternoon, we boarded the buses and headed back to the studio.

I got back to the house too late for dinner, so I walked down 28th Street (fraternity row) to Woodies, a local food joint. While dining on a burger and fries, I reviewed the long day. Although the work lacked the glamour that one might expect in filmmaking, I found being on the set exciting. Even as a grunt waiver, I loved being part of the process. On top of that, the pay was great. Including overtime, I had just made more money in one day than in two days at my airport job. By juggling my class schedule, I could work as an extra two or even three days a week and have plenty of time for studying on the set between shots. It was a perfect college job. The only obstacle was gaining membership in the union, said to be a near-impossible task without connections. I didn't know who or how, but by the time I downed the last fry I was determined to find a way.

※ ※ ※

The days leading up to Christmas break were rather hectic. There were parties and festivities all week, yet classes continued as normal. As an overture to the holiday, I began the break by attending a Bob Dylan concert. Although already into his music, I had no idea of how powerful Dylan could be in person. He was in command of every moment, and his songs and mannerisms were mesmerizing. He opened the show accompanied only by his acoustic guitar and harmonica, and then later his band, The Hawks, joined him for an electrified set. The show was simply stunning. Whereas hearing Elvis for the first time was like being hit with a bass note that awakened some deep primordial instincts, seeing and hearing Dylan in concert was like being hit with a barrage of stimuli that rattled the whole psyche. My date and I drove back to campus feeling overwhelmed.

The next day, after a solid night's sleep, I gathered my essentials, loaded the car, and started my journey home for the holidays. The trip began with a detour to see my mother's parents, who lived in Desert Hot Springs, a small town just northwest of Palm Springs. As a kid, I had spent many Easter vacations with my desert-dwelling kin. I'd roam the empty lots and open landscape searching for horned toads and desert iguanas. Sometimes, my grandfather, Harry—or Papa, as I knew him—would take me to his real estate office, where I'd meet his cronies and learn the subtleties of small-town ways. My grandmother, always inspiring, was a fountain of creativity, a fine artist and craftsperson, especially competent in media featuring rocks, sand, and other natural objects. She, more than anyone else in my family, encouraged an artistic approach to life.

On this occasion, I was stopping by to attend a Christmas party with them and to pick up packages for the rest of the family. The party was a highbrow coat and bolo-tie desert wingding. It was a cool winter night, but the party was warm and cheerful. Before the evening was over, my grandfather and I even stepped outside and smoked cigars together.

I rose early the next morning wanting to be on the road before dawn. Quiet as I tried to be, my grandfather stirred from his sleep to come out and see me off. Pleased that I was following his custom of hitting the road early, he slipped me a twenty and told me to fill up the tank and have breakfast on him. As I was walking out the door, he suggested that, if I wasn't in a hurry, to cross the high desert as it could be beautiful this time of year.

I followed his advice and took the back road toward Lancaster and Palmdale. If it wasn't the exact day of the winter solstice, it was close. Daybreak was slow in coming. By the time the sun managed to make an appearance, I'd gained enough altitude to watch a snow-dusted landscape unfold around me. Scattered about the powdered plains of Yucca Valley were cartoonish Joshua trees, snow-draped prickly giants with arms bent and extended, pointing meaninglessly in all directions. Undeterred by the cacti's comical confusion, I held the course and followed the road north.

Less than three months later, my sister Kathy called to tell me that Papa had died. She tried to keep her composure but broke out sobbing before I could learn any details. A few minutes later, my dad called and filled me in: Papa just sat down in his recliner for a routine afternoon nap and never woke up. That, at least, was comforting.

The next morning, I picked up my favorite aunt, Sissy, at the L.A. airport and drove out to the desert to gather with family. Everyone exchanged hugs and tears, then went about the business of helping my grandmother with arrangements and details. My job done, I headed back to campus. Tangled thoughts were racing through my mind as I cruised the freeways back to Los Angeles. Memories of my grandfather were interwoven with amorous longings for a girl that I had recently met. In an eerie way, the events seemed connected.

Denise and I had been dating since meeting at a Sigma Chi-Kappa Alpha Theta "exchange" at an off-campus beer hall a few weeks earlier. Along with another couple, we had been planning to spend the upcoming weekend in Palm Springs. Logistically everything fit: I was going to be in the desert for Papa's service on Friday morning and could easily meet Denise and our friends in Palm Springs that evening. But I had conflicted feelings about a romantic interlude so soon after burying my grandfather.

Throughout Papa's life he had maintained a sense of balance. He had learned to roll with the punches and to take good fortune with grace. He had been on his own since he was fifteen, moving about from Louisiana to Texas before meeting my grandmother and settling in Southern California. When his business failed and he bottomed out in the Depression, Papa had found refuge in Christian Science, a discipline he adhered to the rest of his life. Though modest in most things, he enjoyed good cigars and thought nothing of taking a road trip cross-country to pick up a new Studebaker (or in later years a Chrysler) at the factory. Be it a real estate sale or a car purchase, to Papa business transactions were personal transactions and meant to be enjoyed. By the time I pulled into the fraternity house parking lot, I had resolved my dilemma. Papa's life had been about seizing the moment, not bemoaning the past. Of course he would want me to go ahead with my plans. After all, Denise would eventually become the mother of his great-grandchildren.

My spring fling with Denise blossomed into a full-blown romance. By the end of the semester, I was taking her home to meet my family. We arrived in the midst of a premature summer heat wave. The skies were clear and blue—it was the Bay Area at its best. I was not surprised that Denise was an immediate hit with my family. She was beautiful and charming. Moreover, she was a gifted golfer. The one-time Southern California junior girls champion and member of the USC women's golf team put us both to shame when my dad and I naively dared to challenge her skills at the local links.

After the get-acquainted visit we drove back to Los Angeles to get on with summer. Denise was going home to spend the break with her folks in La Habra, and I was moving into a Playa del Rey beachside apartment with some fraternity brothers. I had just received notice that I had been accepted by the Screen Extras Guild and could start getting jobs in mid-June. Membership in the union was secured through the intervention of a person that I had never even met. My dad had casually mentioned that I was trying to find a way into the guild to company president George Killian, who was also chairman of the board of MGM Studios. Having connections, I discovered, is sometimes the way the world works.

Elvis

Calling Central Casting for day jobs is like going fishing and tossing a line into the water. One never knows what, if anything, is going to take the hook. One day I'd catch a job as a cowboy, another as a student or a soldier. Some days all I'd get was a disheartening "no work." The unpredictability of daily employment made the work exciting. By fall semester of my junior year, I was working regularly and finding my way around most of the studios. As I got to know my fellow extras, I began spending more time socializing than studying between takes. It was a tight community. Whether pursuing "the business" as a career or as a temporary calling, there was a shared passion for the filmmaking experience. It was a world so apart from my university reality that it was like having a dual life.

One afternoon in early October, I put in a routine call to Central Casting. After I announced my name, a casting director picked up the call and gave me instructions to appear at Paramount Studios the next morning to work in an Elvis Presley film, *Easy Come, Easy Go*. Since I had worked in a Presley picture earlier in the summer, the mystique of Elvis the outlaw had lost some luster. My onetime hero of rebellion had become a compromised commodity manipulated by his ever-present manager, the infamous Colonel Tom Parker. However, it must also be said that even with his creative impulses dampened, Elvis' charisma remained intact.

While working on the previous picture, *Double Trouble*, I had met a couple of Elvis' ever-present buddies, known as the Memphis mafia. One of them recognized me when I arrived on the Paramount set and called me over to where he and the rest of the "boys" were engaged in a lively discussion about the weekend football games. He remembered that I was attending USC and asked if I knew any of the players. I did—a couple of my fraternity brothers were on the team and I knew a few of the other players from around campus. My credentials seemed acceptable and I was introduced to the rest of the guys.

After the lunch break, I had just settled in with my studies when the "mafiosi" returned to the set. They were in a jovial mood, joking and laughing about some matter unknown to me. Then I saw the reason for the commotion: The big dog was conversing with his pack. The group was gravitating my way when one of the guys saw me and called me over to meet Elvis. I dropped my book, stumbled to my feet, and met The King. From what I can recall, little was said, but I had the impression that Elvis liked knowing that I was supplementing my college education by working in his movies. As the entourage moved on toward Elvis' dressing room, I got back to my book, but it took a while to refocus.

※ ※ ※

Monday is formal-dinner night on fraternity-sorority row. The coat-and-tie event is generally followed by the weekly chapter meeting. It is also the evening when guests are invited to join the brothers for dinner and offer a few thoughts after the meal. Usually the guests are distinguished alumni or a prominent relative of a chapter member. On very special occasions when the guest is a celebrity, a limousine is dispatched, a red carpet is rolled out for the arrival, and a Hollywood-style searchlight is employed to alert everyone that something big is happening at the Sig house.

A few days after my experience on the Paramount set, I was having a discussion with some of the brothers about selecting guests to invite for Monday-night dinners. I don't quite know what got into me, but I brashly suggested that we invite Elvis. The others looked at me like I was nuts. Why would Elvis even consider coming over to the Sigma Chi house for dinner? I responded, again seemingly of nowhere, by suggesting that we present him with an award. The brothers began sensing there might be something to this. I pointed out that in my brief meeting with Elvis, I had found him surprisingly accessible and friendly, and he seemed to have a genuine interest in USC. A plan started to form. To entice Elvis, we decided to offer him the first annual Youth Leadership Award along with a day of service we would contribute to a local charity of his choice, which would also be good public relations for the fraternity.

The next morning, I called the Easy Come, Easy Go production office. I was directed to Colonel Parker's office, where an assistant informed me that all requests for access to Elvis must be in writing, and that the letter announcing the award be addressed to the Colonel. I hastily composed a congratulatory letter citing Elvis' service in the military, his public stand against illicit drugs (pharmaceuticals would become another matter), and his well-known generosity as reasons for his selection as the first recipient of the Sigma Chi Youth Leadership Award. My associates agreed with the text, so I typed the letter on official fraternity stationery, signed it in my capacity as social director, and dropped it in the mail.

About a week later, I got a call from the Colonel himself to let me know that Elvis was honored to be selected for the award, and he wanted to know when we could come over to the studio to present it to him. This was definitely not in the script. I answered that we intended to present the award at our fraternity house at a formal Monday-night dinner. "Oh, Elvis, he don't make no personal appearances," the Colonel replied. "You boys come on down to Paramount Studios and you can give Elvis his award right here on the movie set. How about next Tuesday morning, 10 o'clock?" I was trapped and answered that there would be four of us making the presentation. Parker said that was fine and told us to go to the studio gate on Melrose and a pass would be waiting for us. He ended by saying that Elvis was looking forward to meeting us. Perplexed, I hung up the phone knowing that I'd been had by the Colonel.

My brothers, who had not yet met Elvis, did not share my disappointment. They were excited and pointed out that even without the

Monday-night appearance, we would still benefit from the positive PR. I agreed, and we quickly went about ordering the plaques and preparing for the big day.

At the designated time, brothers Pat Larkin, Bill Brown, and I (the fourth member of our delegation was stuck in a class) picked up our pass at the gate and were directed to Colonel Parker's office. There, with a cigar in one hand and a cane in the other, he waved us into his lair. With Elvis movie posters slapped indiscriminately on the walls, and scripts and papers scattered all about, the place had the overall appearance of a too-long-lived-in motel room. The Colonel offered us seats and briefly rambled on about how deserving Elvis was and how much he appreciated us college boys being smart enough to recognize him as such an outstanding role model. After the Colonel's benediction, we were led out of the room to make the presentation.

We walked into a setup. This was not to be a casual affair. Parker had engaged the Paramount public relations staff, who saw the event as a photo opportunity. A press agent started asking us questions about the criteria for the award, why Elvis, and so forth. Though not prepared for the unexpected interview, we winged it and were having fun with the questions when Elvis entered the room. The publicity director ushered us over to a corner of the set where we stood in front of a seamless backdrop, already lit and ready for a shoot. Elvis joined us for introductions and small talk; then, with little fanfare, we gave him our first annual Youth Leadership Award plaque along with our commitment to a day of community service in his honor. Elvis thanked us for the award and presented us with an autographed poster suitable for framing and a prominent display in our frat house. Group photos of the four of us were taken, and we were done.

We drove back to campus, not quite sure what had happened. We had invited Elvis to join us for dinner for our purposes and, as we would soon find out when the photo and story hit the fan magazines, we ended up being used for his. It was my first effort in what would become a career in productions and promotions. I had been bamboozled by one of the craftiest in the business, but when we received our personal copies of the photos with Elvis a short time later, the whole experience became well worthwhile. The photo would have been even more amusing if the fourth member of our presentation committee, brother Tom Selleck, could have gotten out of his class that morning.

Presenting Sigma Chi Youth Leadership award to Elvis at Paramount Studios. From left, Author, Elvis, Pat Larkin and Bill Brown on set of *Easy Come, Easy Go*. October 1965.

Decisions

It was Saturday, November 11, and I was on campus to take the law school entrance exam. I would much rather have been with my friends listening to USC–Oregon State football on the radio. The team was undefeated and on their way to a national championship.

Promptly at nine, the proctor opened the door and I, along with my fellow law school candidates, filed into the room and selected our desks. I picked one in the back row near the door. As the morning session wore on, I realized that I was just going through the motions, casually answering questions that would largely determine my law school options. I tried to knuckle down to the task, but my mind kept wandering. Looking around the room, I saw the determined concentration on my colleagues' faces and felt like an interloper. At the lunch break, I took a long cathartic walk around campus.

The plan was that Denise and I would marry after graduation and I would continue on to law school and Denise would begin her career as a dental hygienist. Everyone, especially Denise and her parents, thought this to be a prudent course of action. I did too until the reality of three more years of intense education set in. But it was more than the prospect of law school that was causing my distress; when it came right down to it I just didn't see myself as a lawyer. The day of reckoning was upon me. I kept walking until it was time to resume the exam.

The afternoon session was an exercise in contradiction. Part of me was already out the door and another part, perhaps out of guilt, was committed to finishing the test. The proctor didn't help matters when he started posting the USC game scores as they came in from Corvallis. I suppose watching my team lose on a chalkboard was better than hearing it live on the radio, but a loss is a loss, which only made me feel more morose. Finally, time was called and we put down our pencils, picked up our papers, and handed them to the proctor as we exited the room.

As I passed the business school on my way back to my apartment, a new consideration crossed my mind. As a business school undergraduate, I could continue on and get an MBA in just one additional year. That appeared manageable, as I seemed to have an aptitude for business and academically was on the dean's list. The change would mean two fewer years of study, earlier entry into the workforce, and less of a burden on Denise as sole provider. With no victory party to attend, Denise and I would have the whole evening to talk things out.

With both families in attendance, graduation day was like a prelim to the wedding. After the formalities and speeches, we were given our degrees and, with hoots and hollers, were unleashed to find our place in the great game of life. I still had another year of studies before me, but it was a milestone to be savored nevertheless. After the perfunctory on-campus reception, our families convened for lunch at a tavern not far from campus. The lunch chatter was more about the forthcoming wedding than the just-concluded graduation.

We were married on June 21, 1968, the longest day of the year. It was also the hottest. The wedding was in a gothic-style Episcopal church in Whittier, California, not far from Denise's family home in La Habra. The ceremony was to begin at five in the afternoon, but due to a last-minute mix-up in logistics, the wedding march did not commence until closer to six. By then, the heat was taking its toll on the guests—like the bouquets, they were beginning to wilt.

The reception at the nearby Hacienda Country Club was reminiscent of a scene out of *The Graduate*, a film that I had worked on a few months earlier. The only mishap was, when changing out of my tux into getaway attire, I discovered that my street shoes were missing. Denise looked so radiant when we departed the reception in a shower of rice and good cheer that no one seemed to notice that the groom was barefoot.

Best man Doug chauffeured us to a hotel near the Los Angeles airport where we spent our wedding night. The next morning, I would take my bride to Hawai'i.

Wedding at Episcopal Church in Whittier, California. June 1968.

First Visit

A chance encounter on the second night of our honeymoon set the stage for my first visit to Hāna. While sitting on the oceanfront veranda of the Halekūlani Hotel, we got into a conversation with an Episcopal minister who, when learning that we were newly married in an Episcopal church no less, took to us like a shepherd tending his flock. When he found that Maui was next on our multi-island tour, he encouraged us to take the drive out to Hāna, referring to it as the most beautiful place in all of Hawai'i. Neither of us had heard of Hāna, and given the short length of our stay on the Valley Isle, we were skeptical of spending an entire day on the road. Nonetheless the kindly cleric made a persuasive case, and two days later we embarked at dawn on a road trip to Hāna.

Driving through Kahului, we turned onto the Hāna Highway and headed toward Pā'ia, then a sleepy little seaside hamlet half-hidden in a thicket of sugar cane and pineapple fields. A quick stop for "last chance" provisions and we were back on our way. Searching the rental car's AM radio for music to accompany our journey, I happened upon a live broadcast of a game between the New York Mets and the Houston Astros with Tom Seaver, a fraternity brother from USC, pitching for the Mets. We headed into a serene rainforest accompanied by the surreal soundtrack of a baseball game being played thousands of miles away.

The well-tended agricultural landscape soon became a forest with trees, vines, and miscellaneous flora barely contained. Our pace slowed as we ascended the mountainside, winding our way along steep canyon walls. Oncoming vehicles were few but never without challenge. There were places where one driver would have to pull over, or even back up, to allow the other vehicle to pass. The road, completed in 1926, felt as if its surface was original issue—mostly paved but well worn and in places not much more than compressed cinder.

It was rugged but drivable, a small price for a ride through a tropical wonderland.

The jungle waterfalls were indeed stunning, and the views of the sea cliffs holding strong against the pounding blue sea were breathtaking. But it was the sensual mix of forest fragrances, sea breezes, and passing showers that made the experience unforgettable. It was like being cradled in Mother Nature's nursery. We drove onward, the radio lost to static, awe muting our conversation.

The jungle eventually receded into rolling pastures, and a scattering of houses appeared along the road. Tired and hungry, we followed the road to Hāna Bay. Unbeknownst at the time, we drove right past the land that would, nearly two decades later, become my home.

We parked the car, stretched, and walked toward the pavilion that housed a small sandwich shop and placed an order for lunch. When Denise went to the restroom to freshen up, I was left to consider the daunting thought that the trip was only half over and the journey back wasn't going to be any easier. Denise returned as our number was called. We picked up our lunch, picnic ready in a paper bag, and walked out toward the shore. We found an empty table and sat down to enjoy our meal and contemplate our surroundings. Looking out over the bay within sight of my home to be, I leaned over to Denise and vowed that, beautiful as the place was, I was never going to drive that road again.

Career and Family Life: Part One

While most of my fellow students in graduate school were dedicated to their pursuit of an MBA as a means of securing a high-paying job, I had not yet focused on a career in business. As an undergrad, I found marketing to be the one business class that allowed for, even encouraged, imaginative thinking. I had an inspirational professor, Dr. Burton Marcus, who opened my eyes to the prospect of a business career that would foster creativity. As a marketing major, I became Dr. Marcus' teaching assistant and eventually worked with him on several outside marketing research projects.

Following graduation, I went to work for a very small company in Santa Monica that manufactured polyurethane ceiling beams. I had met the owner on one of my marketing research projects, and he suggested that I call him when I was ready to enter the job market. I didn't think much of it at the time, seeing his business as having rather limited potential. My opinion changed after several interviews with campus recruiters for large corporations. Suffice to say that very early on I realized that my independent nature was not conducive to a career as a company man. I called back the poly beam maker after deciding that I was better suited to being a big fish in a small pond than a minnow in a large lake. I started work upon returning from a quick road trip up the coast with Denise in our new Porsche. With her career as a dental hygienist well established and mine about to begin, we were fast-tracking right out of the gate.

Alas, the small pond dried up by the end of summer. Unemployed just months after receiving my MBA was an inauspicious start to a career. My fortunes turned when I received a call from Dr. Marcus asking if I would be interested in going to work for one of his clients, Craig Corporation. I could hardly have asked for a better opportunity. I was well versed in automotive sound systems, having already installed an aftermarket record player (yes, there was once such a thing) in my

Chevy. Craig, a leader in the emerging 8-track car stereo industry, was going through a transition from being a family-owned West Coast photographic distributor to being a publicly held national distributor of its own brand-name products. The company was putting together a new marketing team and looking for an MBA graduate to inaugurate their management-training program. I knew I was their man.

The initial interview with the newly recruited executive vice president of marketing went well, but I was forewarned that the next interview would be a challenge. Derwood (Kit) Carson, vice president of sales, was an old-school, hard-charging, heavy-drinking carryover from the time when the sales department ruled and marketing did little more than provide literature and advertising materials. Kit didn't see much use for higher education, believing that success was a product of dedication, determination, and personal character. He was at odds with the whole idea of elevating the role of marketing and even less enthusiastic about hiring someone still wet behind the ears as a potential marketing manager.

Surprisingly, I found Carson more likable than threatening. He asked the routine questions like why should I be hired and what were my personal ambitions. Then, unexpectedly, he asked me what my father did for a living. I told him that he was a freight sales manager for a steamship company. That appeared to be the icebreaker. Once he learned that my grandfather Harry had his own real estate company, he seemed satisfied that I had an aptitude for sales, at least genetically. With that, he escorted me back to the executive vice president's office, where they offered me the job. I accepted without hesitation.

I started work the following Monday. It was early October, and Denise and I were living in a beachside apartment a short distance from the Venice pier. My orientation program began at Craig's headquarters on the west side of Culver City, a short commute by Los Angeles standards. A month later, I was transferred to the products division, temporarily located in downtown Los Angeles. The drive was longer, but products was where the action was and where I would begin my ascent up the corporate ladder as assistant product manager. With my responsibilities, I was given a voice in the selection of our new advertising agency. We gave the nod to Needham, Harper & Steers, a large international firm with a particularly creative Los Angeles office. Together, Craig Corporation and NH&S would soon be setting new standards for consumer electronics advertising.

I've heard it said that success is often as much about being in the right place at the right time as it is about hard work. In my case, I would like to think it was a measure of both. I loved my job. I'd been infatuated with consumer electronics since building a crystal-set radio as a Cub Scout project. Getting paid to play with innovative products, even sometimes taking them home for personal-use evaluation, was almost too good to be true. As an eighteen-to-twenty-four-year-old male, I was precisely the primary target market for car stereos. Preparing marketing plans often meant just drawing on my own desires and motivations. I got along well with my coworkers and superiors and, except during crunch time in preparing for sales meetings and conferences, the job required little after-hours or weekend work.

About a year and a half later, the company went through a major upheaval. Both divisions consolidated into a single complex in a new industrial park in Compton, and territorial disputes and personality conflicts were rampant. The biggest problem was integrating the long-established sales division with the newly created marketing department. It was becoming clear that the aggressive Harvard Business School model of a product-manager marketing structure didn't fit with the family-style atmosphere that had been a Craig tradition since the company was founded in the 1930s. Robert Craig Jr., son of the founder, decided to stay with what had made the company prosperous and brought in Peter Behrendt, a highly respected sales executive from the photo industry, to take the reins as president. Behrendt dissolved the product-manager marketing structure and folded most of the marketing functions into the sales division. All that remained of the marketing department was advertising, and the only marketing department employee still standing was me. By default, I became Craig's new director of advertising at the age of twenty-four.

♠♠♠

A year earlier, Denise and I had purchased a small duplex on the Venice Peninsula. It was a new building with a large, high-ceilinged two-bedroom second-story suite entered from a grand spiral stairway. The downstairs rental generated nearly enough income to cover the monthly mortgage payment. It wasn't our dream home, but it served our needs well at the time. We were both beach people and spent most of our weekends and free time at the shore. Denise, always the competitor, became a regular on the two-person beach volleyball courts, and I enjoyed fishing for halibut and corbina from the breakwater. We entertained frequently: beach parties, dinner parties, or just small get-togethers with the neighbors. Most of all, we enjoyed being young and believing that the world was at our command. It was one of those golden times that seem to pass too quickly.

I readily adapted to my new position. As advertising director, my job was to interface with the agency, my primary contacts being the account executive or account supervisor. I would work with Peter Behrendt and Craig's sales department to develop a marketing and advertising plan and budget. From the plan, I would draw up a copy platform to present to NH&S. A well-written copy platform defines the purpose and objective of the advertising, identifies target demographics, sets the budget, and may even include a preferred tone or attitude. Beyond that, the agency is free to propose a creative strategy and media mix as long as it fits within the established parameters. The key to most successful advertising is a clear, tight copy platform. Conversely, the agency might well claim that bad advertising is often the result of too much micromanaging from the client side. It was a fine line and I thrived on pushing the limits.

Craig's sales rose dramatically during the next couple of years. The advertising budget doubled, and my responsibilities expanded to the point where I was able to hire an assistant. Tim Hendrick, a smart, enthusiastic young man fresh out of college, learned the system quickly and was soon handling many of the ancillary marketing details. With Tim taking care of new product releases and literature production, I was able to spend more time with the agency working on broader-base advertising campaigns and promotions. In the process, I was forming an understanding about the nature of really good advertising.

Effective advertising is often more about triggering emotional feelings than appealing to rational thought. We made exceptional products, technically more advanced than most of our competitors', but to anyone other than a small population of techies, our products were simply stylish devices that played the music people wanted to hear. The sex appeal was in the software. We needed a strategy to sell, as Peter Behrendt was fond of saying, "the sizzle rather than the steak." Advertising, the fine art of manipulating words and images to create the desire to purchase a product or service is, to put it bluntly, a modern form of sorcery. Consciously or not, the sorcerer within me was awakening. I knew instinctively that we could make an emotional connection with our target audience by forging an identity with the creative side of the music industry. Implementing that plan would take time, determination, and some shuffling of personnel.

NH&S was located on the corner of Wilshire and Westwood Boulevards at the edge of Westwood Village. One afternoon after a meeting at NH&S, Tim and I had to stop at Robert Craig's corporate office on our way to an advertising function later that evening. After hiring Peter as president, Craig had kicked himself upstairs to the position of CEO and relocated to Century City. While waiting for our appointment, we passed the time conversing with his secretary, Denise, who appeared to have captivated Tim from the moment he set eyes on her. Uncharacteristically, Tim seemed to have forgotten where he was and invited the boss' secretary to join us for the dinner event at the nearby Playboy Club. Denise hesitantly accepted Tim's bold invitation and that daring first date lead to matrimony a year or so thereafter.

🔺🔺🔺

As I began to establish myself, I became increasingly dissatisfied with the creative direction of the agency. We had just begun airing our first commercials on late-night television. *The Dick Cavett Show* was considered the hippest of the late-night talk shows, but I didn't feel the same about our commercials. We were running a series of animated spots with the theme "Craig, fun to be with." The commercials were pleasant to watch and perhaps even had some emotional appeal, but to me they were too soft. To get the attention of our target audience, I felt that we needed a campaign with more of an edge. I wanted our image to be cool, not cute. Levi's jeans were cool; I wanted our image to be like theirs.

I was convinced that a creative platform aligned with popular music was what we needed, but changing the direction of an advertising campaign is never easy. This is especially true when the redirection comes from the client. When I first presented the agency with the idea that we find a way to tie in with the music industry, I faced a wall of polite resistance. It was no surprise that the creative department was not receptive to my idea, but I was disappointed at the lack of support from the account team. Being young and relatively new to the job, I may have been perceived as lacking the political clout to implement such a change. I would have to find someone within the agency to pick up the idea and run with it as if it were their own. Until then, all

I could do was hope that what I thought to be such an obvious connection between artists and sound systems wouldn't be picked up by a competitor.

Tim was also a music fan and enthusiastically accepted the idea of associating with the music industry. We would occasionally go to concerts with our wives or talk over lunch about favorite artists and acts and how they could tie in with our product advertising. Even though it was the mid-seventies, there remained a stigma from the sixties that music and commercialization didn't mix. I wasn't sure that it was possible (or even proper) to get musicians to do direct product endorsements. What we needed was an association that linked our products with celebrities without appearing to be a sellout.

One late winter afternoon I got an unexpected call from Denise suggesting that we meet for dinner at a new restaurant we had been wanting to try in the Marina. I said I would meet her there at six. Denise was already seated at a table when I arrived. She had a calm, almost blissful look, while at the same time appearing confident and in complete control. I sat down feeling curious and not knowing what to expect. After ordering our meal, Denise matter-of-factly announced that, ready or not, our family was about to expand. Though we had been doing nothing to prevent a pregnancy, we weren't planning for one either. The sudden realization of imminent fatherhood was like experiencing every emotion from fear to jubilation in one instant.

A baby on the way wasn't the only change afoot. About a month after Denise's announcement, Peter called me into his office to say that Brad Roberts, his counterpart at NH&S, called to inform him that the agency had just lost Continental Airlines. Brad wanted to know if we would be opposed to a change in our account team. Specifically, he wanted Sam Morgan, who had been Continental's account supervisor, to take over our account. I welcomed the news. I already knew Sam from various agency and media functions and always thought that he would be a delight to work with.

A week later, Roberts brought Sam down to our offices to meet Peter and our sales and advertising personnel. Before leaving, Sam asked what I thought about making some changes in our creative personnel. He felt that a young art director and copywriter team he had been working with on Continental might be better attuned to our target demographics. I told him that I looked forward to meeting our new creative team at the earliest opportunity.

Career and Family Life: Part Two

Sam was the man. The moment he took over our account, things began to change. As advertised, Sam's new creative team was first rate. Copywriter Kaye Lewis and art director Gary Acord were fresh, bright, and energetic. Most importantly, they wholeheartedly supported the idea of positioning our car stereos with music celebrities. Sam was a seasoned advertising executive, and Gary and Kaye were talented young hotshots who weren't bound by convention. Finally, we had a team ready, willing, and capable of taking our advertising in a bold new direction. Moreover, we all worked well together. Late-afternoon meetings would often begin in the NH&S conference room, then shift to the upstairs cocktail lounge, where the real work got done.

We saw our relationship with the artists as a professional association. Our premise was simple: We made the equipment that made their music sound its best. The fit seemed natural and obvious. The challenge was to convince the musicians of the benefit of doing our ads. Money alone wasn't the answer. We didn't have the budget for (or interest in) buying endorsements. The tie-ins had to have an integrity that would also benefit the artists.

The answer was media. Our impending campaign included an expenditure of about a million dollars for print and late-night television advertising. Not a huge amount, but, if directed primarily at our target audience of eighteen-to-twenty-four-year-old males, it was enough to make an impact. Our target audience also happened to be frequent music purchasers. Thus, our strategy was to cross-promote our car stereos with the musician's most recent record release. Using the leverage of our advertising, we could offer the artists the equivalent of a million dollars of media exposure for their own product. Even if the acts didn't get the connection, their managers certainly would.

Enter Bob Colvin. Bob was a partner in an independent talent agency with close ties to the music industry. We didn't have to convince him of our plan—he immediately saw the mutual benefit. Tim and I had prepared a list of acts that we thought would be ideal candidates for our advertising. Not all had chart-topping hits, but all were respected as talented and demanding musicians. Near the top of the list was Billy Preston. Billy was known as a musician's musician. He had recorded with the Beatles and had just finished a worldwide tour with the Rolling Stones. Bob's agency had some history with Preston's management, so we decided to approach him first.

We were so confident about the quality of our product that we authorized Bob to open discussions by offering to install a Powerplay car stereo in Preston's vehicle without obligation. If, after evaluating the performance of the equipment, he agreed with our tagline, "Billy Preston has the best sound in car stereo, and Billy Preston knows sound," then we would proceed with the ad. If he didn't agree, then he could keep the stereo with our compliments. A week or so later, we arranged to have a Craig Powerplay installed in Preston's classic Bentley.

We started cautiously with a television commercial that just featured Billy's Bentley. He liked the spot enough to agree to appear in the print ad himself. We did the shoot early in the morning at A&M records. Billy had been recording all night but still looked dapper in a stylish red satin vest and jacket. The layout called for him to be standing in front of his stately classic on the A&M lot. The problem was his trousers. They were white, about the same shade as his car. To make matters worse, the old Bentley had an unfortunate dent in the right front fender. Gary tried to solve the problem by posing Billy with his right leg resting on the bumper to cover the blemish. In doing so, Billy's lower torso seemed to blend with the car, creating a slightly grotesque image of Billy as a gigantic hood ornament. Finally, as the sun rose, the photographer was able to set the reflectors to cast just enough shadow to make the shot work.

Our ads broke with the release of Billy's biggest hit, *Nothing from Nothing*. Our ads may or may not have contributed to the making of

Mr. Preston's first number one hit, but they did cause a ripple within the music industry. Billboard magazine did a feature story about our celebrity tie-in campaign, and Bob Colvin was soon receiving unsolicited inquiries from other agents wanting to get their clients into the act. It was too soon to measure the immediate effect on our already strong product sales, but dealer feedback told us that we were off to a great start.

On a Monday morning in mid-September 1973, Denise woke me at dawn and announced that she had started labor. I tried to be calm while jumping into my clothes and scrambling around looking for the car keys. I helped Denise into the car and dashed across town to Cedars-Sinai Medical Center in record time only to find it to be a false alarm. Late that afternoon, Denise called my office to say that the contractions had increased in strength and frequency. I hurried home and again we raced across town, only this time Denise was immediately wheeled into the maternity ward and prepped for childbirth. Three hours later, after summoning the OB from the season-opening *Monday Night Football* game, daughter Tiffany entered our lives.

As every new parent has been forewarned, the first few weeks (or even months) at home with a newborn are usually not conducive to sleep. Friends from college, Tim and Mikie Rossovich, however, managed to beat the odds with their daughter, who was born a couple of years earlier. They did so by employing the services of Gladys Hendrick. Gladys wasn't a nurse or nursemaid—she was a baby whisperer. She would come to your house and essentially take charge of the first week home with the baby. For her to accept a job, the prospective parents had to read her book, My First 300 Babies, and agree to follow her program, no exceptions.

Her approach involved getting the baby onto a feeding schedule that by week's end would have the child sleeping through the night. Gladys would move in with the baby even if it meant sharing a room with the parents. If the baby cried, it was Gladys who tended to her. If the time was right, she would take the child to the mother for feeding. Otherwise, it might mean letting the baby cry. Had it not been for Tim and Mikie's success with Jamie, I don't think that Denise and I would have been willing to try such a course. We did, and Gladys delivered as promised.

Over dinner conversation the evening before she left for another engagement, we discovered that Gladys was the woman who had counseled my grandfather Harry and had introduced him to the lessons of Christian Science at a difficult time in his life. Amazing as the coincidence was, it didn't seem so surprising. Of course, Papa would want his presence known at the birth of his first great-grandchild.

By springtime, we were looking for a new nest. Our Venice Beach duplex had served us well, but Malibu seemed to be the place to raise a family. The timing was right. The real estate market in our neighborhood was taking off, while Malibu, still considered too remote for most commuters, was less affected by the local real estate boom. Our happy family of three (plus our Afghan hound, Jenny) spent several weekends looking at homes and undeveloped land. Building a home was our dream, but we weren't having much success finding available land to our liking. We had just about resigned ourselves to buying one of the existing homes that dotted the ridge above the coastline, when our real estate agent suggested that we take a look at a brand-new oceanfront townhouse. Denise was skeptical, as it was only a two bedroom home, but it was on the beach and I was interested.

I fell in love with the place the minute our agent opened the front door, exposing a twenty-five-foot-wide glass wall of open ocean and sky. The townhouse was one of ten side-by-side homes aligned along the shore. The complex was on a point between the Los Flores and La Costa beaches and was built on pilings that led out to the edge of the sea. At high tide, the surf would roll in several feet under the building. Looking out across the ocean from the deck reminded me of being back on board a steamship. I was definitely sold. Denise was equally impressed with the prospect of living on the shore, but also noted the shortcomings: The townhouse was only slightly larger than our current home, did not have a fenced yard (which had been a priority), and lacked the closet space she felt we required.

We compromised and purchased the townhouse as a temporary home until the right property became available to build our dream house. Once the decision was made, everything fell into place and we were able to relocate to Malibu in late spring. The extra fifteen minutes of daily commute each way to and from Compton was but a small price to pay for coming home each evening to an environment that brought me such pleasure. It wasn't just the sea that made Malibu so remarkable. The hills were full of wildlife, and the land seemed to be connected to another time when a harmony between man and land prevailed. Although I was unaware at the time, the move to Malibu was the beginning of an awakening that would call into question the direction and purpose of my life.

With Denise and Tiffany in our new home on the beach in Malibu. Spring 1973.

Showtime

Arriving late to work one morning due to heavy traffic, I found a message on my desk to call Sam immediately. Sam wanted me to join him for lunch with Bob Colvin. He wouldn't say what the meeting was about, only that he thought that I should be there. I trusted Sam's instincts and told him I'd meet him at his office just before noon.

Sam drove us to a trendy West Hollywood café where we met Bob, who was already sitting at a corner table. As we sat down, Bob introduced Sam Riddle, a popular L.A. disc jockey from the days of KHJ Boss Radio. Riddle had recently launched a television production company and had a project in the works that he thought would interest us. The show, hosted by Hoyt Axton, would be a one-hour television special featuring an array of musical acts. Riddle was quick to point out that Hoyt had many friends in the music business, and if we signed on as a sponsor early, we could have a say in the selection of the guests, some of whom might even work into our advertising. As a favor to Hoyt, his friends would be paid only at scale, and as a syndicated production, there would be no network airing fees. In short, sponsorship of the production appeared to be an offer we couldn't refuse. Lunch concluded, we agreed to meet the next week in the Riddle-Walton Productions office and have a talk with Hoyt.

No wonder Hoyt had so many friends. It was impossible not to like him. Full of life and rich with stories, Hoyt would have won us over even without the presence of his intended cohost, Arlo Guthrie. With Arlo on board, *The Hoyt Axton Country Western Boogie Woogie Gospel Rock and Roll Hour* became a done deal. A few days later, we met again, this time with Tim and the NH&S account team, to work out the details of the television commercial that Hoyt agreed to do for the show. Regarding the selection of talent, my only suggestion was Linda Ronstadt, whom I had had a crush on since seeing her belting out songs barefoot while onstage at the Troubadour early on in her career.

Hoyt assembled so many quality musicians for his one-hour show that it resembled a mini-Woodstock. As if Arlo Guthrie, Rita Coolidge, Buffy Sainte-Marie, Doug Dillard, Tanya Tucker, Kris Kristofferson, Paul Williams, and Linda Ronstadt weren't enough, Hoyt even managed to add a Beatle to the roster. Ringo Starr would close the show by singing his hit, *The No, No Song*, written for him by Hoyt. The special was scripted in the format of the variety shows of that time, a mixture of musical acts and skits, only it was a whole lot funkier.

It was rock and roll meets vaudeville, the slapstick skits intermingled with performances by musicians from a variety of genres. More like ringmasters than hosts, Hoyt and Arlo held all the acts together with song, humor, and charm. And the closing Ringo Starr–Hoyt Axton sing-along lived up to its promise. Hoyt and Ringo had invited a hundred or so of their close friends to stop by for the wrap party. The stage was packed with rock and roll royalty, all singing, whooping, and hollering the lines, "No, no, no, no I don't drink it no more, I'm tired of waking up on the floor....," while partying like it was 1999.

Before going ahead with the next phase of celebrity ads (Leon Russell and Arlo Guthrie were in the pipeline), Sam and I took to the road to get a reading of dealer reaction to our new campaign. The dealers that we spoke to were unanimous in their support for the celebrity tie-ins. Many of them were young themselves, so it was not surprising that they gave us high marks. What was unexpected was their enthusiasm for Hoyt's special. Some wanted to know if we were planning a follow-up. They particularly liked being mentioned in the local advertising that was included in the show as it aired in each market. The big dealers got prominent exposure, but all the dealers in the area got listed on the scroll at the end of the commercial. Most dealers had never used television advertising before and enjoyed seeing their name appear on the screen, even if only as a momentary flash.

Bob Dylan's *Blood on the Tracks* was playing in the background as Sam and I talked about the possibility of doing another television special while driving back to Los Angeles. It seemed to us that the next step should be a national network special that would also provide the opportunity for local dealer participation. Traffic was backing up, so we decided to stop for a bite to eat while waiting out the rush hour.

Over dinner, we carried on our conversation about doing a network TV special. Sam mentioned that NH&S had an executive, Dick McCue in New York, whose sole job was to deal with network relations, and suggested that we meet with him the next time he came to town. Then Sam asked if I had ideas about whom we would want to headline the show. Even though I knew it was all but impossible, I answered yes, Bob Dylan. One of the things that I most enjoyed about working with Sam was that he never flinched, no matter how outrageous the proposal.

Tim Hendrick, Sam Morgan, Linda Ronstadt, Author and Hoyt Axton during taping of Hoyt Axton's *Country Western, Boogie Woogie Gospel, Rock and Roll Hour* at KTLA Studio Lot. Late Fall 1974.

Family Foursome

Malibu in the mid-1970s was still a small beach town populated by an eclectic mix ranging from surfers living in vans at Topanga Beach to bohemian millionaires living in the Colony. In between was an assortment of the gainfully employed (like us), who sought refuge from the congestion of the city. The common bond was a love of the beach and the rural lifestyle. This would rapidly change over the next few decades, when many of the modest beach houses occupied by year-round residents would be replaced with opulent holiday homes for the rich and famous. At least for a few more years, Malibu would remain an iconic bastion of the sleepy little beach communities that once dominated the California coast.

Late spring of our second year in Malibu was overcast and dreary. June gloom, as it is commonly known, is a condition caused by warm air interacting with cooler-than-normal ocean temperatures. The result is a layer of moisture that moves in at night, then normally burns off by early afternoon. In some years, particularly during La Niña conditions, the marine layer hangs around all day, occasionally for weeks or even months. 1975 was one of those years. On the bright side, Denise was almost full-term with our second child. This time we really were ready.

On a Tuesday evening in mid-June, Denise went into labor. Our friends Tim and Denise arrived a short time later to sit with Tiffany, and we again raced off to Cedars-Sinai Medical Center. By the time we reached the hospital, the contractions had become so strong and frequent that Denise was taken directly to a delivery room. The OB was on his way and initially it looked to be a quick and easy birth. A short while later, the situation took a turn for the worse.

The labor intensified into the evening, yet nothing happened. During the first few hours, we were assured that everything was normal and the baby was doing fine. Then suddenly Denise was stricken with excruciating pain and the baby's pulse rate soared with every contraction. With little said, I was escorted out of the room as the doctor and his staff shifted into emergency mode. Waiting helplessly outside the delivery room, I could hear sharp and hurried talk among the medical staff, but I couldn't decipher what was being said. Then, after what seemed like an eternity, a nurse appeared and invited me to come meet my new daughter, Melanie.

Denise looked worn out but relieved. Melanie was on her back next to her as the anesthesiologist cleaned up the last of the gastric meconium that Melanie had inhaled when becoming stuck in the birthing canal. The doctor had no choice but to deftly use forceps to rescue Melanie from her entrapment. Though heartbreakingly bruised, Melanie survived the ordeal with no apparent long-term damage.

We were advised that, although unlikely, there was still a risk of a bacterial infection, and as a precaution, Melanie would have to spend the next few days in an incubator. Denise and I could only touch her hands as the nurses placed Melanie in her new quarters of confinement and wheeled her away to the infant intensive care unit. Denise was exhausted and there was little to say. I squeezed her hand and kissed her on the forehead as she drifted off to sleep. Before leaving the hospital, I stopped by to look in on Melanie. There she was, a giant among the preemies, breathing deeply and steadily, looking content. I was so overwhelmed by the strength of her spirit that I could barely keep my composure as I turned away from the window and left the room.

My mood lightened when I walked out of the building and was greeted by the rising sun. I took the end of June gloom as a good sign. Even more so, when I got into my car and turned on the ignition, the radio came on with Ringo pounding out the opening downbeat on the song "Birthday," with Paul wailing, "You say it's your birthday, it's my birthday, too, yeah..." My amusement at the appropriateness of the song turned to astonishment when the DJ came back on the air and announced, "and today, June 18, is your birthday, Paul McCartney, happy birthday to you!" Happy Birthday indeed.

After Melanie's birth, the rest of the summer was a dream. Denise nurtured Melanie as only a mother can do, while I spent more time with Tiffany, who was evolving from a toddler into a small child. Vacation days that summer were spent at home playing on the beach, picnicking in the canyons, and enjoying the simple pleasures of being with family.

In early August, I had to leave for a few days to go east and prep for the forthcoming Arlo Guthrie ad. While I was away, Denise began researching local real estate availabilities since we were again in the market for vacant land. I accepted that we were outgrowing our townhouse, but I wasn't in any great hurry to leave the beach. Presuming that affordable land to our liking was still a scarce commodity, I was counting on time being on my side.

Not so. When Denise picked me up at the airport, she couldn't wait to give me the news. She had found a local developer who was about to build two spec houses in Serra Retreat, a location that was high on our priority list. She had gone over the plans and found that one of the homes fit our requirements as if drawn to our own specifications. The property was a half-acre lot located about a quarter of a mile inland from Surfrider Beach and the Malibu pier. The home was positioned well off the road, and there was plenty of room for a yard. Construction was to begin in September and we still had time to select materials and finishing components. And, she concluded, it was priced within our budget. Case closed.

Portrait by Chuck Estavan with Tiffany, Melanie, Jenny. Malibu, 1977.

What If?

Media maven Dick McCue came to town not long after Sam and I first discussed the idea of sponsoring a network television special. We met in Sam's office and presented our idea to McCue. We mentioned Bob Dylan as our ideal choice but acknowledged that Dylan's tendency to avoid mainstream media might make him unreceptive to doing a network special. Dick was not as skeptical. He had been around since the early days of television and recalled that in the 1950s, many of the most popular shows were produced by sponsors rather than the networks. He suggested that this approach might especially appeal to an artist with a penchant for creative control of his own work. We briefly discussed some other considerations but kept coming back to Bob Dylan as the standard by which everyone else was measured. Dick said that he would explore the idea with some of his associates and get back to us within a couple of weeks.

Autumn that year was as bright and cheerful as spring had been dark and gloomy. On a warm Monday morning near the end of September, we broke ground on our new home. A mild Santa Ana wind was blowing in from the desert and carried with it small swarms of migrating monarch butterflies. The building site was nestled in a clearing next to a grove of eucalyptus trees. The butterflies seemed attracted to the trees and fluttered around them like shedding leaves refusing to fall to the ground. Oblivious to the dance of the butterflies, the construction crew was busy at work laying out string lines and building the forms for the foundation. Witnessing the rudimentary beginnings of our dream house was exciting, but it was the wind and trees and butterflies that made the day unforgettable.

No sooner was the house underway when, early one morning, I got a call from Dick McCue in New York. He reported that there was talk of Bob Dylan wanting to do a television special at the end of his Rolling Thunder Revue tour of New England. McCue added that he had been given the information from an insider at the talent agency who was representing the project and that we should respond immediately before word of the special reached the street.

When asked about the cost, McCue estimated that the total package including production costs, media time, and public relations would be about a million dollars, which amounted to almost half of my advertising budget for the year. It would have been prudent to discuss the project with Peter Behrendt, but he was out of the office and I was not going to let the opportunity pass. I gave Mr. McCue the green light. A week later, with Peter's blessing, Sam and I went to New York to work out the details.

We unexpectedly found the New York office excited about the event. The Rolling Thunder Revue was generating considerable media attention. People magazine had just done a cover story, and there were continuous news reports about "Dylan's band of gypsies" traveling from town to town, making surprise appearances at unannounced venues. There was a buzz about the project and our little West Coast account was suddenly getting the attention of the big brass at NH&S headquarters.

McCue assembled his team of media and production executives for a status update. In consultation with Dylan's agency, they had selected a director and reserved the Ed Sullivan Theater for the taping in early December. The media department was still in discussions with one of the networks about airtime and date, working toward a 9 p.m. time slot in mid-April. Everything appeared to be going so smoothly that Sam and I wrapped up our work a day early and headed back to L.A. We had work to do reformatting our entire spring advertising platform around a one-hour television show.

🔺🔺🔺

Denise and I decided to squeeze in a long-delayed return trip to Hawaiʻi the week before I was to go to New York for the taping. We flew into Honolulu, then on to the small Waimea-Kohala airport on the Big Island. It was November 29. We landed only a few hours after a 7.2 magnitude earthquake struck the southern end of the island. The tremor generated a tsunami that flooded the island's east coast and triggered a short but powerful eruption of the Kīlauea volcano. It was an inauspicious start to a holiday that would end with an eruption of an entirely different kind.

We spent the first few days at the Mauna Kea Resort on the Kohala coast, then moved on to finish the week in Kāʻanapali on the island of Maui. Unlike our honeymoon, when we had traveled the island from one end to the other, we were content just staying in one place and being pampered tourists.

We spent the last evening of our all-too-short vacation leisurely enjoying a dinner on the veranda of a waterfront restaurant in Lahaina. The sun was slowly setting behind the neighboring island, Lānaʻi, when we caught sight of a breaching humpback whale just outside the harbor. It was always difficult to leave the Islands, but feeling relaxed and rested, I was excited to get on with the show in New York.

We were about to go upstairs to our room and start packing for our respective early-morning flights, when I stopped by the front desk to check for messages. There was one from my folks wanting to confirm the time of Denise's arrival, and one from Sam telling me to cancel my flight to New York. The special had fallen apart. Dismayed, I raced up to the room and called Sam at his home, asking for details. He didn't have much information other than there had apparently been some miscommunication and Dylan wasn't comfortable with the setup. He simply was not willing to go ahead with the show. I asked Sam to contact Dylan's lawyer and schedule a meeting as soon as possible.

It wasn't just the unraveling of the special that was a problem. The whole spring advertising campaign would have to be revamped once again, and I was going to have a lot of explaining to do with my superiors. Our vacation may have flown by, but the flight back to Los Angeles seemed to take forever.

Hard Rain

David Braun, the lawyer for Bob Dylan and an assortment of some of the biggest names in music, wasn't able to meet with us until the second week in December. I was anxious for the meeting but needed the time to cool down and formulate a proposal to try to resurrect the project. Mr. Braun received us cordially and seemed receptive to our proposal. We asked him to assure Bob that we saw the special as an opportunity to do something extraordinary in network broadcasting, and that our commercial participation would be as unobtrusive as possible. Our approach, should the show move forward, would be to take only three (rather than the customary six) commercial breaks, and to format a copy platform compatible with the content of the show. We added that we had no interest in creative involvement in the production and that we would do what we could to curtail network interference as well. Lastly, we recommended that we bypass the New York agents and agency producers and, at least initially, confine communication to the three of us in the room. David promised us that he would discuss the matter with Bob but was unable to suggest when he might have an answer. Timing, he emphasized, was everything.

By early March 1976, the job site in the canyon was beginning to look like home. To save construction costs and to partially fulfill my desire to build my own home, we had negotiated with the contractor to do the interior paneling ourselves. Trading my coat and tie for Levi's and a T-shirt, I took time off from my job and became a carpenter for a week. My crew consisted of my brother, Rick, and my fishing buddy and printing broker, Dick Acker.

Early Monday morning, the three of us met at the beach house, collected our tools, and drove to the canyon. We were slightly overwhelmed when we arrived at the site to find an enormous pile of cedar planking and seemingly endless empty walls in need of paneling. We didn't have time to grumble, so after a quick assessment of the situation, we each took a position and got to work. By midday, we were into a rhythm and the magnitude of the task became much less daunting. We wrapped up the job early Friday afternoon and returned to the house to cap off the week with some hard-earned beers. While enjoying the moment, I got a call from my office with a message from David Braun. Bob Dylan was reassembling the Rolling Thunder Revue for a spring tour and wanted to proceed with the television special.

The RTR ensemble reconvened in April for rehearsals at the Belleview Biltmore Hotel in Clearwater, Florida. The special was to be taped in the hotel's Starlight Ballroom, a somewhat incongruous setting for a concert by a band of gypsies. The Victorian-style hotel was built in 1897 by Henry B. Plant, an industrious railroad tycoon. The four-story 820,000-square-foot wooden structure is an architectural work of art known for its fine wood craftsmanship and Tiffany glass embellishments. Since its opening, the hotel has hosted numerous foreign heads of state, US presidents, and an array of historical luminaries, including Thomas Edison, who I would learn later was a friend and associate of Hawaiʻi's King Kalākaua. The grand old place was also said to be haunted.

The Revue was out doing a show in St. Petersburg when Sam and I checked into the Belleview the evening of April 20. David Braun met us in the lobby and walked us over to the ballroom, which was being set up for the taping scheduled two days later. There were to be two shows: a run-through performance in the afternoon and the production version later that evening. The stage was positioned near the center of the room and surrounded by two stories of scaffolding-like bleachers for the audience. The configuration, besides being a clever way to pack a sizable crowd into a rather small venue, made the set intimate, though a bit claustrophobic.

The next day was spent working out details and going over contract amendments and clarifications. I was given open access to photograph both shows for possible promotional use. Burt Sugarman, producer of the popular NBC late-night program *Midnight Special,* was prepping the production crew, while the RTR roadies were on the street selectively distributing tickets for the shows (which no doubt accounted for the preponderance of young and beautiful Floridian females in attendance for both concerts). We ended the day by catching the concert in Tampa that evening.

The Clearwater performances were abbreviated versions of the nearly four-hour Rolling Thunder Revue road show. There was no script, although Dylan's song selections were similar in sequence to those performed in concert the night before. Between shows, Sam and I were taken backstage to meet Bob. The meeting was brief, cordial, and professional. Bob expressed appreciation for our support, and we reiterated our commitment to make the special a major media event. Satisfied with the direction of the project, we agreed to reconvene in Los Angeles after completion of the tour.

The tour moved on the next morning as Sam and I headed home. Relieved that we finally had the show in the can, we still had a big task ahead of us. We had only six minutes of commercial time to justify our investment. The commercials had to promote our products and, at the same time, be sensitive to the content of the show. Sam assured me that our creative team was ready for the challenge. The special, to them, was more than just an occasion to make stylish commercials. They saw it as an opportunity to make advertising history. Bob had done his part, now it was time for us to do ours.

After a series of meetings and "what if" sessions that progressed from the NH&S offices to the upstairs lounge, we came up with a plan. Given that we were committed to taking only three commercial breaks, we decided to take advantage of the two-minute segments to tell a three-part love story. Following the basic boy-meets-girl, boy-loses- girl, boy-gets-girl story line, each segment would feature a Craig product conspicuously placed in the background to subtly set the mood like a strolling violinist in an Italian restaurant. It was a daring approach that defied conventional wisdom that the product must always be the star. Our strategy, however, was not so much to pitch our products as it was to enhance Craig's brand image. It was a risky proposition; however, with product sales already high and inventories low, Peter and his bottom-line sales staff accepted our premise that a soft-sell approach today would generate stronger sales tomorrow. Timing was, indeed, everything.

Our family of four plus Jenny the dog started moving into our new home in late May. The garden had been laid out a few months earlier, but finally, after nearly nine months of construction, our dream house was about to become home sweet home. Our plan to spend the weekend preparing the house for occupancy was interrupted by a call from David Braun. The RTR tour was closing with a big outdoor show at Hughes Stadium in Fort Collins that weekend, and Bob wanted to tape the event for possible inclusion in the special. Although my attendance was not absolutely necessary, David suggested that I might want to be there to represent our interests. I agreed and called Sam to inform him that we would be spending the weekend in Colorado.

The Hughes Stadium concert was the antithesis of the Starlight Ballroom shows. The Clearwater performances were, if not scripted, at least tightly produced. The Fort Collins production was loose and, at times, borderline chaotic. The weather was foul. Intermittent rain and gusting winds made conditions miserable onstage and off. Unlike the preselected comfortably attired studio audiences tightly clustered around the set for the Florida shows, the congregation of Dylan stalwarts, draped in blankets and rain gear, braved the elements to watch the event in the open stadium.

If just putting on the show under adverse conditions was not enough, taping it for broadcast was another challenge altogether. TVTV, the edgy Los Angeles–based television production team brought in at the last minute to tape the event, barely had time to gather equipment and set up command before show time. Only three of their four cameras were operational, communication between videographers and the makeshift production team in the trailer was spotty, and keeping the stage and equipment dry was a constant struggle. The saving grace was that the camera operators had already worked with the Revue, shooting much of the fall tour for the film *Renaldo and Clara*. They not only knew what to expect but also had Bob's trust and were able to tape the outdoor stadium concert with the intimacy of being onstage with the band.

What the Fort Collins crowd lacked in comfort was more than made up for in high-altitude attitude. The musicians felt it as well. The band played loudly and energetically, as if in defiance of the dreary conditions. Dylan, first harmonizing with Joan Baez, then as frontman for the Revue, was spirited and intense. He concluded his set with an electrifying rendition of *"Idiot Wind."* The stage curtain had fallen, but the rowdy audience was not going to let the show end, as it roared for an encore. Cast and crew hastily reconvened onstage as Bob led the ensemble into a raw and unrehearsed version of *"Hard Rain."* The onstage camera was angled out over Bob's shoulder as the curtain rose and exposed the drenched but not yet spent audience devotedly hanging on for one more song. By a simple twist of fate, *"Hard Rain,"* the unplanned concert encore, became the opening segment and title for the television special when it aired nearly four months later.

We stayed with the tour and spent the night at the Stanley Hotel in Estes Park. The Stanley, another of the grand old wooden-structure hotels that hark back to another era, was a perfect bookend for the tour that began at the Belleview Biltmore. Like the Biltmore, the Stanley, constructed at the turn of the twentieth century, has housed and hosted a variety of historical movers and shakers, and it, too, is said to have its own resident ghosts.

The lobby and adjacent bar were buzzing with cast and crew. The tour was all but over, and everyone knew that the concert that day had gone well. Some of the troupe had family in attendance, which added to the warm and cheerful atmosphere. Sam and I wandered into the bar and joined Ramblin' Jack Elliott for a beer. We listened with amusement as Jack recounted his version of the same shaggy-dog story Hoyt Axton had told about him a couple of years earlier. It was late by the time we retired to our rooms. Whiffs of music and laughter permeated from up and down the hallway throughout the night.

Within days of returning from Colorado we had a major issue with which to contend. The differences between the shows were too great to allow for integration into a single one-hour production. The television special was going to have to be one show or the other. NBC was pushing for the Clearwater production and the Dylan camp favored the Fort Collins performance. All parties except Bob convened for a Sunday afternoon get-together in Malibu (spouses included) to watch clips and lobby for their respective interests. NBC was represented by Sugarman and its late-night programming executive who had been assigned to the production. Filmmaker and longtime Dylan associate Howard Alk joined the TVTV team to represent the Hughes Stadium show. About the only thing that everyone agreed upon was that the shows were incompatible and, of course, no one was dissuaded from the belief that their production would make the better show. The gathering was cordial and pleasant, but little was accomplished.

Craig Stereo, as the sponsor contracted to both parties, was caught in a bind. As a fan, I found that the Fort Collins tapes more accurately reflected the spirit and energy of the Rolling Thunder Revue and more intriguing to watch. But as advertising director, I had to consider that the Florida coverage, in a more traditional television format, might appeal to more viewers. After further discussion with Sam and the NH&S media department, we concluded that we would be better served airing the show that had the greater appeal to Bob Dylan fans more likely to buy our products than trying to appeal to a slightly larger viewership outside our target audience. We notified NBC of our decision to go with the TVTV production.

※※※

As soon as we unpacked and moved into our new home, I was back on the road, traveling to Maine to supervise production of the commercials, then to New York to finish up the shoot. While I was in the city, Dick McCue arranged a meeting with a public relations firm hired to publicize the special. Frank Goodman, an old-school publicist, was a bit perplexed about the lack of approved photos and stories available for distribution to the press. Nevertheless, he felt that a *TV Guide* cover story was within reach, but it would require an exclusive photo from the show and an interview with Bob. It seemed to me to be a reasonable request. Persuading Bob to do the interview, however, might be a challenge.

The rest of the summer was hectic. My workdays were spent juggling the ongoing responsibilities of my job with the pressing demands of the television special. After hours, I was always on call, from shuttling artwork and copy out to Bob's home for approval to interrupting weekend social functions to look at a new edit.

The project seemed to have a life of its own. Despite numerous obstacles and setbacks (not the least being NBC's rejection of the first edit), in the end everything somehow worked out. The revised edit, reshaped to open with *"Hard Rain,"* was reluctantly accepted by the network, Bob's first interview in seven years garnered a *TV Guide* cover story, and we were generating good local press coverage even with limited material.

September 14, the air date for the special, was also Denise's thirtieth birthday. On learning of the coincidence, David invited us to come over to his house for dinner and to watch the broadcast. He added that he had also invited Bob, but his attendance was uncertain. I accepted the invitation, telling Denise only that we were going to have dinner and watch the show with David and Merna Braun at their home in Beverly Hills. Not long after our arrival, Bob and Sara Dylan showed up bearing an iced bottle of Dom Perignon to commemorate the evening.

After dinner and a happy birthday cake, the six of us gathered around the Brauns' bedroom TV and watched NBC's broadcast of *"Hard Rain."* As the closing credits rolled over the ensemble performing *"Knocking on Heaven's Door,"* I felt a wave of relief and contentment. Knowing that I had contributed to a unique television experience witnessed by millions of viewers was humbling in a most gratifying kind of way.

As the evening wore on, some of David's and Bob's friends trickled in to offer congratulations. Soon a small congenial group had gathered, and the party carried on into the early-morning hours. Arriving home in the middle of the night, I tried to grab a couple hours of sleep before heading back to the office. Tomorrow would be just another working day.

From an overall ratings standpoint, the show came in third among the networks. Within our demographic, however, the show was a solid success. Many retailers set up TVs and made the broadcast an in-store event, and dealers around the country reported strong sales from tie-in promotions. Reviews varied, with some acclaiming it a television milestone and others who seemingly didn't get the point.

Surprisingly, the commercials also garnered critical attention. *The Washington Post* did a whole piece on the "soft focus" style of the commercials, and *Rolling Stone,* in its review of the special, stated that "Craig Corporation turned in the most remarkably erotic series of commercials ever seen on TV." It certainly wasn't our intention, but we appreciated the attention. The advertising industry took note as well and awarded *"Last Summer"* a Cleo Award as best long-form commercial of the year.

Bob Dylan in rehearsal for taping of TV special in Clearwater FL at the Belleview Hotel, April 1976. Show never aired as Fort Collins concert taped a month later was selected for broadcast on NBC as *Hard Rain* on September 14, 1976.

Storm Warnings

The heart of our new home was the family room. Located between the kitchen and bedrooms, it was the hub of activity. We took most meals at the kitchen counter next to a large sliding glass door that opened onto the garden patio. Denise, who was very exacting on furnishings for the living and dining rooms, deferred to my preferences for the family room. Arcade Americana was my chosen motif. Two jukeboxes, one a restored "bubble light" Wurlitzer that played 78 rpm records, the other a commemorative version of the 1946 classic that played 45s, flanked the walls, and an antique nickel slot machine sat on an old sewing machine table off to the side of the room. Denise drew the line at pinball machines.

My favorite weekends usually started with a pancake breakfast and a side of jukebox music. The weekly playlists were drawn from my extensive collection of 45s and a smaller assortment of 78s. I like to think that exposing my daughters to an eclectic mix of many musical genres during their formative years was an early lesson in the pleasures of diversity. At the very least, their musical horizons were expanded beyond top-40 radio.

If the weather was good, we would follow the meal with a family outing, often hiking the canyon and hills or walking down the road to the beach. On one such hike in early spring, we found a brown-and-yellow-banded king snake sunning itself on the side of the trail. Excitedly, I reached down and picked up the subdued serpent and held it out for the girls to examine and touch. After a few minutes of studying the curious legless creature, we gently put it back on the ground and watched it slither back into the brush. Each outing was an adventure. We never tired of exploring the terrain and discovering new inhabitants that populated our canyon.

Our routine began to change when Denise took up distance running. While the girls and I continued to find pleasure traversing the familiar foot trails, Denise preferred to strike out on her own and jog along the highway. Eventually, running became her passion and our weekend family outings became the exception rather than the rule.

▲▲▲

Craig Stereo was starting to feel the pinch of increased competition, and management was moving into a more aggressive marketing mode. Our advertising budget remained intact, but the focus had shifted to traffic-building events that produced immediate sales at the dealer level. We were able to continue with the celebrity tie-in ads that were already in the works, featuring the Beach Boys, Emerson Lake and Palmer, Dave Mason, and Ray Charles (the car stereo was installed in his airplane). Beyond that I was requested to come up with a new campaign focused more on product and less on lifestyle and image association. The soft-sell celebrity tie-in campaign had served well when product inventories were low, but competitive pressures were dictating that advertising be more directly accountable for product sales. The challenge would be finding a creative way to put a harder push on Craig's products without tarnishing its brand image.

Sam was having his own difficulties with NH&S. The agency had brought in a new creative director from New York who considered account management subordinate to the creative department. Things came to a head when we prepared to leave for London for the EL&P shoot. Sam had supported my objection to the expense of bringing an art director and copywriter with us for a format ad when the NH&S London affiliate could easily supervise the production. In doing so he crossed a line that would lead to his termination.

The trip was scheduled to be short, but due to bad weather and timing (it was the queen's silver jubilee and London was at a standstill for several days), the two-day shoot stretched out to be a week. By the time we returned to Los Angeles, the new creative director had poisoned the well regarding Sam's tenure with the agency. I had been the antagonist, but it was Sam who took the sword.

Later that summer Denise and I spent a week on Kaua'i while my folks took care of the girls. We rented a condo at Poipu Beach on the southern side of the island, spending the week playing tennis, snorkeling, and catching up on recreational reading on the beach. But our time together felt flat and without spark. Only learning of the death of Elvis from a local radio station while having lunch one afternoon seemed to stir any emotions between us.

Like a dark omen, Elvis' passing seemed to be a harbinger of things to come. After returning from Hawai'i, Denise began to cultivate a new circle of friends, mostly fellow runners. Our relationship remained functional; emotionally we were drifting apart.

Win the Car of Ringo Starr

In early autumn Bob Meyrowitz, producer of the *King Biscuit Flower Hour* radio concerts, called to inquire if Craig would be interested in sponsoring another television special. I answered that I was, of course, but doubted that management would be receptive to the idea. Besides, after Dylan, who else could fill the bill? Bob suggested that a Beatle might do, offering that Ringo was interested in doing a special and that they were meeting in Toronto the next week to discuss the project. He invited me to join them to kick around the idea just to see what came of it.

I presented the proposal to Peter, who, as expected, was not enthusiastic about sponsoring another TV special. He did, however, leave the door open to the possibility of sharing sponsorship with another advertiser if we could come up with a retail tie-in that would excite the dealers. Dick McCue accompanied me to Toronto to meet with Bob and Ringo. Over dinner, Ringo expressed his interest in doing something more like a song-and-dance musical than a live concert. The idea was intriguing, especially since it opened the possibility of working a sales promotion into the storyline. By evening's end, we all had a good feeling about how a sponsorship association might work.

A couple of weeks later, Bob Meyrowitz called to say that Ringo was enthusiastic about a musical version of the Prince and the Pauper story in which he would play himself as Ringo Starr as well as a lovable loser named Ognir Rats, who sells maps to celebrities' homes. The show would be filmed like a short movie in studio sets and on the streets of L.A. The promotional hook was that Ringo/Ognir would have a car in the story that could be equipped with a Craig stereo. I took the idea a step further. Why not have George Barris, "the King of Kustomizers," deck out an old classic for the show and then promote "Ringo's car" as the grand prize in a dealer sweepstakes. We had been providing George with stereos for his show cars for years. This project was right up his alley.

George picked up on the idea immediately and proposed using a 1957 Chevy painted black with flames adorned across the hood and decked out with lake pipes and chrome rims. Ringo, who needed a little education regarding the mythos of the '57 Chevy, accepted the "Win the Car of Ringo Starr" promotion, and Dick McCue lined up Nissan as a cosponsor. With everything in place, I took the package to Peter, who, after a quick check with the sales department, gave the project his approval.

Ringo was taped in Los Angeles in January 1978. Starr called on Keith Allison of Paul Revere and the Raiders fame to put together his all-star band assembled an A-list of guest stars including Art Carney, Angie Dickinson, Vincent Price and Carrie Fisher as his supporting cast. He even recruited fellow Fab Four alumnus George Harrison to act as on-camera narrator. My contribution to the ensemble was John Ritter, who played the part of Ringo's slick, fast-talking Hollywood agent. John and I had been friends in college when he was dating one of Denise's sorority sisters. We had been in different schools and- friends in college when he was dating one of Denise's sorority sisters.

Taking a break from the "Win the Car of Ringo Starr" sweepstakes shoot at a dreary and barren location inland from Los Angeles. The Badlands look of the landscape gave the poster its punch.

We had been in different schools and had differing interests, but the one thing we had in common was that we were both huge Beatles fans. We had lost contact since college, then reconnected some years later when John met, dated, and married Sam's daughter, Nancy. It was pure serendipity that we wound up working together with a Beatle.

On a Saturday morning in late January, I took Tiffany to the set to watch Ringo and Carrie Fisher tape a choreographed production of Ringo's hit *"You're Sixteen."* Their routine was taped in front of a seamless backdrop, later to be Rotoscoped into a montage of colors, images, and animations. The process was cutting-edge at the time, and it turned out to be one of the highlights of the show. During a break, I took Tiffany over to meet Ringo. At four and a half, she knew of Ringo only in an abstract way, more as someone with whom I was working than as an icon of a generation. Ringo was at his charming best, but Tiffany's attention was elsewhere. She was much more interested in Princess Leia.

The TV Special Sweepstakes was selected by *Advertising Age Magazine* as one of the best sales promotions of 1978.

All Things Must Pass

One evening around the time of my thirty-second birthday, Denise announced that she wanted a separation. I should have seen it coming, but as it was, I felt blindsided. After an awkward discussion about the state of our marriage we decided to table our talk to give us both time to think things over.

I eased out of a sleepless night early the next morning and left the house quietly without waking Denise or the girls. Getting the jump on the Friday morning rush-hour traffic, I detoured to Hermosa Beach to meet Dick Acker for breakfast. I needed to share my plight with a friend before facing the day at the office.

Worthless at work, I came home early and found Denise sitting on one of the patio lounges while the girls were playing in the yard. Tiffany and Melanie came running up to greet me, then rushed back to their toys that were scattered around the walkway. It was a beautiful spring day, and I was glad to be home regardless of the reason. I sat down next to Denise. Clearly not a time to talk, I was relieved to be just sitting, still absorbing the moment. My daze was broken when the phone rang. Denise got up and took the call in the kitchen. She cupped the phone saying it was one of her best friends calling from the East Coast.

As the girls chased and played on the lawn, Melanie seemed to notice something and started walking toward the eucalyptus trees at the far side of the yard. The object of her attention looked to be a stick that had fallen from one of the trees. When it moved, I raced over and caught her just as she was approaching a young rattlesnake spread out across the walkway. Denise, watching from the kitchen, dropped the phone and ran outside to steer Melanie and Tiffany into the house while I went in search of a shovel to dispose of the threatening viper.

That incident shelved further talk about separation, at least for the time being. I was confused with complicated emotions, not the least of which was guilt. What was I thinking when I pointed out a king snake as a harmless creature without mentioning that other kinds of snakes could be very dangerous. At the same time, had it not been for Denise bringing up the idea of a separation the night before, I wouldn't have been there when she went inside to take the phone call. Traumatic as my situation appeared to be, it also seemed that something akin to a guardian angel was watching over all of us while the deck was being reshuffled.

In April, I attended the company sales meeting in Scottsdale, Arizona, alone. Ringo's show aired on the closing night of the meeting, and we integrated the event into the program. After dinner, our sales representatives and their wives gathered to watch Ringo on the numerous televisions set up around the conference room. It was a rousing success, with most attendees staying on for questions and cocktails long after the show concluded. Apart from the show itself, the sweepstakes had driven more than 160,000 potential customers to Craig dealerships and garnered recognition as one of Advertising Age's best sales promotions of the year.

Our marriage essentially came to an end on a Saturday afternoon in early June when Denise packed her car and moved into a cottage in Venice. The rest of the summer was spent shuttling the girls back and forth and trying to avoid facing the inevitable. We tried a short stint with a marriage counselor, but it was too little, too late. In September divorce papers were filed, the house was put on the market, and I was suddenly adjusting to my new role as a single parent with a part-time family.

Once change starts, it sometimes snowballs. Just as our new product-focused ad campaign featuring the forthcoming gull-winged DeLorean DMC-12 sports car was breaking, I was offered and accepted a position as account supervisor at the Los Angeles office of Dentsu Advertising. The pay was great and the location on mid-Wilshire Boulevard was a welcome change from the confines of industrial Compton. Most of all, it was a fresh start.

I left Craig on a high note. Our joint promotion agreement with John DeLorean led to Craig stereos becoming standard equipment in all DMC-12s. After a personally fulfilling and professionally satisfying nine-year stint, I tendered my resignation to Peter and passed my title to Tim. Shortly thereafter, I stopped by the local Porsche dealership and treated myself to a new 911 SC Targa to start the new year with aplomb.

On the Rebound

Dentsu Advertising occupied one-half of the top floor of a thirty-two-story building on a stretch of Wilshire Boulevard known as the Miracle Mile. The 5900 Building (the Variety Building today) is located across the street from the Los Angeles County Museum of Art and a block away from the La Brea Tar Pits and the Page Museum. As one of two account supervisors, I was responsible for a couple of small industrial accounts that were mostly directed out of Japan, and a medium-size consumer electronics client that was content with a conservative approach to product advertising. My job lacked challenge and was undemanding, but it was a godsend. I needed the energy to recalibrate my personal life.

Most pressing was adjusting to a new relationship with my children. Their primary residency remained with their mother, but they stayed with me two nights a week and every other weekend. I had two lives: the active father who would fix the girls' meals, play games, and take them out to movies and activities; and the inactive father, adapting to a new life as a single. The one activity common to both worlds was hiking in the canyons and hills. Alone or with my children, there was something about being surrounded by the natural world that made life seem more authentic.

※※※

Tom Bergen's House of Irish Coffee, a Los Angeles institution since opening in 1936, was located just around the corner from my Dentsu office. More a pub than a restaurant, the place drew an eclectic crowd from throughout the city. It was a particularly favored watering hole for the advertising community.

I stopped by one evening to join a couple of my new colleagues for some after-hours beers and found myself sitting next to a striking young woman that I had recently seen in an elevator as we were being whisked up to the thirty-second floor. She gave me a quick curious glance as she exited, then hurried down the hall and darted into the RKO Radio suite. It happened in an instant, but the fiery flash of her deep brown eyes gave my heart a little jolt it hadn't felt in a very long time.

Now, with the opportunity to converse with this intriguing woman, I was tongue-tied. While I was trying to come up with a clever opening, she nudged me in the shoulder and, with a slight New York accent, asked me to pass the peanuts. The conversation that ensued led to an on-and-off relationship that would span three years. Her name was Barbara. She had come to Los Angeles on a lark after college and was starting a career in radio sales. Besides being beautiful, she was quick witted and had the exalted air of a New Yorker just biding her time in the California sun.

The house sold in late spring. My share of the proceeds enabled me to buy back our old beach townhouse from the Englishman who had purchased it as an investment. The current tenant's lease, however, ran for six months, causing me to take temporary residence in a rickety old apartment in a four-unit building on Los Flores Beach. Fate, it seemed, was knocking on the door the day I moved in.

As I was unpacking, Jim and Nancy, the couple who lived in the apartment above, stopped by to introduce themselves and invite me to the party they were hosting that evening. Jim and two of his longtime friends were in the process of making their first feature film. The party was to inaugurate the start of production. The guests were all involved with the project in some capacity, and the energy in the room was electric. I never got over the thrill of working on a set, and the party awakened in me a longing to be back in the business.

The next morning, while drinking a cup of coffee on the beach, I saw Julie, the female lead in Jim's movie, stretching by a large rock perched on the shore. She recognized me from the party and waved me over to say hello. In the kind of direct conversation that is sometimes easier with strangers, I asked her what motivated her to get into acting. She said that she never saw herself as anything other than an actor. It wasn't a matter of choice, but of answering a calling that she had known since childhood. Later that summer, I took Tiffany and Melanie to Hawai'i for the first time. I was beginning to recognize a calling of my own.

In early October, I moved back into my old townhouse. Even with new furnishings, it felt more like an old memory than a new home. At the same time, it was the comfortable, familiar, and safe place that I needed for some overdue soul searching. As part of the process, I started running regularly on the beach and resumed taking my inflatable Zodiac out for some offshore fishing.

One brisk morning, I packed and tied down my gear and braced for one last launch before the winter weather set in. I charged into the water and pulled the craft out until I was chest deep, jumped in, and power-rowed to get past the surf line before the next break. Out of danger, I pull-started the four-horsepower engine and headed upwind along the coast. I killed the engine at Carbon Beach, baited the hook with a frozen anchovy, tossed the line in the water, and began a slow drift south. I was drifting for halibut and fishing for answers.

It wasn't just the uninspiring nature of my job that had me down; I was beginning to question the whole direction of my life. I felt done with advertising. I was satisfied with what I'd accomplished but unmotivated to follow that career path any further up the corporate ladder. I envied Jim and his friends, who had just finished filming their picture. My heart was in production and I could no longer deny my yearnings. One way or another, I vowed to get back into the business.

Reeling in the empty hook, I got out the oars and power-rowed the boat home.

Feeling liberated and relieved with my resolve to take a new path, I started assessing options. I had just updated my résumé to emphasize my television and commercial production experience when I got a phone call from a college friend who was with a New York-based management consultant firm. Bill was conducting an executive search and asked if I knew of anyone who might be interested in running the western sales office for a large magazine publisher. He wasn't at liberty to mention the name of the company at the time but added that the job paid very well, included a car, a very generous expense and entertainment account, and some rather interesting perks.

I revised my résumé once again and was on first-class flight to New York a week later. Shortly after checking into the hotel, Barbara's sister, Patty, came by to take me out to New Rochelle for a Sunday-night dinner with her family. I had hosted Patty when she was visiting Barbara over the summer, and she insisted on returning the hospitality.

Over dinner, Barbara's mother was curious to know the nature of my mission but didn't press me when I replied only that I was interviewing for an executive sales position with a company headquartered in New York. After a most enjoyable home-cooked meal, we excused ourselves and headed back to the Big Apple. As we pulled up to my hotel, I finally confided that my interview the next morning was with *Penthouse Publications*. As Patty began to drive away, she blew me a parting kiss and teasingly said that I was perfect for the job, "Mr. Penthouse man."

By appearances, I had sold out. Truth was, the position was just too good to pass up. In one swift move, I jumped up the corporate ladder that I once shunned and landed in a corner-office executive suite in a prime location in Westwood Village with a salary and expense account commensurate with the trappings. It wasn't all a mercenary decision. My responsibilities also included advertising sales for Bob Guccione's other publication, *Omni*, a science-genre magazine that featured speculative fiction. I had been a science fiction aficionado since my youth. The chance to meet and converse with some of the writers who were prophesying the future was, to me, a special bonus.

The first *Omni* event that I attended was a small gathering of Silicon Valley luminaries at a very exclusive restaurant in San Francisco in early February 1980. *Omni* publisher Kathy Keaton had set up the dinner to establish a relationship with the emerging personal computer industry. The guest list included not only key executives but also the brightest visionaries of the valley. As host, I was privileged to dine at the table with those who were both.

Though it was my job to entertain, I spent most of the evening just listening to the conversations between the guests, the most memorable being a young Steve Jobs in a passionate discussion with two of his colleagues about artificial intelligence. I asked if this was possible in our lifetime. Oh, yes, they all agreed. Jobs went so far as to say that we would probably see it happen within thirty years. That moment came back to haunt me thirty-one years later, when Steve Jobs died the day after Apple introduced its first product embedded with artificial intelligence, the iPhone 4.5 with Siri.

Barbara turned a planned dinner date into a surprise birthday party. Malibu, March 1981.

New Horizons

It didn't take long to get into the rhythm and routine of my new employment. I had a competent staff of three *Penthouse Magazine* sales reps, two *Omni* reps, two secretaries, and a receptionist whom we shared with the editorial department that occupied the other half of our floor. In a very peculiar arrangement that I had nothing to do with, the sales reps and secretaries, as well as my direct bosses at *Penthouse* and *Omni*, were all women. I got along well with everyone, but I sometimes had the notion that I was merely a male figurehead in a world run by women.

By early spring, Barbara and I were seeing each other frequently enough to bring friends into the picture. On a hunch, we invited Fayla from her office and my fishing buddy Dick to meet us for an after-work get-together at Bergen's. The four of us were soon spending weekends together on camping trips and hanging out on Dick's boat, Destiny. Tiffany, Melanie, and I decided that we needed a beach dog and picked out a rambunctious Golden Retriever puppy to join our family. We named him Shooter.

On a sunny summer afternoon while the girls were playing on the beach with Shooter, I climbed into my hammock and started reading Tom Robbins' *Still Life with Woodpecker*. From the opening line, I was hooked. Forty pages later, I had an epiphany that almost knocked me out of the hammock. I saw the book as a movie, and suddenly realized that it wasn't a job that I needed to start a new career; it was just finding the vehicle to take me there. By the time I finished reading the book a week later with my daughters on the beach on Maui, I was convinced that *Still Life with Woodpecker* could be a milestone film, and I wanted to make it happen.

While the girls played in the gentle shallows with the local keiki (kids), I savored the last few pages until the story simply ran out of words. Everything about the story, the characters, the locations, the attitude, and especially the philosophical musings of Robbins, resonated with my life. Since our arrival we had dined at the Blue Max restaurant and listened to some rowdy good music in the Pioneer Inn bar. Days earlier, I had read of both venues in the story. In a peculiar way my life seemed to be intersecting with a fictional storyline.

With the clarity gained from a week on Maui with my daughters, I returned to Malibu refreshed and determined to find the ways and means to make a movie. Tiffany and Melanie came home with an accomplishment of their own as well: While playing with their newfound friends at Napili Bay, they had learned how to swim.

The traditional route to acquiring film rights is to approach the agent who represents the author. I didn't think this would work in my case. Lacking the credentials to impress his agent, and sensing that Mr. Robbins would be more concerned about the treatment of his work than the status of the producer, I figured my best shot would be to meet him directly, preferably in an informal setting. As Tom Robbins lived in the Seattle area and I had client friend who was well connected in the Pacific Northwest creative community, I started my search with a sales call in Seattle.

Steve Smith was the owner of a small but sharp ad agency that had a consumer electronics client who was a steady advertiser in *Penthouse*. We had been friends since meeting at a summer Consumer Electronics Show in Chicago and finding that we were both big fans of Jimmy Buffett's music and lifestyle. I filled him in on my ambition and asked if he had any connections to Tom Robbins. Having recently read *Still Life with Woodpecker* himself, Steve thought it would be a great movie, but he didn't know of any direct sources to reach Robbins. Later, over dinner, Steve told me that he would put the word out, assuring me that he would come up with something.

The next big upheaval also started with a call from a friend. This time it was Scott, a Malibu real estate agent I had known since he was a sales representative with Craig. Scott was representing a client who was interested in buying one of the townhouses in my complex and wanted to know if I'd consider selling mine. He added that his client was a wealthy widow willing to pay top dollar to be near her sister, who had just purchased one of the other units. To tweak my interest, Scott told me of a very attractive little two-story house on Las Tunas Beach that had just come on the market at a price lower than what I would get for the townhouse. The idea of moving to my own beach house, located closer to town and with some money in my pocket, was more than appealing. I met Scott at the property later that afternoon. The place felt like home the moment I stepped inside the door. Scott put both deals together the next day, and I moved into my new quarters three months later.

I wanted the inaugural weekend in our new home to be especially fun for the girls. The small fenced yard that opened onto the beach looked like the perfect place to find buried treasure. I found a couple of small wooden jewelry boxes at a local import store and filled them with old coins from my childhood collection, then topped them off with add-a-pearl starter bracelets. Barbara came over Friday night to be part of the inauguration. After dinner and table games, I gave Tiffany and Melanie each a hammock, which we strung low to the floor across their new bedroom. I kissed them goodnight and told them to pretend that they were sleeping under the stars on a tropical island.

Barbara and I retreated to the moonlit downstairs deck and leisurely sipped a bottle of champagne. Later, after the girls had fallen asleep, we quietly sneaked out to the yard and buried the boxes. We drew a map that marked the location of the treasures, burned a border around the edges, and smudged up the rest of the map with the ashes. We rolled up the map, inserted it into the depleted and labelless champagne bottle, and sealed it with a cork. The next morning after breakfast, Barbara suggested that we take a walk on the beach. As she escorted Shooter and the girls to the back stairway, I held back and rushed to the closet, grabbed the bottle, and flung it into the surf before they reached the beach. By the time I caught up with them, the bottle was just washing ashore. Excitedly, we fished out the map and followed it to our yard. After a couple of misses, the treasures were uncovered and, to the amazement of all, we had apparently moved into a house once visited by pirates.

In late spring, I got a call from Steve Smith. He had found a contact at the *Seattle Times* who was in regular communication with Tom Robbins. Steve was told to have me write a letter outlining what I had in mind and how I planned to make it happen, and he would forward it to Tom. I addressed the letter to Steve as a friend asking a favor of a friend. As the words formed on paper, the vision took shape. In a three-page synopsis, I poured out my accumulated thoughts of what the film should and should not be. I made comparisons to landmark films and emphasized that I wanted it to be a film version of the story rather than just an adaptation of the story to film. The film had to be true to the outlaw ethos of Robbins' unconventional love story and cinematically express the wit and wisdom of Tom's masterful interplay of words.

Steve called back a couple of weeks later to say that Tom had read the letter and wanted to talk. Tom invited us to come up and meet at his home in a small town north of Seattle. As we were getting off the phone, Steve chided me not to get a big head, as he thought it might have been the Penthouse letterhead, more than my letter, that got Robbins' attention.

I flew up to Seattle on a Friday toward the end of July and met Steve and some of his friends for dinner at a restaurant near Lake Washington. The place was a hangout for trendy young professionals, and Steve seemed to know everyone in the room. Word of our forthcoming meeting with Robbins had proceeded us, and a small group of film buffs had gathered for a lighthearted discussion. Sharing ideas about who to cast, who to direct and so forth, made for an enjoyable evening and a perfect benediction for the road ahead.

After a late breakfast at a nearby coffee shop, Steve and I headed north up Highway 5 and arrived at Robbins' home in early afternoon. Tom met us at the door and gave us a quick tour of his eclectically furnished home before settling down for business. Tom speaks like he writes, slowly and methodically. After some embarrassing early interruptions, I curbed my enthusiastic outbursts and started listening to the man who would, over the next few years, have a profound influence on my life. We talked and exchanged ideas for the rest of the afternoon. Tom wrapped up our discussion by giving me the contact information for his agent in Los Angeles. Then, as Steve and I got up to leave, Tom bestowed upon each of us a *Still Life with Woodpecker* promotional T-shirt as if to cinch the deal.

Pot of Gold

I was still in a euphoric daze when I boarded the flight back to Los Angeles. Proudly wearing my Woodpecker T-shirt under my open jacket, I puffed up like a peacock when the welcoming flight attendant gave me a knowing smile and said how much she loved the book.

I welcomed the two-hour flight as a chance to put my thoughts together. Although I still had to work out details with Tom's agent, Phoebe, in Los Angeles, the option deal was essentially done. The next big step was finding seed money to pay for a screen play and start-up costs. Due to the timely and fortuitous consequence of my recent real estate transaction, I had enough money in the bank to pay for the option and initial legal fees. Beyond that, I would have to find an investor. With that daunting thought, I closed my eyes and drifted off to sleep.

A couple of weeks later, I was back at the airport, this time with my daughters. We were returning to the Islands for what was becoming our annual visit. Only this time, after our week on Maui the girls were going to the Big Island to spend a few days with their mother. Arriving at the airport in Kahului, we picked up a rental car and drove straight to our favorite spot on Napili Bay.

Although I was there to relax and enjoy time with my family, the matter of raising seed money was weighing heavy on me. It takes a special kind of backer to invest a couple hundred thousand dollars in a picture without even seeing a script. Motion pictures are a high-risk investment under any circumstances, and those willing to speculate on a film upfront expect a high return if the film makes it into production. The payback often includes a significant percentage of ownership of the picture. *Still Life with Woodpecker* was an unconventional story about unconventional characters told in an unconventional way. Why not unconventional financing as well? I couldn't quite put my finger on it, but I knew there had to be a way.

The answer came to me in a dream. On our last night on Maui, we went to Lahaina for a shopping spree at the tacky souvenir, trinket, and T-shirt shops that line Front Street and topped off the evening cooking our own dinner in the Pioneer Inn courtyard restaurant. Back at our condo, we packed our bags and turned in early since our flight to Kona was first thing in the morning. Just before dawn, I had a vivid dream. In it, I was prospecting for gold in a desert landscape that looked like the cover of *Still Life with Woodpecker*.

This was, in dream terms, understandable. The cover art for the novel was a stylized rendering of a woodpecker carrying a stick of dynamite against the background of a Camel cigarette pack. The Camel pack becomes an integral part of the storyline in a delightfully concocted way. As noted on the cover jacket, *Still Life with Woodpecker* is a sort of love story that takes place inside a pack of Camel cigarettes." In my dream, the connection couldn't have been more obvious (at least to an ad guy). The pot of gold was to be found at R.J. Reynolds Tobacco Company, the manufacturer of Camel cigarettes. It would be to their benefit if the film was made; seemingly they would be willing to put up some money to help get it started. It appeared to be so obvious, all I needed to do was knock on the door. Waking from my prescient dream, I rousted the girls for breakfast, then headed for the airport.

Finding the right door to knock on was more difficult than I had anticipated. I went through a labyrinth of departments at RJR before finally speaking to someone in their copyright legal division who was attentive to my pitch. The contact was noncommittal, offering only that he would forward the information to the Camel brand product manager and get back to me. I was beginning to understand that a big part of producing a film is learning how to hurry up and wait.

In the meantime, I had given a copy of the book to my former neighbor, the filmmaker Jim Abrahams, and asked for any advice that he had to offer. His picture *Airplane!* had been a huge success, and he and his partners were being lauded as the next big thing in the business. We met at the Baja Cantina in Malibu, and over margaritas and nachos, he gave me his short and concise critique that I had a gem on my hands and to treat it like one. I asked if he would be interested in directing the film. He declined, citing obligations to his own projects. He did, however, offer to participate in an advisory way.

Next came the lawyer. Close friend Dave Levene, a rising star at a prominent Los Angeles-based law firm, steered me to a young lawyer who had recently joined his firm's entertainment division. Jeff, my new attorney, set me up as a California corporation and took over negotiations for the option agreement with Phoebe and a respected theatrical agent whom she brought in to give more clout to the project. I was finding not only that the business of filmmaking lay in the hands of the agents and lawyers, but also that the success of the venture very often depended on the reputation of those representing the package.

Just after Labor Day, I got a call from my contact at R.J. Reynolds saying the Camel product group was interested in my proposal and asked me to submit a personal résumé complete with professional references, the name of my lawyer, accountant, and anyone else associated with the project. After receiving the material, a meeting was set for a Monday morning in early October to coincide with a *Penthouse-Omni s*ales conference that I would be attending the prior week in New York.

The conference concluded late Friday. I stayed over at Patty's apartment and flew down to Winston-Salem the next morning. North Carolina's southern charm was a pleasant diversion while I mentally prepared for the meeting. On my way to breakfast Monday morning, I picked up a newspaper with a front-page headline about some kind of incident in the Middle East. The accompanying photograph was of a jet fighter on an airfield with the Great Pyramid of Giza prominently looming in the background. With so much synchronicity already taking place around the project, I took the photo of the Camel pack pyramid as a good omen and confidently headed off to my appointment at RJR.

The meeting focused more on my capability to make the film than on product exposure in the movie. Due to legal restrictions and public perceptions, they wanted nothing to do with the making of the film and had decided to participate only if they believed that the film would be made even without their involvement. By their reasoning, they were more interested in protecting against any negative product exposure than promoting product usage in the storyline. In short, they offered to buy the right to review the script and omit any mention or use of their product they deemed unfavorable. I had approached them with a promotional opportunity; instead, they bought an insurance policy. That worked.

Endings and Beginnings

A couple of days after returning from North Carolina, I met Barbara for lunch at Bergen's. We had been spending less time together as I had become preoccupied with the film project, and Barbara had some pursuits of her own. Nonetheless, it was an upbeat and happy lunch. She congratulated me on raising the money and lifted her beer to toast the success. I accepted the toast but cautioned that the devil lay in the details, which still had to be negotiated. While walking back to our building, I challenged her to a small wager on the forthcoming World Series between the New York Yankees and the Los Angeles Dodgers: Loser buys dinner, winner chooses the place. She slapped my hand, "You're on, sucker."

There is a maxim in filmmaking that a picture can be no better than the screenplay. The next challenge was to find a screenwriter up to the task of adapting a Tom Robbins story to film. My hope was that Tom would do his own cinematic treatment of the book, but he didn't have the time or initial interest. His agent, Phoebe, who had earlier tried to make a movie of Tom's second novel, *Even Cowgirls Get the Blues,* offered some suggestions, but no one seemed quite right. Over the next few weeks, I spent my after-hours and weekends watching so many movies and reading so many reviews that I felt more like a film critic than a producer.

Bronco Billy, a rather quirky Clint Eastwood film, caught my attention as it had a lighthearted touch that made the offbeat picture quite charming. I looked up the screenwriter and found that he had also penned another endearing film oddity, *Wanda Nevada,* with Peter Fonda and Brooke Shields. Tom was coming down for a visit that weekend, so I picked up videos of both films to watch with him while he was in town.

Jim Abrahams came by on Saturday to meet Tom and share his thoughts about making the film. Jim made suggestions about which parts of the book he thought should be left out of the picture and about how to structure the cinematic storyline, while Tom offered insights into the characters and some of the metaphorical underpinnings embedded in the story. Little by little a vision of the film was forming.

That evening after previewing the videos, Tom had little to say one way or another. Responsibility for selecting the screenwriter would have to be mine alone.

Tiffany, Melanie, and I stopped by the Colony Coffee Shop for breakfast one morning and sat in a booth next to Kris Kristofferson and his daughter, Casey. The girls were all friends, and Kris and I knew each other as fellow single fathers who frequented the same ballet classes, horseback riding lessons, and school events. I gave Kris a copy of *Still Life with Woodpecker* (I always carried at least one), saying that as a songwriter he might enjoy Tom's lyrical play with words. I also noted that I had optioned the film rights and, as an actor, he might be interested in the lead. He took the book and said he'd give it a read.

The Dodgers won the 1981 World Series, and Barbara took me to dinner at La Scala in Malibu on a cold Saturday night in early November. Barbara had a flair for dramatic moments and announced over dinner that she was returning to New York City in early December. She had always been up-front about L.A. being only a temporary situation, and I was truly happy for her, yet I couldn't help but feel a sudden sense of loss. To lighten the mood, she suggested that we have a parting fling on Maui over Thanksgiving.

I saw Barbara one more time after Maui. We dined again at Bergen's on the day before her departure. She was leaving by train and neither of us wanted a cheesy farewell at the station. After lunch, we took a walk around the neighborhood where we had met and worked and said our goodbyes over a long, lingering kiss in Bergen's parking lot.

⁂

A few days later, Jeff called to say the deal had been completed and to come by the office to sign the papers. I left home early the next morning, planning to stop by Century City to sign the contract, then to the office to hand in my resignation. On the way, I pulled into Gladstone's on the Pacific Coast Highway for breakfast. The hostess, an effervescent young woman with a mischievous smile, escorted me to a booth, then reappeared a short time later to comment that she liked my hat. Leaving Gladstone's well fed and flattered, I forged on to face the big day ahead.

My resignation was accepted, though I agreed to stay on through the Las Vegas Consumer Electronics Show in early January, in exchange for taking the week off between Christmas and New Year. Returning home that evening, I received a message from the answering service saying that Kris had called to say that he finished the book and was looking forward to talking about It. The events of the day would affect changes in my life that I could not then imagine.

⁂

Working the last CES as an employee was more like a party than a job. When not staffing the suites or escorting models to clients' booths for autograph sessions, I made the rounds signing off with friends and acquaintances that I knew from years in the consumer electronics industry. On the last evening, Tim Hendrick, Dick Acker, and I enjoyed dinner together, after which I took my friends upstairs for a cocktail in the *Penthouse-Omni* hospitality suite. As we were about to leave, Jackie, one of the models that I had worked with at previous events, asked if she could join us as we made the rounds. She was off duty and wanted to play.

I awoke alone in my suite to find a note on the table next to the bed thanking me for a fun evening and wishing me luck with my "woodpecker." Chuckling at Jackie's amusing choice of words, I showered and went downstairs to check out. My advertising career behind me, I caught a cab to the airport and headed for home.

Part Two
Letting Go

"We must be willing to get rid of the life we've planned, so as to have the life that is waiting for us. The old skin has to be shed before the new one can come."

—Joseph Campbell

The Smith Brothers

On the day after Christmas 1981, Steve Smith, the screenwriter Dennis Hackin, and I rendezvoused on Maui, picked up the last available rental car on the island (or so we were told by Tom of Tom's Car Rentals), and headed straight to the Pioneer Inn. The PI, as it is known to locals, has been a fixture on the Lahaina waterfront since its inception in 1902. Though much smaller than its stately cousins, the Stanley and Belleview Biltmore Hotels, the old wooden structure was born in the same era and still holds the allure of that time. It also happens to play a prominent role in the *Still Life with Woodpecker* storyline. The reason for the visit was to familiarize Dennis with Maui and the places that figure into the story. It was also a kind of payback to Steve for his help setting up the meeting with Tom Robbins.

The plan was to spend a few days scouting around Maui, then return to the Mainland before year's end. Instead, we kept extending our stay and ended up greeting the new year in Lahaina. On our first night in town, we stopped by the Blue Max for dinner. While Steve signed in on the waiting list at the reservations desk, Dennis and I staked out an empty table in the lounge.

Steve had no sooner caught up with us in the lounge when a hostess appeared to announce that the table for the Smith brothers was ready. We glanced at each other for a quick moment and recognized that we all had the same impulse. Smith brothers? Why not? we thought, as she led us to our table.

We fell into a quick and easy routine. By day, we drove around the island visiting beaches and taking in local attractions. By night, the Smith brothers took to town. Steve and I did our best to blend in with our simple attire of shorts, flip-flops, and vintage aloha shirts. Dennis was another story. Too slick-looking to be a local and too hip-looking to be a tourist, he had the look of someone who surely must be up to something. The ever-present toothbrush that protruded from his shirt pocket like a vacancy sign and his John Lennon–like wire-rim tinted glasses only added *to* the mystery. The oddity of our appearance and joviality of our collective persona seemed to attract attention wherever we went. By New Year's Eve, we had made enough new friends and acquaintances to host a party at the Pioneer Inn.

🌲🌲🌲

We had a welcome surprise when Kris Kristofferson, who was vacationing with his family at the Hotel Hāna Maui graciously agreed to meet with us to go over his take on the Woodpecker. The next morning, we boarded a small eight-seat aircraft at the old Kāʻanapali airport and headed off to Hāna. Recalling my honeymoon vow to never again drive the notorious road to Hāna, I was relieved that I was returning to Hāna by air. Kris met us at the tiny airport and whisked us away to join his family at Hāmoa Beach.

Unexpectedly, Kris took a detour on the way to the beach and drove us up a barely paved road to the top of Lyons Hill. There, with a panoramic view of the tiny hamlet fronting Hāna Bay, is anchored a massive stone block cross. The cross, erected in 1960 to honor Paul Fagan, the founder of Hāna Ranch and the Hotel Hāna Maui, stands strong and silent as if protecting the peaceful village below. The vista is breathtaking. Even without knowledge of Hāna's rich and relevant past, I sensed a timelessness about the place and was humbled just being there. In a very peculiar way, I also felt a sense of belonging.

Hāmoa Beach, noted by James Michener as one of the most beautiful beaches in the Pacific, is located about two miles south of Hāna town. It was a bright and sunny day in the midst of the holiday season, and the renowned beach was well populated by a diverse mixture of visitors and locals alike. We followed Kris to his family's encampment on the southern side of the cove. After being introduced to his ʻohāna, we took up positions in the sand and got down to business. Our session was so easygoing it was hard to think of it as a business meeting.

Kris and Dennis agreed on most things about the character, and we concluded the overall discussion about the book in less than an hour. With time to spare before our late-afternoon flight back to Kāʻanapali, Kris had thoughtfully arranged for his longtime friend Jim Meeker to give us a tour of Hāna.

Texas native and part-time Hāna resident, Jim Meeker was most generous with his time and seemed to delight in escorting us through his magical kingdom. After inviting us into his home near Hāna School for refreshments, Jim drove us south through Hāna town to Kīpahulu. Throughout the excursion he shared stories of the area's cultural history with reverence and admiration. At Oheʻo Gulch we paused to savor the roaring waterfalls cascading into stepped pools and gushing out to the sea. The sensual impact was so stunning I felt giddy, like I was drowning in beauty. On the way back to town we stopped to look at a house on an expansive bluff above the sea that Jim was considering buying. The place was exquisite. The view extended out across the ʻAlenuihāhā Channel with the triple volcanic peaks of the Big Island looming in the distance. The house had been built by a retired sea captain and reflected the meticulous attention to detail one would find on a well-crafted ship. As we piled back into the car, Steve asked Jim what he planned to do with two houses in Hāna. Jim replied that one house would be for friends when they came to visit.

The Hāna airport is just a landing strip with an open-air lobby about the size of a small cottage. Jim pulled up to the check-in counter just as our plane was taxiing up to the gate. As we gathered our belongings and exited the car, we tried to thank Jim for his hospitality, but he just brushed our words aside and insisted that the pleasure had been his. Sporting a Texas-size grin, Jim reminded me that I had a place to stay anytime I wanted to come back for a visit. Bidding us aloha, he got into his car drove away.

Shortly after returning from Hāna, the Smith brothers acquired a sister. Mystica was a New Zealand native, a resident of New York City, and on her way home from a long trek across India. We met her in the PI lobby as we were checking for messages at the front desk. When learning that she was traveling alone, we suggested that she join us for dinner and our nightly tour of the Front Street bars and night spots. She accepted the dinner invitation but implied that she had other plans for later that evening. Her after-dinner intention, we soon found out, was to visit the local Buddhist graveyard under the nearly moonless night sky. She asked if we would be interested in accompanying her. Dennis' trepidation notwithstanding, the Smith brothers accepted her invitation.

The four of us quietly walked up Front Street toward Māla Wharf. The cemetery was located on a side road behind a Buddhist temple not far from the shore. The night was overcast, and the flickering illumination from the nearby rooftop "Jesus Coming Soon" sign (famously mentioned in the Eagles' song "*The Last Resort*") cast a surreal pall over the grounds. Mystica gathered us in a circle and, in a whispered voice, instructed us to breathe deeply, clear our minds of any negative thoughts, and be of the moment. She took my hand and beckoned us to follow her into the yard. Steve gave Dennis, by now pale enough to haunt the place himself, a reassuring nudge, and the four of us took a momentary leave from the land of the living.

On the first morning of the new year, we met in the Pioneer Inn's streetside restaurant. Some of the other hotel guests, including Mystica and a Tom Waits-like character named Jack Thomas Fly, had already found a table for our departure breakfast. Dennis, his toothbrush conspicuously missing from his shirt pocket, was accompanied by his date from the party the night before. Steve, not quite ready to throw in the party towel, ordered a round of Bloody Marys to start things off. After the meal, Mystica clanged her coffee cup with a spoon and offered an invocation that we all find love and good fortune in the year ahead.

Followed by a round of hugs and kisses, we said our goodbyes and went our own ways.

Tom was still at the desk when we returned the rental car. I was a bit startled when he asked with a wink how the Smith brothers enjoyed Maui. Apparently, our exploits had been a topic of conversation on the island's coconut telegraph.

⁂

The holiday week in Maui was a life-changing experience for all of us, but only Steve was aware of it at the time. The midnight walk through the graveyard had awakened him to the realization that he was spending precious time tied to a desk when he could be out sailing. He was returning to Seattle to wind down his advertising business and find a new career more compatible with his passions. Dennis began a long-distance romance that led to marriage, and I had returned to Hāna and heard the future calling.

Smith brothers Steve Smith and Dennis Hackin with Tom Robbins. Seattle, December 1981.

E J Productions

The *Woodpecker* odyssey began in earnest when I, along with Margot, my assistant from *Penthouse*, opened a storefront office in a fashionable building on the corner of Hill and Main Streets in Santa Monica. We set up shop in mid-January shortly after I contracted Dennis to write the screenplay. On Friday, a sign painter stenciled our logo on the window, and *E J Productions* officially opened for business. A small reception for friends, associates, and neighbors followed later that evening.

It wasn't the most financially prudent thing to do. I could have operated out my house and contracted secretarial services as needed, but the ease of obtaining the film rights and start-up money had given me a false sense of confidence that the film would swiftly move into production. Financial misgivings aside, it was a very cool office, and the location was prime. Numerous restaurants and shops were within walking distance, and the commute from Malibu was an easy drive along the coast. Learning that Tom's agent, Phoebe Larmore, lived just two blocks up Hill Street and worked out of an office a few blocks down on Main Street was a startling coincidence indeed, but I was getting used to the fiction-like reality that seemed to surround the project. Phoebe, with her prior experience pitching another Tom Robbins novel to the film industry, became a ready adviser and confidante.

🌲🌲🌲

One night in early February, I stopped by the Baja Cantina to attend a friend's birthday party. I hadn't planned to stay long but became so mesmerized by the cocktail waitress, who kept restocking our table with beers and shots of tequila, that I was among the last to leave. Her name was Paula. She was quick to flirt but in a playful way. She said she was living with someone but seemed to enjoy my attention. Her contradictory ways were both alluring and confounding. Driving home, I sensed that I'd seen her before; I just couldn't make the connection.

Dennis delivered his screenplay later that month and, by most accounts, it fell short. In fairness, the script captured the storyline and had its moments, but it lacked the soul of the novel. The missing ingredient was Tom Robbins, and Mr. Robbins was not happy. He asked me to meet him in Seattle that weekend. Knowing it was going to be a difficult day, I brought Margot along for moral support.

Tom and Phoebe were seated at a table near the back of the Virginia Inn, a Seattle mainstay since opening in 1903. It was mid-Sunday afternoon and the place had only a scattering of patrons. Margot and I pulled up chairs, and I braced for the lecture that was certain to follow. Not to disappoint, Professor Robbins rose as we sat down and let loose with the kind of virtuoso tongue lashing that only a pissed-off poet could deliver. The critique stung, but Tom concluded that the only way to save the project was to write the screenplay himself. It was a costly route to have taken, but the early misstep led to Tom doing what I had hoped he would from the beginning. Much as I'd like to think it was a shrewd move on my part, it was just another strange twist of fate that was clearly beyond my doing.

Margot and I landed in L.A. early the next afternoon and drove out to Malibu to pick up her car and stopped by the Baja Cantina for a late lunch. The dining room had closed, so we took seats at the bar. To my surprise Paula suddenly appeared with menus and a welcoming smile. After greeting me and meeting Margot, she inquired about what brought us in at such an odd time of day. I explained that we had just gotten back from a Seattle meeting with the author Tom Robbins and asked if she happened to have read his book, *Still Life with Woodpecker*. She hadn't, so I handed her a copy, told her that we were making it into a movie, and that I'd be interested in her take on the story. She said she'd get right to it after finishing the Alan Watts book she was currently reading. Apparently, we had a shared interest in esoteric philosophy.

In mid-March, while Tom was at work on the new script, I decided to take Jim Meeker up on his kind offer and returned to Hāna for a few days of R&R. The night before leaving, I stopped by the Baja hoping to see Paula. She was working but busy. She said that she was thoroughly enjoying the book and suggested that I stop by some afternoon when she would be more at liberty to have a conversation. When learning that I was heading to Maui for a short visit, she took out a pen and scribbled her address on a piece of paper. Handing it to me with an impish grin, she asked me to send her a postcard.

🌲🌲🌲

It was late afternoon when I landed in Hāna. Jim picked me up and drove to the Hotel Hāna Maui. His house in town was being worked on, and he had a lady friend staying with him at his new home outside of town, so he decided to put me up in a suite at the hotel. As he dropped me off, he suggested that I relax and freshen up, and he and Liz would meet me in the dining room around seven. What a surprise! Back then, the hotel was small, and the staff was known for treating guests like family. The lobby and lounge were open-air, and the one-story guest bungalows were discreetly placed in small clusters throughout the lush and extensive grounds. After a shower and short nap, I wandered through the meticulously tended gardens.

Over dinner, Jim announced that he had some work to do in the morning, but he had scheduled a horseback ride for the next afternoon. I welcomed the free morning with nothing to do beyond getting out of bed. After breakfast, I visited the hotel gift shop and picked up a couple of postcards. While selecting the cards, I noticed a small paperback Hawaiian dictionary and was struck with a thought. I bought the cards and book and went back to my room. After writing conventional cards to Margot and my daughters, I got out the Hawaiian-language dictionary and composed a note to Paula. Even without translation, vowel-heavy Hawaiian words seem to ooze sensuality. I figured that she would get the message.

Jim and Liz brought a local friend to join us on our horseback ride. Leona was pure Hawaiian and had never been off the island. I was the novice in the group and lagged behind as the trio galloped ahead, Leona's long black hair trailing in the wind like a silken cape. It was like being in another world, a simpler world, as we rode through the pastures and along the bluff that fronted the sea. A few days later, my generous host took Liz and me over to Lahaina for some deep-sea fishing. We didn't catch any fish, but spending the day at sea in sight of five magnificent islands rising out of the deep, dark Pacific Ocean was reward of its own.

My sojourn ended the next day when Jim and Liz dropped me off at the airport as they returned to Hāna. The visit may have been short, but the experience was causing me to again question what I was doing with my life. Whereas my focus had been on finding direction and place, I was now having reservations about the very purpose of life. What I had seen and felt those few days on Maui seemed to have no real connection with what I would face when returning to the Mainland. Other than my daughters, the rest of my life felt inauthentic. I was still passionate about making the movie, but I was beginning to have serious doubts about the fundamental values governing the socioeconomic environment that I was living and working within.

I pulled into my garage late that evening and picked up the mail on my way into the house. On top of the stack of bills and junk mail was a note from Denise wishing me a belated happy birthday and reminding me that she would be dropping off the girls early the next morning. I didn't need the reminder. The weekend had been on my mind throughout the flight home. We were going to make a surprise visit to see great-grandma Dodo. There is no more beautiful way to experience the renewal of spring than by witnessing a floral bloom in the desert.

Essential Insanities

I stopped by the cantina a few days after returning from my travels and once again found Paula on duty. She was amused by the card though quizzical about the message. I quipped that it had something to do with a Hawaiian princess. With little time to talk, Paula said she had loved the book and confided that she was moving out of her "situation," offering that perhaps we talk about it sometime apart from work. I took the lead and suggested we talk about it over dinner, proposing at we take an early-evening excursion up Malibu Canyon to an out-of-the-way dinner joint favored by connoisseurs with a taste for adventure. She was game.

Located on Mulholland Highway near Malibu Lake, the Old Place was a no-frills bare-bones restaurant in a weathered old building said to have once been a pony express station. It was owned and operated by a couple. Barbara ran the bar and served the meals, and Tom cooked the steaks and steamed the clams over his signature Oakwood fire in the back kitchen. I'd been a patron for some years—the appeal was its authenticity. It didn't try to create an atmosphere; it just was.

My Porsche days behind me, I picked up Paula in my newly acquired Jeep Scrambler, a sort of hybrid Jeep–pickup truck. Even off-duty Paula seemed to be in perpetual motion. Her hands, constantly aflutter punctuating her playful chatter, made it hard to keep my attention on the road. We parked the Scrambler off the dirt driveway adjacent to a hitching post for horses. Walking up the stairs, we opened the screen door and stepped into a time warp.

With only four booths, a couple of tables, a twenty-foot-long bar occupying most of one wall, and a well-worn piano in a corner near the doorway, the place had the air about it of an old saloon. Barbara greeted us with a couple of beers as we took seats at the empty bar. I introduced Paula and asked how things had been. Barbara, a stout woman who kept order in the place, sarcastically remarked that there hadn't been any recent fights or brawls if that was what I was asking about. She added that Cowboy was coming by that evening and asked if I wanted to stake him a dinner. I told her I would with pleasure and directed Paula to a booth where we could accommodate my old friend.

Tom Pruitt, aka Cowboy, was an old codger who had lived near Malibu Lake since childhood. He claimed he was in his mid-sixties, but he looked older. His past was sketchy. He made occasional references about working for Hughes, but it was unclear if he meant the eccentric billionaire or his company. When I met him, he was selling handmade neckties out of a battered old briefcase. A woman named Pearl made the ties, but Tom liked to say he built them. He would case thrift shops and yard sales in search of distinguished patterns and prints. He was especially fond of frogs. I not only bought Tom's ties, I wore them to work in my waning days in advertising.

Cowboy, dressed in his usual rumpled Salvation Army–issue business suit and well-worn boots, tipped his signature rattlesnake-skin-banded hat at Paula when he sat down at the table. He asked me how I was and, with a twinkle in his eye, inquired if I had any magazines for him. I had to explain that I no longer worked for *Penthouse* and, no, Paula was not a model. Paula flashed me an inquisitive "Is that something I should know about?" look as Tom opened up his satchel and laid out his inventory of ties on the table. He pulled out his flashlight and started the presentation with his standard pitch, "I don't build cemetery ties." He then picked up each tie and told a brief story about it. Paula was drawn to a bright floral print that looked like it was made from an old aloha shirt. I slipped it out of its cellophane wrapper, draped it around her neck, tied a loose half-Windsor, and proclaimed it a perfect choice for a Hawaiian princess.

After our dinner of steaks and clams, Cowboy suggested that we go dancing at a honky-tonk just over the hill in Calabasas. I went to the bar to pay our tab as Cowboy led Paula around the back to use the restrooms. Barbara gave me a thumbs-up sign as I left the money on the counter.

The three of us piled into the Jeep, Paula and Cowboy sharing the lone passenger seat, and headed out into the night. We arrived at the crowded roadhouse just as the band was taking a break. Cowboy was in his element; he was treated like a celebrity the minute he walked into the room. While a small circle of admirers formed around Tom, Paula and I slipped onto the dance floor and gently swayed to Jimmy Buffett crooning on the house jukebox about stars falling on Alabama. We were cheek to cheek and kissing by the time the song ended and decided to take our leave before the band returned to break the mood. Waving goodbye to Cowboy, who would have no problem finding a ride home, we left the joint and drove home to Malibu.

I made pancakes for Paula the next morning. We enjoyed them with coffee and juice on the deck and mulled over the day ahead of us. Paula had arranged to move in with some friends later that day. Her new location was crowded, but it would have to do until she could find something more suitable. I told her that I had space and that she could stay here at least on a temporary basis. Looking out to the crashing surf on the beach below, she answered that she guessed she could, for the time being anyway.

Paula had barely moved in when we took a day trip to Santa Barbara. It gave us a chance to talk and learn more about each other outside the home in which we were suddenly cohabiting. On the way, we stopped at Kelly's Coffee Shop in Oxnard for a midmorning snack. Over coffee, Paula shared her story. She had driven out to California in September with her college boyfriend. They had intended it to be a short road trip, but neither was eager to return to an East Coast winter. They had both found jobs and decided to stay on for a while, even though their relationship was fading. She said that she had started work at Gladstone's as a breakfast hostess but had moved on to cocktail waitressing at the Baja Cantina so she could take some morning classes at Santa Monica City College. That's when it hit me. I asked if she could have been the hostess who seated me for breakfast one morning, then came back to my table to say she liked my hat. She answered that it could have been her—if I was the guy who drove up in a silver Porsche.

The impromptu coastal drive became an unexpected shopping spree. After picking up a pair of decorative kites in a specialty store on Santa Barbara's State Street promenade, we moved on to an antique store located in an old house in a residential area a few blocks away. My big find was an old buggy seat with attached mounting springs. I borrowed a carpenter's tape from the shopkeeper and measured the bed in the back of the Jeep. Finding that the seat would fit, I negotiated a price with the proprietor and went in search of Paula to tell of my score.

I found her on the second floor in a fit of laughter. She was pointing to a carved Woody Woodpecker on a brass pole that had once graced a merry-go-round. How could I resist? The cartoonish artifact would be a perfect adornment for the office. The last oddity that we picked up was a decorative artificial parrot in a small hanging birdcage. Paula thought "Polly" would be a splendid accessory to have dangling in the cab of the Jeep.

"So what's with the name *E I Productions*?" Paula inquired as we were driving back to Malibu. I asked her if she recalled Tom writing about the distinction between inessential insanities, which are rooted in ambition, aggression, and anxiety, and essential insanities, which are instinctive impulses that ring true in the heart even if others think they are crazy. She said she did but didn't see the point. I elaborated, saying that many would think quitting a successful advertising career to pursue making a movie about an idealistic redheaded princess who wanted to save the world and a renegade redheaded bomber who liked blowing things up, to be insane. I added that, to me, the decision was essential. I could tell by her stifled laugh that she was impressed.

The next morning, I bolted the rear-facing buggy seat in the Jeep's bed while Paula perched Polly the mascot near the passenger-side sun visor. That afternoon I drove into town where Rich, a graphic designer I had worked with in advertising, stenciled the *E I Productions* logo on the midnight-blue Scrambler's doors, branding the vehicle as the official *E I Productions'* company car and public persona of the spirit behind the name.

A week later I picked up my kids and brought them home to meet Paula. I had told them of our new housemate over pizza earlier in the week while Paula was working her shift. Paula prepared for the introduction by livening up their bedroom with the lightweight nylon kites that we had found on our day trip to Santa Barbara. We placed the kites at the high point of the vaulted bedroom ceiling and crisscrossed and looped their long multicolored tails across the room. One kite featured the face of a purple unicorn and the other was adorned with a bright rainbow. Matched with the various hues of the hammocks below, the room became a playfully inviting enclave full of color and whimsy.

Tiffany, Melanie, and Paula took to each other from the beginning, forming a relationship where Paula became more like a wise older sister or special auntie than a substitute mother. On our first morning together, the girls helped Paula make sandwiches before setting out for a hike into the hills. We had just gotten home when a sudden squall set in. Paula roused the girls to don their bathing suits and follow her to the beach before the showers passed. Sensing what was coming, I went to the deck and turned on the hot tub. In an instant, the three of them bolted onto the beach, holding hands and dancing in circles under the falling rain until tumbling into the wet sand. Paula led the brigade into the still chilly surf for a quick rinse, then raced back up the stairs to the awaiting tub. I joined the them in their warmup soak but felt like an intruder. They had already formed an alliance of their own.

A short time later, Paula quit her job at the Baja Cantina and became full-time housemate and cheerleader in chief for *E I Productions*. Paula's frequent visits to the office provided levity, comfort, and encouragement during the long wait for Tom to craft his screenplay. At home, she made my day every day. As our first date stretched into months, we eased into a groove as smooth and soulful as an Al Green love song.

Flanked by Paula and Melanie, proudly displaying yellowtail I caught while fishing in Zodiac with first mate Shooter. Malibu, Spring 1982.

The Waiting Game

In late May, Phoebe delivered Tom Robbins' screenplay over breakfast at Cora's Coffee Shop near the Santa Monica Pier. Phoebe said little, but her manner assured me that Tom had hit the mark and we had a workable script. I hurried to the office and unbound the manuscript so Margot and I could read it together. We finished just in time for lunch and scurried across the street to claim a table at Merlin's, a popular restaurant/bar known for its eloquent stained-glass windows depicting the great magicians of lore. Sharing our initial thoughts over lunch, we concurred that Tom's screenplay captured the essence of his book with nuance and style. Most important, the screenplay was written through the same magical lens from which the novel was crafted.

Getting a workable screenplay was only the first step in a long, arduous process. Finding a director who could relate to Robbins' offbeat material was no easy matter. Phoebe, Tom, and I discussed numerous prospects, but protocol dictates that a screenplay be submitted to only one director at a time. Every submission of the script to a director became an investment of time, and time was money. Even after careful scrutiny of our preferred candidates, it took almost a year to find a director with the credentials, availability, and willingness to make the film. By that time, my working capital was barely working.

🜲🜲🜲

A fringe benefit of having a storefront office is that the door is always open to the unexpected. Perhaps that is what kept me coming in to the office each morning even when little else was happening. Some drop-ins like Rebecca, the networking actress, and Fred, the pataphysician, had been referred by Tom. Others, like an old baldheaded Turk named Constantine, just wandered in off the street. Each visitor seemed to have a purpose or reason for stopping by. Rebecca and Fred were both players in an emerging circle of New Age aficionados and were themselves Tom Robbins–like characters.

Constantine was something else entirely. He walked in one afternoon, and we ended up talking for hours. When he spoke of his past, a good part of which was apparently spent in a Greek prison, he harbored no bitterness or anger. Instead, he was cheerful and kind with a modest sense of self-assurance. By the time he left, Margot and I had committed to helping him procure food for the homeless shelter up the street. Margot collected donations from neighboring merchants, and we presented the proceeds to Constantine the next time he stopped by the office. He smiled broadly and thanked us profoundly but humbly offered that he had no means of picking up the food.

I met Constantine in front of his residence at the Santa Monica YMCA before dawn the next morning. He directed us to the wholesale produce market in downtown Los Angeles. He knew his way around the place, and in less than an hour the Scrambler was loaded to the limit with fifty-pound bags of rice and beans topped off with boxes of fresh fruits and vegetables. This became a monthly routine for some time until Constantine inexplicably vanished. When I later became familiar with the tradition, I recognized Constantine as being similar in style to a Sufi who anonymously appears, does his work, then quietly disappears. Regardless of who he was, he was a crafty old character who deftly transmuted our abundant idle time into productive service to others.

At the end of June, I brought my ʻohāna to Hāna. Jim generously offered us his house in town, which made us feel more like guests of the community than tourists. The house, located on the Hāna Highway, was distinguished by a mature plumeria tree in the front yard. Each morning Paula and the girls gathered the delicate blossoms that had fallen onto the lawn during the night and strung them into lei using long needles and fishing line from the Hasegawa General Store. My flower-clad ladies and I spent our days at Hāmoa Beach and our evenings simply hanging out together in our lovely Hāna home.

Jim hosted us along with Leona, her husband, Lawrence, and their two small children with a July 4 barbecue at his house outside of town. America's Independence Day is largely a non-event for many Hawaiians, but Lawrence brought along pyrotechnics from his New Year's Eve stash for Tiffany and Melanie to enjoy. None of us were eager to leave the next morning, but we had reserved a suite in Lahaina, and Paula had yet to see the rest of the island.

We stopped for lunch at Hats, a local-style coffee shop in Pā'ia. After our meal, we wandered into the adjacent antique store. I was immediately drawn to a small framed picture of a figure sitting at the foot of a bridge that arched over a body of water. Across the bridge loomed a beautiful wooden palace. There was a golden aura to the work that, on closer inspection, was light reflecting off the tiny pieces of straw-like material from which the picture was intricately constructed. The proprietor knew little about the piece, but speculated that it was from the Philippines. It was inexpensive, mysterious, and small enough to fit in my carry-on bag. I decided to buy it and take it home.

While paying for the picture, I asked the shopkeeper about the Hawaiian artifacts in the display case next to the cash register. She seemed pleased by my interest and took them out of the case for my inspection. The items included a couple of fish hooks, a stone poi pounder, and a flat-edged disk-shaped stone that was used in gaming. I expressed admiration for the pieces, saying that I felt connected to another time just by looking at them. She then handed me a small stone bowl and told me to put it in the palm of my hand. The bowl, she said, was used by a kahuna to grind herbs. It had been recently found on the ocean floor along with a few other items, likely the result of a canoe accident. Kahuna, she added, were powerful spiritual practitioners, adept at everything from the healing arts to counseling high chiefs. The bowl did, indeed, feel old and even wise, like it held a history of its own. Sensing that it belonged to someone else, I handed it back to the woman and thanked her for sharing the bowl and the story. Years later I would meet the rightful owner.

The fortuitous stop in the antique shop was just the beginning of a very unusual day. We unloaded our belongings at the Lahaina Shores Resort on the southernmost end of town, then drove up to Napili Bay for a swim and some snorkeling. Paula took to the aquatic pastime like a mermaid to water, though I think it was the colors more than the creatures that held her fascination. Later we returned to our hotel to prepare for dinner and a show not soon to be forgotten.

I had made a reservation at the Lahaina Broiler specifically for the oceanfront table at the southern end of the open-air patio. It was the best spot in the place to watch the moon rise. On this particular night a rare supermoon lunar eclipse was poised to begin at sunset. Seated at our table, from cocktails through dessert, we witnessed the spectacle of the rising blood-red moon reflected on the ocean like a river of fire being slowly devoured by Earth's shadow. By the time we left the restaurant, the moon had been consumed, leaving only a ring of fire to light our way home.

The day before our scheduled departure I read a newspaper article about a tribute dinner for Charlie Fern, aviation pioneer, newspaper publisher, and founder of the Barefoot Football League on Kaua'i. For reasons unknown I felt compelled to go to the dinner and decided to stay on a couple of days to attend the event. The next morning we parted at the airport, with Paula and the girls heading back to Los Angeles while I caught a flight to Kaua'i. I welcomed the time alone in Kaua'i and the chance to digest the events and discoveries of the past few days. The banquet on Saturday night was the grand finale to a remarkable week.

One morning during the midsummer doldrums, I got a call from a director that we were especially interested in, to say that he was passing on the project. Being a redhead himself, he was fascinated with the material and had read the book as well as the script. However, he was at a critical point in his career, and taking on a project such as ours was just too much of a risk. I understood and greatly appreciated his consideration and encouragement, but it was yet another in a growing string of disappointments. As I got off the phone, Margot handed me a card that had just arrived in the mail. It was from Paula, another of her thoughtful postings of inspiration and support. It not only made me smile when I needed a lift, but it also reminded me of the gentle ease with which Paula had become such a big part of my life. I took a walk down Main Street and came back with a bouquet of flowers. I told Margot that I was leaving for the day. I had business to tend to at home.

Weathering the Storm

In early November, Margot and I met Rebecca for coffee at the Rose Café, a popular gathering spot for the local creative community, just a short walk from the office. Rebecca brought with her a young producer she knew from a loose association of media professionals who were working to bring a higher consciousness to television and film production. Shawn was a Tom Robbins fan and considered it quite a coup for me to get the film rights option for *Still Life with Woodpecker*. At the time, he was scouting for a network television executive who was looking for high-quality material for TV movies. He asked me if I had any ideas. I didn't have a project to pitch but I did have a story to consider.

I told him about Charlie Fern starting the Barefoot Football League on the island of Kauaʻi in the 1930s. In autumn, weekly games were played in fields and schoolyards around the island. Players, predominately Asian plantation workers, could weigh no more than 135 pounds and wore only sweatshirts, cutoff jeans, and sailor hats pulled down over their ears for protection. The league lasted until about the time of statehood in 1959 and at its peak was so popular that a featured game was carried live each week on Charlie's radio station. US Senator Spark Matsunaga played in the league as a youth and was the featured speaker at the banquet honoring Mr. Fern. I summarized that the story was about how camaraderie and character held the league together for more than two decades, even during the adverse military-imposed restrictions in World War II.

Shawn liked the concept and asked if I could come up with a treatment to present to his associate. I told him I would collaborate on a treatment, but I wasn't interested in taking on the project on my own. He was agreeable to that, and we decided to start with a quick research trip to Hawaiʻi to visit Mr. Fern and interview some of the former players.

We met on the Monday before Thanksgiving at the Honolulu airport. Shawn had just arrived from Los Angeles, and I had flown in from Hāna, where I had spent the previous couple of days. We went directly to our scheduled meeting with Charlie Fern at his residence in a downtown assisted-living retirement home. Charlie was just as gracious and full of wit and charm as he was the night he was honored for his lifetime contributions to the modern history of the Islands. He shared stories, starting with his arrival on Oʻahu in 1919 as an aviation veteran of World War I. Charlie was vague on exactly when the league began. He said that plantation-sponsored teams were playing games on a casual basis since the late 1920s, but it took almost a decade for a league to form. He was less evasive when I asked if it was true that part of his motivation to develop the league was to have something to cover as the sportswriter for *The Garden Island*. "Well, it did make good copy," he replied with a wry smile. He gave us some names of people to look up on Kauaʻi, some with phone numbers, most without. "Don't worry, Kauaʻi is a small island. When word gets out that you want to make a movie, the people still around will find you."

A slight misty rain was falling when we arrived on Kauaʻi later that evening. We picked up a rental car and drove north a few miles up the eastern coast to the Kauaʻi Beach Resort. We had a full day ahead of us, so we grabbed a quick meal and retired to our rooms early. I awoke before sunrise and was back in the dining room just as daylight was breaking. A strong breeze had come up during the night, and there was a strange feeling in the near-empty room. Shawn joined me a short time later. He anxiously asked if I'd heard about the hurricane that was expected to hit Kauaʻi later that afternoon. I hadn't and was dismayed that it could just appear so quickly without warning (it was attributed to a down weather satellite and an abnormally warm El Niño condition). He felt we should abandon our plans and head for the airport right away. We finished our breakfast in a hurry and returned to our rooms to pack. I turned on the TV and learned that

Hurricane Iwa was coming from the south and was tracking north up the corridor between Oʻahu and Kauaʻi. I paused to assess the situation.

The storm was expected to parallel the coast and, since the hotel was inland some distance from the shore, a storm surge didn't appear to be a danger. The hotel was built of concrete and my room was on the second floor of the three-story building. If need be, I could brace the bed against the sliding glass door. I called Paula to let her know that a hurricane was approaching, and I had decided to ride out the storm rather than trying to catch an early flight home. I added that Iwa was expected to pass during the night, and I would meet her and the girls in San Francisco the next evening as planned. Paula, rather than worry, found the whole thing exciting and asked that I call in with regular updates. I met Shawn in the lobby and told him I'd take him to the airport, but I had decided to stay. He looked at me like I had lost my mind when I said I thought the adventure might even be fun.

The Lihue airport was so congested with cars and people that I had to drop Shawn off about a block away from the lobby. Outside the airport, residents were busy taping and boarding up their windows and tying down their belongings against the ever-increasing winds. Back at the hotel, I stopped by the gift shop and picked up a cheap transistor radio, a flashlight, and some batteries and went to my room to catch up on the news. Heavy winds and surging surf were already battering the southern coast of Oʻahu, and the hurricane was expected to hit the island full force by late afternoon. Kauaʻi could expect the same about an hour later. I called Paula with an update, then took a walk out to the beach while I still could. The wind had gone from gusting to a strong, steady blow, and the surf was running sideways, whitecaps cresting and breaking but never reaching shore. The roaring and rattling through the coconut palms sounded a warning, like that of a serpent ready to strike. I got the message and headed back to the hotel.

Later that afternoon I decided to go to the bar for a drink and hang out with some of my fellow grounded guests. Passing through the lobby, I was surprised to see Shawn back at the registration desk. He looked upset and disheveled. He had waited in line for more than an hour to change his reservation, and then the airport had closed down before his midafternoon flight could get off the ground. Trying to make the best of the situation, I suggested we meet in the bar for a cocktail or two during happy hour. I don't think he got the joke, but he agreed to meet me there after checking back into his room. In the meantime, I returned to mine to file another dispatch to Paula. She was giggling when she answered, saying that with coverage of the hurricane being all over the news, she thought it very cool to have her own personal reporter on the scene. I was charmed but told her that branches were already flying off trees and I didn't expect the phone lines to last much longer. Realizing that this would likely be the last chance to talk, we exchanged some sweet talk and vowed to meet on the morrow in San Francisco.

Shawn and I had no sooner sat down at a table in the lounge when a plate-glass window across the room blew out. A security guard appeared and directed everyone to a windowless banquet room on the other side of the lobby. The hotel staff was setting up a dinner buffet, and it would be the safest place to weather the storm. I told Shawn I'd meet him there, then dashed back to my room to get the radio. I turned it on and found only one Kaua'i station still on the air. The reporter was saying that all lines were down, they had lost contact with Honolulu, and the eye of the storm was heading directly toward Kaua'i. The realization that I was isolated on an island under siege by a hurricane and completely disconnected from the world was chilling; even more, it was exhilarating.

The open-air lobby was a mess. Water was everywhere; chairs and tables were sliding around like they were on rollers. I stayed tight to the wall, trying to reach the entrance to the banquet room without being hit by debris or drenched by the rain. I heard a loud explosion just as I reached the door and turned to watch the huge A-frame skylight lift off the roof and tumble to the lobby floor. I felt no fear, only a hypnotic fascination as the event seemed to unfold in slow motion. Fortunately, no one was hurt, so I entered the room and found that I was right back where the adventure began. It was the very same room where the Charlie Fern tribute banquet had been held.

The storm weakened around nine o'clock that evening. I paid my tab for dinner and was heading back to my room when I heard music coming from a dark corner of the lobby. I approached the area and saw a small group of women sitting around a table harmonizing with songs blaring from a portable cassette player. One of them saw me and waved me over to the table. I sat down and accepted a beer that another pulled out of a large cooler. Shawn suddenly appeared and pulled up a chair to join the party. They paused the music long enough for a round of introductions. All were entertainers-one woman was a fire dancer, another was her apprentice and younger sister. The other three women were men, all members of a *mahu* (transgender) singing group. The music started back up, and we ran out the evening singing along with our newfound friends to *The Carpenters' Greatest Hits*.

The sky was clear the next morning as we departed for the airport. Without functional stoplights or law enforcement, the drive was an anarchist's delight. Nevertheless, traffic flowed smoothly with everyone seemingly tuned in to a collective mind, a practice I would later find commonplace in places like Manila and Bali. Unlike my colleague, who had to wait in a long line to rebook his canceled reservation, I boarded my flight as scheduled, made the connection in Honolulu, and arrived in San Francisco in time for Thanksgiving. The lasting memory of the day was taxiing out to the runway amid the clutter of overturned small aircraft and the cartoonish sight of a blown-out wind sock. All the while the Carpenters' tune "*Top of the World*" was playing over and over in my mind like a broken record.

Progress

Tom Robbins had become a frequent house guest ever since his first visit, when I was still working for *Penthouse*. One weekend in April 1983, Tom had come to town to attend a dinner party with Timothy Leary, so we invited Phoebe to join us for an informal dinner meeting at home the night before. Paula's simple but scrumptious meal and the soothing beachside atmosphere set the tone for a relaxing discussion about progress on the film. We were all somewhat mystified that we were still without a director, yet everyone remained confident that it would be just a matter of time before the pieces fell into place.

Over dessert, Phoebe brought up the name of a director that we had not previously considered. Graeme Clifford was just beginning his directorial career, having come up the ranks from being a highly regarded film editor and assistant director. His stylish and well-crafted directorial debut, *Frances*, had garnered two Academy Award nominations. Phoebe's sources said that he would be interested in reading the screenplay. Tom and I agreed that Clifford sounded promising and recommended that he be sent the script.

A few weeks later Fred stopped by the office to further enlighten me about pataphysics. On his previous visit he told how his association with Tom began when he noted pataphysical inferences in *Still Life with Woodpecker*. Fred followed up his hunch by sending Tom a pataphysically encoded postcard, which led to a lunch between fellow pataphysicians. This visit Fred filled me in about the term *pataphysics*, coined in the late nineteenth century by the French writer Alfred Jarry to denote a branch of philosophical science that accounts for a world beyond metaphysics. He described pataphysics as, among other things, the science of imaginary solutions. As if to clarify, Fred noted that pataphysics was best comprehended when not taken too seriously. Before leaving, he handed me a copy of the May-June 1960 issue of the *Evergreen Review* titled *What Is Pataphysics?* and suggested that I read the issue cover to cover, but in no particular order. He added that the rare magazine was only a loan and he would stop by to pick it up the next time he was in L.A.

In late June, Tom returned to Malibu to meet with Graeme. He was interested in doing the film, but he had another project in his native Australia tentatively scheduled for production in early 1985. We had a window of about six months to put something together. Graeme had some concerns with the script but felt they could be resolved in a second draft. He also offered a different take on casting the leads. Although he thought Kris would be ideal as the Woodpecker, Graeme felt the chemistry between the romantic leads was so important that the parts should be cast in tandem rather than individually. He suggested Malcolm McDowell and Mary Steenburgen, who were then married and happened to be friends of his. They also happened to have been Tom's example of ideal actors for the parts while we were kicking around ideas with Jim Abrahams at the very beginning of the project. We also addressed the sticky subject of financing. Graeme felt that the material would be a difficult sell to studio executives. He suggested that we should try to secure at least some partial independent financing to make the package more attractive. I was already in need of additional development funds, so it made sense to think big and go for production funding as well. Where to start was the question.

A short time later, I put pataphysical thinking to the test. I was reading an article about the recent US Festival, a musical extravaganza on the scale of Woodstock but better planned and organized, when an idea started to form. The three-day concert, featuring many of the top musical acts of the time, also served as a showcase for the emerging technology that would soon change the world. The person with the vision and means to create the inspired event was Apple Computer cofounder Steve Wozniak. The part of the story that triggered my "imaginary solution" was that Wozniak sponsored the festivals (the first had taken place the previous September) more as a labor of love than as an investment for financial gain. I didn't know much about computers, but a man who prioritized his passions over his pocketbook was a man after my own heart. I picked up the phone and placed a call to Apple.

The receptionist put the call through to Steve, who answered directly. I introduced myself, briefed him about the project and suggested that a venture into filmmaking seemed to be the next logical step after his US Festival experience. I added that as a metaphorical outlaw himself, I thought he would relate to the story. He was interested enough to let me send him a copy of the book, saying that he would read it and get back to me.

A couple of weeks later, I flew up to San Jose, picked up a rental car, and drove over to Apple headquarters in Cupertino. There, I was escorted to the office of Apple's principal engineer, Steve Wozniak. I knew Steve had to be highly intelligent. What I didn't expect was his sense of humor and almost childlike curiosity. He had read the book and found it much to his liking. We discussed how he might become involved, but only sparingly. Steve still had to read the script and discuss the idea with one of his financial advisers. As I gave Steve a copy of the screenplay, he brought up what might be a potential red flag. He said his wife was not happy with the financial outcome from the US Festival and felt he should confine his investments to enterprises within his area of expertise. Otherwise, he was interested in moving ahead and would give me a call after he explored the situation a bit further.

The follow-up call wasn't from Steve, but from his financial manager requesting some personal information and permission to conduct a background check. He also asked if I had any objections to Steve hiring another producer to evaluate the material and offer him advice about if and how he might participate. I provided the information and told him I was fine with both the background check and the third-party assessment.

Several meetings and phone conversations later, all the players gathered at the US Festival office near the San Jose airport. The meeting concluded with Steve agreeing to put up some development funding and attach his name to the project to help secure studio financing. I flew back to L.A. in a state of bliss. Paula picked me up at the airport, and we headed to Willie Tiffany's, a classy dive bar near my office, to meet Phoebe and celebrate. Unfortunately, our revelry was short-lived. I had barely recovered from the tequila hangover when Steve's business manager called to say that the deal was off. Steve's wife had become very upset upon learning about the venture and Steve didn't want to cause a rift by continuing with the project. I spoke directly with Steve a short time later and asked if there was any way we could get his wife to reconsider. He answered that he didn't think so but to let him know if anything came up that might help change her mind. Progress: One step forward, two steps back.

Wedding Kazoos

Paula and I were married at sunset on the beach the Saturday after Thanksgiving, 1983. The wedding was a spontaneous conclusion to an engagement that had started more than a year earlier. On the day I learned that a director with whom we had high hopes was passing on directing *Woodpecker*, I decided to leave the office early. The constant waiting and depending on others to move the project forward was wearing. I needed some time at home to remind myself that I had another life.

Paula and a mutual friend were just finishing lunch when I entered the house. Kathy, suspecting I must be home early for a reason, helped Paula clean up and excused herself, leaving the two of us alone. I wanted to talk and suggested to Paula that we take a hike up nearby Las Tunas Canyon. We took some provisions and hiked up to a place off the trail where large stones formed a natural amphitheater. We sat down on a grassy spot in front of the massive rocks and settled into a heart-to-heart discussion. My memory is fuzzy about exactly how it came up or what words were said, but by the time dusk set in, we were walking back home, arm in arm, engaged to be married.

We had planned to take the girls and elope to Hāna, but the timing and finances were never right. What finally gave us the nudge to nuptials was a three-day party we attended at the end of October. The event, known as the Mad Scientists and Artists Party, was the brainchild of Marilyn Ferguson, the author of *The Aquarian Conspiracy*. Her book, published in 1980, and companion newsletter, *The Brain/Mind Bulletin*, had become the field guide in New Age and human potential circles and had established her as one of the pillars in the field. Rebecca had taken us to a Saturday-afternoon gathering at Ms. Ferguson's hilltop home a couple of weeks earlier. We had so much fun romping around on her trampoline and playfully engaging with her other guests that Marilyn invited us to the big party. Neither of us had the notoriety or credentials of most on the guest list, but she thought we would bring "good energy" to the wingding.

Conveniently, the party was held at a large estate not far from my parents' home. On Friday evening, Paula and I picked up Tom (who had made the guest list on merit as well as personality) and his fiancée at their hotel in Burlingame and drove up to the gated manor in Hillsborough. There we joined the one hundred and twenty other guests for a briefing on the purpose, format, and rules of the "game." The general purpose of the affair was to mix right-brain artistic types with left-brain scientists and academics just to see what might come of it. Sessions on topics ranging from science and consciousness, to alternative forms of intelligence, to the relationship between psychotropic drugs and creativity were scheduled throughout the weekend. The real party, however, took place during the mingling time between the meetings. The ground rules encouraged eavesdropping and jumping into any discussion that caught our attention. To make matters more interesting, we were given name tags but told to initially identify ourselves only by using three nonverbal symbols. The only symbol I remember using was the circular spiral loosely identified with pataphysics. At least Fred and Tom would get the connection.

The Saturday sessions concluded late in the afternoon and about half of the guests returned to their hotels. The rest of us stayed on to participate in an informal experiment conducted by the pharmaceutical alchemist Alexander Shulgin. "Sasha" was credited with rediscovering the compound MDMA that had been originally synthesized but discarded by Merck in 1912. The drug, more commonly known as Ecstasy, was being embraced by a semi-underground network of approximately four thousand psychologists, who were finding it to be a valuable tool in therapeutic work with their individual patients. Sasha and his wife, Ann, were taking the research further by studying our group's dynamics while under the influence of MDMA. The Shulgins handed out the tiny white capsules and cups of water to the remaining volunteers like priests offering bread and wine at communion. A half hour later, our group formed a circle in the garden and were led in a chant to the beat of a drum as the drug took effect.

Zonked in the most pleasant way, Paula and I wandered around with perpetual smiles, nodding at our fellow psychonauts with a knowing recognition of our common state of euphoria. Inside the main meeting room, we came across a small group of guests in quiet conversation with Rebecca, who was hunched over like an old man, apparently channeling the recently deceased Buckminster Fuller. Vocalizing in a raspy pitch quite different from her normal sweet voice (she was, after all, an actress) Rebecca/Bucky singled us out and asked what we were doing to make the world a better place. Paula caught on to the game more quickly than I did and replied that we were just doing our best to spread a whole lot of love. That seemed to please everyone, and as we moved on, Rebecca/Bucky predicted that a wedding would be forthcoming. Wondering out loud where that came from, I heard Paula whisper to just go with it as she took hold of my arm and led us back to the garden.

The following Saturday, still basking in the love-fest afterglow, Paula and I decided to go ahead with our postponed plan to get married. I told her it was time to put our money where our mouths were and just do it. Paula muttered that she didn't care about the money as she tenderly put her mouth on mine and sealed the deal with a kiss that lasted 'til lunchtime.

Less than two weeks later Paula's mother, father, maid of honor sister, and both brothers shuffled in from Buffalo and took up residence in the beach house with Paula. I moved into a guest room in Jim and Nancy Abrahams' house up the hill on Big Rock, almost directly above the rickety old apartment building we all had lived in only a few years back. Jim and Nancy had married earlier in the year and, despite his enormous success with *Airplane!*, Jim was without formal wear in his wardrobe. We were close in size, and he had married Nancy dressed in a dark three-piece suit out of my closet. The Abrahams generously returned the favor by letting me bunk in their home in preparation for my own wedding.

Though the wedding was not taking place in Hāna as originally planned, we wanted to keep it Hawaiian in spirit. The night before the wedding, we took a chance and called United Airlines in Honolulu with a very unusual request. We asked if there was any way we could get one of the flight attendants to pick up a pair of lei at the airport and carry them over to Los Angeles on the red-eye flight that evening. The sympathetic ticket agent put us through to the employee lounge where we reached the head flight attendant. After hearing our story, she offered to bring us the lei purely on the trust that we would meet her at the gate upon her arrival at six a.m. the next morning.

Paula and I left before dawn and drove to the airport to pick up the lei. After the last of the passengers departed, the flight attendant appeared with a bag containing two traditional maile lei. Her willingness to do something special for two total strangers was a heartfelt beginning to our wedding day. We stopped for breakfast at a coffee shop in Santa Monica and wrote our wedding vows together. We had arranged for minister Rob—ordained in some sort of ancient order and fellow attendee of the Mad Scientists and Artists Party—to officiate the service, but the script was to be our own.

With no time to send out invitations, we just put the word out to our eclectic circle of friends. Some, like Sam, Tim, and Dick, I'd known for years; others, like Paula's fellow teachers at Carden Preschool (where she now taught art), were new acquaintances. Add to this Cowboy (courtesy of Margot and her boyfriend, who provided transportation), my parents, Etta, Paula's family, and a few spectators who just happened to be taking a late-day stroll on the beach, and voilà! We had a wedding party that looked like it had been cast for a Woody Allen movie.

As the group convened on the beach, Tiffany and Melanie handed out ribbon-wrapped kazoos. At the appropriate moment, after best man Dave Levene, Rob, and I had taken our positions on the sand, the all-inclusive kazoo band struck up a rousing rendition of *The Wedding March*, heralding the appearance of the barefoot bride. Escorted by her father, adorned in the wedding dress once worn by her mother, and draped in a green maile lei, Paula was radiant. At the conclusion of the ceremony, we gave our lei to Tiffany and Melanie, who in turn passed them on to Paula's sister, Diane, and best man Dave. By the end of the evening, the two lei had been circulated and worn by all the guests before being returned to us in time to cut the strawberry shortcake wedding cake.

Later that night, after all but very close friends and family had departed, Paula and I picked up our prepacked overnight bags and prepared to take our leave. We were heading north a few miles up the road to our wedding-night suite at the Malibu Beach Hotel. Normally, this would mean driving south on the Pacific Coast Highway, then turning around at Las Tunas Canyon. Instead, since there was no apparent traffic coming in either direction, I pulled away from the curb in front of the house and made a U-turn on the highway. Bad call. Just as I was in the midst of the turn, a sports car came speeding around the curve from the north. Had it not been for the adept maneuvering of the driver, we would have been broadsided with unthinkable consequences.

We had come face to face with our mortality. Our wedding night at the hotel became a transcendental experience, as if we had both been given another chance in life. We held each other tight through the night like there was no tomorrow.

Barefoot bride and giddy groom draped in maile lei. Malibu, November 1983.

Cowboy in one of his finest Pearl ties flirting with guest Anita with Melanie photobombing picture. Malibu, November 1983.

Honeymoon in Buffalo

Paula and I were met with a blizzard when we arrived in Buffalo for our honeymoon. Her parents and sister greeted us at the gate, then whisked us away to the family house for a low-key, late-day Christmas celebration. The big event was scheduled for the next day, when the family would be hosting a second wedding reception. Paula's mother was Lebanese and had a sizable number of relatives living in the area. The clan had gathered and was already preparing food for the feast when we arrived at the house. I was handed a basement-chilled Molson, offered platters of unusual and tasty Middle Eastern food, and warmly welcomed by my newly extended family.

A couple of days after the second reception, Paula's family suggested we spend the night in her grandfather's cabin in the Allegheny Mountains. It should have been an easy drive of a few hours, but we made a wrong turn somewhere along the way. It was one of those "This doesn't seem right but let's go on a bit further" situations. Eventually, we found ourselves on a narrow road in the middle of a vast plain of snow. The cloud cover was so low and thick, we had even lost our sense of direction. Just as we were about to turn around and backtrack, Paula noticed smoke puffing out of the chimney of a tiny speck of a house farther up the road. We turned onto the driveway and followed the rutted trail up the hill to the house. As we were getting out of the car, an elderly couple who looked like Mr. and Mrs. Claus in civilian clothing came out on their porch to meet us.

We told them that we didn't want to impose, but we were lost and in need of directions. They chuckled like it happened all the time and invited us inside for some refreshments. The kind folks insisted that we warm ourselves by the fire as they prepared cups of hot chocolate and a large plate of cookies. After we partook of the snacks, and discovering that we were not as far off course as we thought, we found it difficult to leave. Our hosts were apparently without nearby kin and seemed to relish having company, especially newlyweds. Finally, after eating the second plate of Mrs. Claus' special holiday cookies (most of which Paula had discreetly stashed in my jacket pocket), we were able to politely take our leave and reach the cabin before dark. We talked about the incident later that night while snuggling in our sleeping bags in front of a roaring fire. By Paula's logic, we were never lost, just taken on a detour that brought a little holiday cheer to some lonely people. I suggested that maybe it was us who were meant to meet them and learn the secrets of a long and happy marriage. Either way, it had been an extraordinary day.

The Party

The new year brought new vitality to the *Woodpecker* project. Graeme called in early January to say that he had met with Malcolm and Mary over the holidays and they were both interested in playing the leads. He added, however, that they still had some questions and recommended that we take a drive up to their home in Ojai and talk things over. A few days later, we arrived midmorning for a brief get-acquainted meeting while their small children were sleeping. Afterwards, Malcolm, Graeme, and I slipped away for further discussions over lunch at a café near the town square. Malcolm, no stranger to offbeat films, was concerned about financing and distribution. Having been party to enough good projects gone bad, he was wary of even the most promising independent productions. I brought up Steve Wozniak as someone with the interest and means to assure financing but pointed out that his involvement in the project had already been vetoed by his wife. Nevertheless, Malcolm encouraged me to give it another try.

I called Steve to give him an update. He was impressed that we had an Academy Award–winning actress and her cult-status actor-husband lined up for the leads but was uncertain whether it would change his wife's mind. I asked if meeting them might help. He said it was worth a try and to let him know if I could set something up. I next called Phoebe and brought her up to date. We agreed it was time to bring Tom back to town to meet Malcolm and Mary and to start thinking of ways to introduce the Wozniaks to the McDowells without it being an awkward situation.

A short while later Sam Morgan called to tell me that he had just spoken to his nephew, Michael Fitzgerald, about my involvement in *Woodpecker* and suggested that I give him a call. Michael and his brother had written a screenplay adaptation of Flannery O'Connor's novel *Wise Blood* and had managed to make it into a successful independent production directed by John Huston. They had done it on a shoestring budget, and Sam thought Michael could give me some useful advice.

Michael was more than helpful. He shared his story, which was even more serendipitous than mine. After writing the screenplay, he got ahold of John Huston's phone number and called him at his home in Puerto Vallarta. The film legend happened to be a Flannery O'Connor fan and told Michael that if he could round up three million dollars, he'd do the film. With Huston directing and a budget all but guaranteeing a profit, Michael had no problem securing the financing. I asked how he had been able to make a quality film on a B-movie budget. His answer was Tom "Tommy" Shaw, the best production manager in the business. He gave me Tommy's number and told me that if I could get him on board, the film would come in on time and within budget.

I called Shaw and made an appointment to meet with him at his home in the San Fernando Valley. I was told that he had been John Huston's right-hand man for years, but I was surprised to see how much he resembled the master. With white hair and beard and piercing blue eyes, he looked like a smaller and slightly less weathered version of Huston. Tommy was friendly in a gruff sort of way and got right down to business. I gave him a copy of the script and told him that, as an independent production, we needed to keep the budget to a minimum. He pointed out that by shooting on location in Maui and Seattle, we were already looking at a significant bump in production costs. He said that he would look at the script and prepare a tentative below-the-line budget and boards. Below-the-line costs are the fixed production costs to make the film, and boards outline the daily filming schedule. Above-the-line costs include variable fees for actors, the director, screenwriters, and producers.

Graeme was pleased to learn that Tommy was available and already working on a budget. On his end, Graeme had been talking with his agent, Lou Pitt of ICM, about packaging the film. Conveniently,

Pitt also represented Malcolm and Mary. Graeme recommended that I meet with Pitt and offered to set up an appointment.

The stars finally seemed to be aligning in our favor. Though tenuous, we had the makings of a package that just might see the light of production. I had lunch with Phoebe before my meeting with Lou Pitt and we worked out a strategy to tie everything together. Tom was coming down to meet with Malcolm and Mary on the second Saturday in February, so we decided to up the ante by inviting everyone to meet at a dinner party that evening at the beach house.

Mr. Pitt told me that after reading the script and discussing the project with Graeme, he had made some preliminary inquiries within the industry. His initial research was not promising. He had found more resistance to, than interest in, doing a film based on a Tom Robbins novel. He said the word on the street was that Tom's colorful use of language and narrative style made for great reading but wouldn't translate well to film. Nonetheless, he respected the judgment of his clients and said he would do what he could to package and sell the film, adding that he would represent me as well if we got something going. I told him about the party, which he thought was a great idea, pointing out that bringing Steve Wozniak to the table, even just as an initial backer, was my best shot at getting a production deal going.

The next day, I called Steve to invite him to the party. The event was only a couple of weeks away, yet his busy social calendar happened to be open that evening. He said he would still have to check with his wife, but they would likely attend. Fortunately, the date worked equally well for everyone else. The party was on.

🌲🌲🌲

On Saturday morning, a week before the party, I picked up a couple more copies of *Still Life with Woodpecker* at the local bookstore in Malibu. Marilyn was having a get-together at her home that evening and hinted that a couple of guests might be potential investors for the film. On the counter, next to the cash register, I noticed a peculiar red book with the cover design of an eye in a pyramid. Curious, I picked it up and thumbed through *The Illuminatus Trilogy* but quickly put it back when I found the volume exceeded eight hundred pages. Another time, I thought; I already had a stack of half-read books on my nightstand.

On the way to Marilyn's house, we stopped by the office and picked up the copy of *The Evergreen Review* to return to Fred, who would also be attending the gathering. Upon opening the door, I noticed a business card that had apparently been dropped through the mail slot. It was Fred's card with a cryptic one-word message, "Fnords," written on the back. I put the card in my shirt pocket, gathered the magazine, and went back to the car. Driving off, I asked Paula if she knew anything about Fnords. "Never been there," she said.

By now we had come to expect the unexpected when attending Ferguson functions. That evening was no exception. The usual assortment of staff, family, and friends this time included a boozy scientist from NASA with photos that he claimed showed a pyramid-size face on the surface of Mars, and an Argentine inventor of a device that recorded three-dimensional sound. It was an interesting mix, but the much-touted investors were nowhere to be found.

We had just about given up on Fred and were planning an exit strategy when the pataphysician suddenly appeared. I mentioned my surprise in finding his card on my office floor, especially since I had stopped by specifically to pick up the magazine he had lent to me. When I asked the meaning of *Fnords*, Fred gave me a dreary look. "You mean you haven't read Robert Anton Wilson's *The Illuminatus Trilogy?*" I meekly answered no but told him I had had a copy in my hands that very morning. Fred seemed amused but not surprised at the coincidence. As I handed the rarefied text back to my esoteric tutor, he implored me to read Wilson's conspiracy-riddled trilogy as a follow-up to my introduction to pataphysics.

Kathy, another *Penthouse-Omni* alumnus, who was a great cook and a big Tom Robbins fan, offered to take care of the catering details for the party. She came by the office on Monday morning to go over the menu and discuss logistics. The beach house was large enough to comfortably host a party of about fifteen guests, but lacked a table, chairs, or space suitable for a formal sit-down dinner. Kathy suggested keeping the menu simple and serving the meal as a buffet. Margot supported the idea and the two of them started putting a tentative menu together. I called the Malibu Beach Hotel and made a reservation for the Wozniaks, then prepared a checklist of everything that still had to be done.

Tom flew in from Seattle on Friday, and we spent a quiet evening in preparation for the events of the next day. I expected the afternoon meeting with Malcolm, Mary, Graeme, and Tom to go well. The big question was the party. All the players essential to getting the film into production would be gathered in one room. Everyone, except Woz, had at least conditionally signed on to the project. Getting him to take the next step would clinch the deal. Not wanting to let my worries get in the way of a good time, I followed Mystica's advice and cleared my mind of negativity, took some deep breaths, and focused on the moment.

The afternoon meeting was more a preparty warmup than a business session. Everyone got along famously and seemed pleased with the prospect of working together. Graeme, Malcolm, and Mary were taking a break to freshen up when Kathy and Margot arrived with the catering supplies. Tom went upstairs to take a nap, while I helped the caterers unload and set up. A short time later, Paula took our weekend rental car to the airport to pick up the Wozniaks. Upon her return, she reported they were at the hotel and preparing for the party.

The first guests to arrive, appropriately enough, were production manager Tommy Shaw and his wife. The rest of the guests paraded in over the next half hour. The party was casual and relaxed. The buffet-style dinner allowed everyone to circulate and mingle. Steve and his wife were obviously the focus of attention, and the rest of the guests managed to keep them engaged throughout the evening. The Shaws and Lou Pitt left not long after dinner, but everyone else lingered into the night. The Wozniaks were among the last to leave.

Paula and I helped Margot and Kathy clean up while Tom warmed up the hot tub. It had been a long and emotionally exhausting week. Having done all that we could do, the five of us capped off the evening by climbing into the tub for a long, relaxing soak.

On the Monday morning after the party, I felt like Cinderella after the ball. The dream seemed real for a little while but faded away with the rising sun. The day started with a brief phone conversation with Steve. His wife had enjoyed the party and meeting the other guests but remained firm in her objection to any financial involvement in the film. He asked me to keep in touch, as he still liked the project, but I took his decision to be nonnegotiable. I spent the remainder of the morning calling the rest of our ensemble with the news. Graeme, I think, was the most disappointed. With his Australian project looming, the window for directing *Woodpecker* was now all but closed. Without Graeme, we no longer had a package.

Head Games

Undeterred, we set out to assemble a new package. Our problem was not so much in securing talent, but in convincing potential financial backers, be it film studios or individuals, that the film would succeed at the box office. That the novel had been a bestseller translated into several languages was apparently not enough to offset the widespread belief that the material would not fare well on the screen. In retrospect, also working against us were the changing times. While the novel had been written in the late 1970s when social and political sensibilities still reflected the spirit of the 1960s, by the mid-1980s Reaganism had taken hold and, as Randy Newman noted, "it was money that mattered." Paula made the connection before I did. One day, arriving home and feeling dejected after another disappointing meeting, I asked Paula how it was that the studio executives, lawyers, and agents didn't get the significance of the material. "Of course they don't," she answered. "If they did, they would have to quit what they're doing."

While making the film remained the focus of my endeavors, other influences were taking hold of my life. By nature, I had long questioned inherited beliefs, be they religious, political, or sociological but had accepted them as norms that just had to be lived with. The quest to make a movie of a Tom Robbins novel had brought to my acquaintance a cadre of writers, artists, and alternative thinkers who looked beyond the status quo, some even questioning the validity of "consensus reality" altogether. Most notably it was the unnerving writings of Robert Anton Wilson that turned my worldview upside down. There should be a label on his books: *Reading this material may be damaging to your mindset.* Following Fred's advice, I dug into *The Illuminatus* and found it to be annoyingly confounding yet absolutely compelling. Tom Robbins is a more lyrical and meticulous writer, yet he shares Wilson's penchant for using humor as cover for the infusion of profound thoughts and esoteric insights. When asked, Tom once told me that he had indeed been influenced by Robert Anton Wilson, ever since reading Wilson's monthly "Forum" column in *Playboy Magazine* in the 1960s. Tom encouraged me to also read some of Wilson's nonfiction writing and suggested starting with *The Cosmic Trigger*.

🌲🌲🌲

By springtime, another *Woodpecker* incarnation started to take shape. This time it was one of the hottest actresses in town who turned up the heat. It started with a routine call to Creative Artists Agency concerning the availability of a director. His agent, I was pleased to learn, was already familiar with *Still Life with Woodpecker* and intrigued with the idea of making it into a film. Although the director in question was not available, his agent said he would like to explore some other ideas and would get back to me. A week later, he called back to say Debra Winger was interested in the project, and he would like to set up a meeting for the next afternoon.

Winger's performance in *Urban Cowboy* had established her as a star. Her role in the just-released *An Officer and a Gentleman* was receiving wide acclaim and would garner her an Academy Award nomination. Winger was on a roll and she knew how to use her clout. Our meeting was cordial but perfunctory. She was forming her own production company and was interested in coproducing as well as acting in the film. It was a twist that I had not previously considered, but it seemed definitely worth exploring. The next step was to discuss the matter with Tom.

A week later, Tom, Phoebe, and I met Debra at her agent's office at CAA. The official meeting was just a rehash of the idea of E I Productions and Debra's company coproducing the film. A more telling meeting took place a short time later at Willie Tiffany's tavern. There, after a couple rounds of tequila shots, Phoebe and I witnessed Tom and Debra cement their newfound friendship with a blood-brother-sister ceremonial bonding at our table. I inferred that Tom was quite comfortable with Debra's involvement.

I was both excited and concerned. No question that Debra had the status and wherewithal to get the film made. My hesitation was about what kind of film our union would produce. I had two problems working against me as a producer. I wasn't in it for money alone, and I wasn't looking to make the film a stepping-stone in my career. I wanted one thing: that the story be as magical on the big screen as it was in the book. I knew Debra only in a cursory way, but it was clear that she was highly intelligent, willful, and undoubtedly had her own vision for the film. Whereas I wanted to share thoughts about the film we were going to produce, my next meeting was instead with her lawyer, Barry Hirsch, one of the most powerful and highly regarded in the business.

I admit I was not properly prepared for the meeting. Had I more clearly understood what was about to take place, I wouldn't have been thrown off balance when Mr. Hirsch opened our session by quoting Dickens, "It was the best of times, it was the worst of times." It may have been a graceful way to get down to business, but his clever efforts made me feel ill at ease. As a result, I became defensive. It seemed I was being given an offer to get the film made, but the price was steep. I would get a credit and a producer's fee, but my involvement in the project would, for all practical purposes, be over. Sensitive to my misgivings, Hirsch tactfully ended the meeting by suggesting that I think things over and get back to him—*if* I wanted to go ahead with the proposal.

Debra called me a week later from her cabin in New Mexico. She was not pleased with the outcome of the meeting, suggesting that, had she known I had an allergy to lawyers, she would have taken another approach. I think we both knew that the moment had passed. Promising as the joint venture had briefly appeared, the deal fell apart when confronted with the details.

On a Sunday evening, not long after the latest *Woodpecker* setback, I had a riveting experience that was like being struck by a paranormal lightning bolt. I was in bed reading *Cosmic Trigger*, Wilson's autobiographical account of deliberately reprogramming his own brain. His experience, moving from dogmatic thinking based on an attachment to (or a belief in) a singular "reality tunnel" to inclusive (or quantum) thinking that embraces the idea of multiple and mutable realities, is heady stuff and not lightweight reading. I had been taking the book in small doses for about a month and had barely covered a hundred pages.

On that particular evening, I had reached the part where Wilson includes his correspondence with Timothy Leary during the professor's imprisonment in the early 1970s. In his letter to Wilson, Leary recounts an ESP experiment he had conducted while incarcerated. As I read his letter, I formed a precise thought wondering when I was going to meet Leary. It wasn't an unfounded question as I had already crossed paths with several people associated with the notorious professor. What was astounding was that the phone rang a few minutes later with Dr. Leary on the line.

Paula, reading something unrelated and unaware of my definitive thought, had answered the call and, after a very brief exchange, cupped the phone and whispered, "It's Timothy Leary. He's looking for Tom's phone number." I picked up the phone, introduced myself, and told Leary what had just happened. He laughed and commented that I must be doing some powerful stuff. I responded by reminding him that he was the one who had made the phone ring. He laughed again, gave me his phone number and address, and invited me to stop by when I was in the area.

Summer's End

The marquee event in the summer of 1984 was the return of the Olympic Games to Los Angeles. It was also the last summer living in the beach house. My financial situation forced me to put the house on the market in early June. Knowing our beach days were numbered made us enjoy the time we had even more. Weekend barbecues with friends were commonplace, and I spent many early mornings fishing with my dog Shooter in the Zodiac.

Paula's side business was creating "coat of colors" flags custom-designed to match the personality of each of her clients. Between commissions, she made an assortment of whimsical flags that were always flapping in the wind from our decks. Viewed from the beach, the house stood out like a parrot in the company of seagulls. To commemorate the Olympic Games, Paula created a five-by-five-foot flag with a cartoonish image of earth as seen from space. She stylishly crafted a smiling, winking face on the terrestrial orb with the phrase "Go Planet!" placed across the top of the banner. Her vision of the Olympics was that it should be more about celebrating the best the planet had to offer than keeping score of medals earned by nations. The term "Go Planet!" was coined by retired Lt. Colonel Jim Channon, founder of the Army's First Earth Battalion and fellow attendee of the Mad Scientists and Artists Party.

The Olympic torch relay had been routed down the Pacific Coast Highway a couple of days before the July 28 opening ceremony. The torch was scheduled to pass our house around six-thirty in the morning. To preview Paula's Go Planet! flag (and perhaps catch some press coverage), we invited a dozen or so friends to join us for an early breakfast buffet on the side of the highway. Ours was not the only roadside party on the route, but we were certainly among the most flamboyant. Our guests, dressed in an assortment of styles from street-legal pajamas to formal business attire to casual beachwear, milled about joking and munching on papayas and croissants while awaiting the big moment.

We heard the runners approach before we could see them. As the cheers grew louder, our team shifted into action. Paula unfurled her flag and draped it from the roof over the garage door. A couple of our guests started warming up with leftover wedding kazoos just as the torch runner and his entourage came into view. By the time the pack of runners reached us, we were in a rhythmic chant of "Gooooo Planet! Gooooo Planet!" bridged with a kazoo rendition of the *Rocky* theme. The sight and sound of our spectacle caught the attention of the passing caravan, producing big smiles and thumbs-up salutes from the amused runners. Unfortunately, the press lay in wait a few miles up ahead, and the photo that made the papers was of USC alumnus O.J. Simpson carrying the torch up the California incline into Santa Monica.

For months, the citizens of Los Angeles had been warned of unprecedented traffic congestion during the Olympic Games. Traffic was expected to be especially heavy opening day when over two hundred thousand spectators would be lining the streets and packing the coliseum. Paula had intended to display the flag at the entrance to the stadium as the torch arrived for the opening ceremonies. With all the dire predictions of traffic tie-ups and massive crowds, however, we thought better of the idea and decided to have a party instead. We had just left the house to pick up supplies when we heard a traffic report that the downtown streets were free of congestion. Struck with the same impulse, Paula and I returned to the house, picked up the flag, left a note for our guests to start the party without us, and headed to the coliseum.

We put our plan in place as we drove. Parking would be a problem, so we decided to stop by my old frat house and see if we could stash the Jeep there for a couple of hours. With little traffic to contend with, the Santa Monica Freeway was a breeze and we reached the Hoover Avenue off-ramp with time to spare. We pulled into the Sig House lot, found a spot, and parked the Scrambler. I wrote "Alpha Upsilon class of '68" on the back of an E I Productions business card and slipped it under the windshield blade, and we continued on by foot.

The quickest route to the coliseum was cutting across campus. While pausing in the quad to pay our respects to Tommy Trojan, Paula decided it was the time and place to unfold the flag. There, in the shadow of the mighty Trojan warrior, Paula debuted her banner of peace and cooperation. I took one end of the flag, Paula took the other and, holding the planet high over our heads, we marched steadfastly onward to the opening ceremonies of the 1984 Summer Olympics.

By the time we reached Exposition Boulevard, we had attracted a small following. By the time we crossed the street, it felt like we were leading a parade. Excitement filled the air. The Go Planet! banner seemed to galvanize the sentiment many were already feeling. Without being asked, volunteers offered to help hold the flag as the crowd cleared the way for us to march all the way up to the stadium entrance. This time the cameras were looking in our direction. The backdrop of a smiling, winking, watching world framed the picture as Gina Hemphill, granddaughter of Olympic legend Jesse Owens, carried the torch into the tunnel that entered the coliseum.

The moment was brief but electric. That sudden inspiration to follow our hearts rather than reason was self-empowering. Driving home to our party, we marveled at how, after giving up on the idea altogether, we ended up at the coliseum for the opening ceremonies as originally intended. Paula concluded that it must have something to do with pataphysics. For lack of a better explanation, I agreed.

🔺🔺🔺

The euphoric mood didn't last. The next morning, I got a call from the real estate agent to say that my counter offer had been accepted and he would be by with the escrow papers later in the day. He added that the buyer wanted a short escrow and we should plan to move out by late September. I told him that we would be ready—summer can't last forever.

Paula test flying a new Coat-of-Colors flag. Malibu, 1983.

Adjustments

The sale of the house was structured in a way that provided only a small amount of cash up front with the balance to be paid in lump sums over the next three years. In the long run it was a godsend, but with limited funds to work with and an abbreviated escrow, we had few options when it was time to relocate. The only place we could find that fit our budget was a small cabin on a hill above a nearby canyon. The rustic charm of our hilltop abode was not without shortcomings. About two-thirds of the six-hundred-square-foot cinderblock structure was an open living space. The kitchen and tiny bathroom were located on one end of the room, and the two small bedrooms opened onto the other. Heating was limited to a single potbelly stove that even at full blaze was insufficient to warm against the chilly autumn nights. The view was expansive, the air was crisp and clear, and there were hiking trails in all directions, but it wasn't the beach. I did my best to adjust to the change in altitude, but as Jimmy Buffet might say, my fin was drooping low.

The move also marked the beginning of a downsizing process. We left behind or sold the living room, dining room, and bedroom furniture. Even one of my two prized jukeboxes failed to make the cut. We furnished the cabin with a foldout futon couch to sleep on in the living area, a picnic table for dining, twin futons for the girls in one bedroom, and a desk and a sewing table for Paula in the other. It took some getting used to, but learning to live with less was surprisingly liberating. Less than two years later the entirety of my earthly possessions would fit inside a four-by-four-by-eight-foot crate.

No longer able to afford the office, I met with the building manager to ask for release from my lease. The building was owned by a major Hollywood celebrity, and the manager understood the financial ups and downs of the business. She offered to stake me to a much smaller office on the condition that I would vacate on short notice if a paying tenant appeared. It was a kind offer that I could not refuse. The new office was just large enough for a desk and a table to house the computer and printer that Steve Wozniak had generously gifted to E I Productions earlier in the year. Downsizing the office was one thing, having to let Margot go was quite another. She was more than an employee; she had become a good friend. Most of all, she had been a believer in and champion of the making of the film. I was beginning to call into question just what I had gotten into.

With funding prospects on the *Woodpecker* front all but dried up, I began looking for smaller, more immediate projects that could generate a cash flow. Borrowing on Mark Twain's advice to write what you know, I turned to consumer electronics as the place to start. I'd been fascinated with holophonic sound recording since first hearing it demonstrated at a gathering at Marilyn Ferguson's. Having spent time over the summer with the inventor Hugo Zuccarelli experimenting with his binaural three-dimensional recording device, I was convinced that his invention had commercial appeal. It just needed the right application.

In late October, I paid a visit to former Craig coworker Reese Haggot, then president of Alpine Stereo. After some initial small talk, I handed Reese a set of headphones and told him to sit back and enjoy the ride. About two minutes into the demo tape, Reese tore off the headset and said he wanted to buy the company. Explaining that the recording device was not for sale but could be licensed for use on a project-by-project basis, I suggested that Alpine could produce the first commercial holophonic sound recording and sell it exclusively through their dealer network. I had barely finished the pitch when Reese called his assistant into the office and instructed him to sign me up as a consultant. While that was taking place, we discussed ideas about the audio product and agreed to a tentative production budget.

I signed the consultant papers as Reese handed me a check and set up a meeting for the following week with his marketing team. Such as it was, E I Productions was going into production.

Reese and I weren't alone in our enthusiasm about the revolutionary nature of holophonic sound. Hugo had already acquired quite a business team. One of his partners was a well-known agent, another was an entertainment lawyer, and the third was a Grammy Award–winning sound engineer. I approached the team on Alpine's behalf, expressing its interest in producing a proprietary holophonic sound tape to use as a retail-traffic builder. Alpine wanted to debut the tape at the Consumer Electronics Show in January, meaning production would have to start by the beginning of December. The group accepted the proposal and assigned the engineer, Ken, to the project, as Hugo would be in Argentina.

In discussions with Reese and his marketing team, it was decided to do one side of the tape as a narrative demonstration of a variety of sound effects and the other side as an original musical recording to accentuate the dynamics of the sound. I approached my former beachside neighbor Lee Oscar, member of the band War and acclaimed harmonica soloist, about producing the music. Lee accepted the challenge and brought in his collaborator, Greg Errico, drummer for Sly and the Family Stone, to help compose the music and assemble the musicians.

For the sound effects side, I turned to a couple of young filmmakers, Brett Leonard and Gimel Everett, who had made a documentary about the Mad Scientists and Artists Party. As filmmakers, they thought visually and wanted to do more than just string a variety of sound effects together. They came up with a rather unique science-fiction scenario that started with the activation of a newly minted robot named Laz. Robot Laz was educated about the human condition through a series of audio excursions and adventures, then blasted into space to take his knowledge to the stars. It could have been a storyline lifted from a comic book, but it worked.

To get the full effect of its recording capacity, we treated the human-head-shaped device like a person, taking it on horseback rides, roller coaster rides, and sailboat rides. We took it on walks by a rushing stream and on busy streets, even surrounded it with children at play, all the while recording the sounds. Not everything worked. Our most ambitious endeavor, taking the equipment up in a hot air balloon to capture ambient sound from six directions, was washed out by the ever-present blasting of the furnace that kept us afloat. After a week of recording, we had enough distinctive sound elements to take to the studio and edit into a story.

Lee and Greg used Hugo's demo tape to recruit eighteen of the best musicians available to take part in the grand musical experiment. A two-story scaffold was assembled, and the musicians were stacked in two rows across the soundstage to maximize sound distribution. Since the musicians were essentially performing for an audience of one, Ken had to mic each performer and do the production mix live rather than after the fact. The duo had composed two songs for the session: "*Feeling That Way*," a breezy upbeat number; and "*Mainland/Island*," an extended percussion-oriented piece that became, in my opinion, the gem of the whole production.

Once everything was in the can, we went back into the studio for the extended editing process. The last session ran through the night, concluding late afternoon on December 24. Totally exhausted, I made it home just in time for a Christmas Eve dinner with Paula and the girls. On Christmas morning, I drove Paula to the airport to catch a flight back to Buffalo. I stayed behind to finish up some production details and would catch up with her a few days later.

While waiting to board the plane I had second thoughts about going to Buffalo. The month had been long and stressful and, though Paula had been involved throughout the production, we were in need of some quality time together. I called her from the gate and suggested that we change our plans and meet in New Orleans to celebrate New Year's Eve Dixieland style. It was snowing in Buffalo and Paula thought it to be a fine idea. I told her I would catch a flight that morning, find a hotel, and pick her up at the airport the next day. I found a quaint little room with a balcony in a hotel just off Bourbon Street and picked up Paula at the airport the next morning as scheduled. As her suitcase came sliding down the luggage chute and hit the carousel, one of the latches sprang open and, as if a prelude to New Year's Eve in the Big Easy, out popped a red lace bra.

Full Circle

By midwinter, Paula and I were ready to vacate our hilltop hacienda. The windows were drafty, the owners were like feudal lords, and we had had enough of the roosters. The lease ran through April, so we had no choice but to ride it out and make the best of a bad situation. Most weekday mornings, I would drive Paula down the hill and drop her off at Carden School, then continue to the office. Her art classes were finished by noon, and she would often take the bus into town and meet me for lunch at Chez Jay, just across the street from the Santa Monica Pier. We had been frequenting the celebrated dive bar since early in our relationship, and it had become our spot to pause and check in with each other. Evenings could be fun and exciting when it was packed with slumming celebrities, dealmakers, hustlers, and colorful wannabes, but we most enjoyed the unpretentious afternoon lunches.

Proprietor Jay Fiondella, like Bogart in *Casablanca*, hosted his restaurant and watering hole on one level and used it as a front for adventure on another. The walls were covered with mementos and posters documenting four decades of exploits and escapades. Jay was always ready for a caper, and he bought into holophonic sound the minute he heard the demo tape.

Paula and I rendezvoused at Chez Jay shortly after returning from the holophonic tape debut in Las Vegas. I had brought Jay some copies of *Touch the Future* even though the segment using his hot air balloon had ended up on the cutting-room floor. Jay, as he often did, sat down with us for a chat and was anxious to hear about how the show had gone. I told him that the tape was well received and that Alpine reported strong initial sales from its dealer network. Along with the tapes, I reminded him that he would still receive residuals for the use of his balloon. Jay was astounded when I stopped by a few months later with a royalty check. The unexpected return on his investment led to a trusting and lasting friendship.

Paula and I walked back to the office and, finding nothing on the answering machine, decided to window-shop down Main Street to the Rose Café for an afternoon cup of tea. Along the way, Paula excitedly pulled me aside, pointing to a flyer in a bookstore window. The poster announced that Robert Anton Wilson would be delivering a pair of lectures at the Santa Monica Masonic Lodge. Better yet, there was a cocktail reception scheduled before the first event to meet Mr. Wilson. A tagline at the bottom said to inquire within for reservations. Unfortunately, the store was closed.

🔺🔺🔺

We took note of the bookstore phone number and headed back to the office. Paula took the Jeep to do some shopping while I went inside to finish up some business. Ken, the holophonic sound engineer, had left a message on the machine saying they had a potential investor and wanted to know if I would be interested in producing a holophonic-sound demonstration film. I called him back and got the details. The investor wanted to do a fifteen-to-twenty-minute movie that would test the effectiveness of holophonic recording in film. He wanted to use the demo film as a means of attracting enough investment capital to finance a feature film. I asked Ken if the feature film could be *Still Life with Woodpecker*. He said it was possible and suggested we arrange a meeting and find out.

A few days later, Ken introduced me to Dave Anderson, the potential investor. I never got a clear reason for his interest in the sound technology, or even why he wanted to make a movie without concern for the subject, but he apparently had funding and was putting money on the table. Dave was easygoing and, in an hour or so, the three of us came up with a tentative deal. He liked the *Touch the Future* tape and agreed to bring Brett and Gimel in to write the script and direct the film. We all worked well together on the Alpine project; it seemed prudent that we should reunite for the film.

When I finally reached Laura, owner of the occult bookstore promoting the Robert Anton Wilson tour, I told her how much I looked forward to the lectures and that I was especially excited about the chance to meet Robert Wilson at the reception. She replied that she was not personally familiar with his writing but was handling the Los Angeles segment of the tour in her capacity as head of the local chapter of the Hermetic Order of the Golden Dawn. After the call I took some deep breaths. Wilson, who then lived in Dublin, Ireland, was suddenly appearing for lectures at the local Masonic Lodge on a tour sponsored by Golden Dawn. I felt like I was being drawn into a magical and conspiratorial realm straight from the pages of *The Illuminatus Trilogy*. Something wonderfully weird was going on.

The Robert Anton Wilson lectures were scheduled for the first Saturday and Sunday evenings in February. On the Friday before the events, Laura called me at the office and asked if I could accompany her to the airport that evening to pick up Wilson. Laura explained that neither she nor her partner felt knowledgeable enough to carry on a conversation about his work and thought that I would be good company on the ride to Timothy Leary's house, where he would be staying.

The Golden Dawn delegates and I were there at the gate to greet Wilson as he stepped off the plane. Laura approached him and introduced the rest of us as his escorts for the evening. Gruff, but less intimidating than expected, Wilson handed me his bag and lit a cigarette. Laura kept the conversation going until we reached the car. As we settled into the back seat, Wilson turned to me and asked if we had met before. I answered that we hadn't but recounted the strange events that had led me to his books, concluding with the time when

Timothy Leary called just minutes after I had read his letter about ESP experiments in *Cosmic Trigger*. Then I boldly asked, "Mr. Wilson, don't you think it rather remarkable that, after that experience, I am now in this car with you on the way to Dr. Leary's house?" His only response was to again ask my name and to please call him Bob.

Dr. Leary was waiting at his front door to greet Bob and company. After a warm embrace between the two of them, the rest of us were introduced. When I started to remind him of our phone conversation, he interrupted to say that he remembered the call well. He thought it interesting that we should meet again in the company of Bob Wilson. Before leaving, I gave him a copy of the *Touch the Future* tape, suggesting that he might find the experience a bit trippy, especially if using headphones.

The next evening Paula and I mingled with the eclectic assortment of guests in attendance for the cocktail reception. Describing this crowd as colorful would be an understatement. Although no one was wearing a tin hat, some of the attendees looked better suited for a comic book convention. Complementing the mix were bow-tied, pipe-smoking intellectuals and a variety of New Age neo-pagans. Bob arrived with Dr. Leary, who would be providing a short introduction to the lecture. When we came upon the dynamic duo in the reception line, Dr. Leary shook my hand and told me that he loved the tape, though his attention was directed at Paula. As I introduced them, Paula blushed when the rakish professor commented on her charm and natural beauty. I made a mental note to keep an eye on the good doctor.

Brett and Gimel had come up with a script, *The Rendezvous*, that was a much more elaborate production than had been envisioned in the initial meeting. The film that we had agreed upon was a bare-bones production meant only to test and demonstrate the use of the recording device. Brett and Gimel saw the project as a chance to make a short film that would, at the very least, be suitable for public screenings at film festivals. Dave Anderson saw value in the idea but wasn't sure if he could convince his backers that the extra expense would be worth the investment. Early on, it was apparent that I would be working with two different factions trying to make two different movies. Dave called back a short time later to say that he had secured the extra funds and told me to go ahead with pre-production.

Fellow Malibu residents Rae Dawn Chong and John Stockwell lent support to the film by agreeing to play the leads. They liked the experimental nature of the project and that most of the filming would take place in Yosemite National Park. We rounded out the crew with family: Ken, Hugo, and I brought our spouses to assist as needed, and Melanie came along to babysit Rae Dawn's young son. After a few days of prepping the equipment, we loaded up the vans and drove all night to our first location, a mini-mansion in Los Gatos.

Brett and Gimel had arrived a day earlier to set up the location, so we began shooting midmorning and continued into the night. We finished up the next morning and drove to Yosemite that afternoon. Then the trouble began. The shooting schedule became more complicated than anticipated, and something had to give. Our cast, who had generously donated their time, had other commitments, and Dave, who had already gone to the well once, was unwilling to do so again. Brett and Gimel insisted that we film all the sequences, so we tried to squeeze everything into what became sunrise-to-sunset shoots. The initial easygoing nature of the production became intense and stressful. We completed primary shooting with just enough time for me to drive Rae Dawn and her son to Fresno to catch their flight back to L.A. Though filming was complete, the success of the project was still to be determined in the editing and sound-mixing process.

After tying up loose ends in mid-April, my job was essentially done. Dave Anderson admirably stayed with the project and provided incremental postproduction funding until completion nearly a year later. I liked Dave and respected his tenacity, but I never got the impression that he was serious about financing a feature film. It had been a worthy effort, but I was glad to be done with the project. At least the small producer's fee gave Paula and me the means to make some changes in our life.

We had given our landlords notice that we intended to move out when the lease expired at the end of the month. We were told, however, that we would not get our deposit back unless we cleared the thick brush that had accumulated around our cottage after the winter rains. The charming one-bedroom loft apartment that we had located in lower Los Flores Canyon wouldn't be available until the middle of May, so we decided to let the brush grow a little longer and take a Hāna respite before working off our indentured servitude. I called Jim Meeker, and we were offered the use of his new guest bungalow. He said it was small, yet cozy and quiet. It sounded perfect. We were used to small; it was the cozy and quiet we were looking for.

Cave with a View

Maui's main airport circa 1985 was small, crowded, and intimate. There was little distinction between arriving and departing passengers, and everyone mingled in the common area. A lei stand and snack shop were located next to the baggage carousel, and a home-style coffee shop was perched on the mezzanine above the boarding gates. I never got over the excitement of disembarking from the plane and walking down the open-air ramp. Even though I was just visiting, in my heart it felt as if I had come home.

The road I had so loathed the first time I drove it had become a familiar friend. We took our time, stopping here and there to stretch our legs and wade in the cool roadside springs. As we wound our way deeper into the jungle, the stresses of winter began to peel away like worn-out skin. We didn't talk much—there would be time for that later. We just let the rhythmic sounds of nature and the fragrances of the forest overtake our senses. We drove through Hāna town late that afternoon and made a stop at Hāmoa Beach before continuing on to Jim's. The sun had dropped behind the kamani trees, and most of the beach was in shadow. I slipped off my sandals, walked across the sand to the edge of the shore, and dipped my toes in the gentle surf. While looking east across the ocean I had just crossed, I had an eerie sensation that the world I had known was coming to an end.

We ate breakfast most mornings in the old Hotel Hāna Maui dining room. Back then, the hotel was still locally owned, and employees were given the latitude to be themselves. There was always an undercurrent of playfulness and gentle teasing in the room. One of the waiters carried a long-spouted pitcher from which he could pour an arcing stream of water and fill a glass from two feet away. He was always laughing, and he never missed. One morning, as we were getting ready to leave, our waitress suggested that we attend the Lei Day celebration at the Hāna School. We thanked her for the tip and went straight to the school.

Lei Day, the Hawaiian version of May Day, is a big event. The whole school, composed of just over two hundred students from kindergarten through twelfth grade, participates in this rite-of-spring festival. The preparation of music and dance routines had been going on for weeks, and dress rehearsals and costuming overrode studies in the days leading up to the presentation. What a privilege, I thought, to be sitting on the school lawn in the company of half the town, watching their children dance and sing, celebrating the renewal of life. The show was tender and touching, setting the right mood for the discussion that we knew had to be faced.

The conversation started with a cleansing swim. Afterward we walked up the beach, found a spot under a shady tree, and settled in for a talk. We began with a stark assessment of our situation. *Woodpecker* was going nowhere, I had been reduced to producing novelty items that were barely covering the bills, and Paula's job, although emotionally rewarding, paid very little. Other than a sizable royalty check forthcoming from the Alpine tape promotion, the path we were on was unsustainable. We needed to think big, even if it meant changing course altogether. Admitting that the *Woodpecker* dream was all but over was like taking a blow to the gut. Feeling my discomfort, Paula suggested we pick up some wine and start anew back at the bungalow.

I went for a run later that afternoon and started seeing things from a different perspective. My dream had also been a burden. Now, at least, I could be open to other dreams and new directions. Contented, I ran mindlessly up the road toward Kīpahulu. I was about to turn around when I came upon a small pond at the base of a roadside waterfall. I took off my shoes and shirt and dove in. I worked my way across the pond until I was directly under the brisk water cascading down from an outcropping high above. I let the torrent pound my back and shoulders, relieving the weight I had been carrying.

Unburdened, I climbed out of the pond, gathered my belongings, and walked home barefoot.

Paula had prepared a picnic dinner and suggested that we dine by the shore. We took our basket and bottle to a grassy spot on the bluff overlooking the churning sea. Across the ʻAlenuihāhā Channel, the volcanic peaks of the Big Island reflected the amber glow of the setting sun. I uncorked the wine, poured us both a glass, and we toasted new beginnings. While nibbling on our provisions, we started playing the "what if" game. Our imagination quickly stretched to the point where we were living in Hāna raising a family. It could happen, we both agreed. As the day dimmed, we lay on our backs and watched the night unfold. Stars began to appear so quickly, we ran out of wishes. Soon the sky was alive with thousands of distant suns whose flickering ancient light filled the night. Caught up in the cosmic scheme, we slowly undressed each other and made love under the diamond-studded sky.

Everyone knows that rebounding from a broken relationship requires caution. So, too, does rebounding from a broken dream. The next morning, a carpenter who was working on Jim's other house stopped by to take care of some minor repairs. I made a remark about the beautiful craftsmanship of the house, particularly the extensive use of hardwoods. He told me that I should meet Sam Eason, a local designer who lived nearby. Sam, he said, was obsessed with the idea of building an entire house out of hardwood. He suggested I walk down the road and give him a holler. He added that Sam would be most receptive if I brought along some beer.

My instincts overrode my reluctance to spend precious vacation time with a stranger talking about hardwoods. I picked up a six-pack of beer and headed down the road to meet Sam. He was expecting me. The carpenter, it seems, had misunderstood my comment and had implied that I was interested in building a house. Eason's disappointment in discovering that I was a visitor rather than a prospect quickly faded when I gave him the beer. He opened a bottle and asked me what I did, where I was from, and what brought me to Hāna. I answered that I was a producer from Los Angeles taking a break between projects. Then, without thinking, added that I would like to live here one day. That was all Sam needed to hear. He had been working on a project that had just fallen through and saw me as its salvation. He handed me a beer, then proceeded to tell me about a remarkable piece of land I might want to purchase.

I tried to explain that my current situation didn't allow for moving to Hāna, but Sam wouldn't have any of it. He said the property was a once-in-a-lifetime find and it wasn't going to wait around for my convenience. It was almost as if he knew my situation better than I did. The first of the lump-sum payments for the beach house was coming due, and either I invest it in another property or squander it away trying to hold things together. Since I didn't have enough capital to repurchase in Malibu, perhaps destiny was pointing elsewhere. I asked Sam to tell me more.

He described the property as a half acre of land unlike anything I could imagine. Located near the shore on Hāna Bay, the parcel had a magnificent lava-rock cliff riddled with caves and lava tubes that surrounded an overgrown fishpond. He then pulled out sketches of a hardwood house that he had already configured for the property. Sam knew he had piqued my curiosity and suggested we take a drive and visit the land. I walked back to the bungalow and told Paula about the property. Without going into detail, I said that it sounded intriguing and we should at least take a look.

We picked up Sam and drove over to Hāna Bay. We parked off the road and walked down a gravel driveway to a bluff that looked out across the overgrown fishpond. Walking toward the shore, Sam led us down a crude stone stairway that connected both parts of the property. There, on a flat stretch of land that backed up against the lava-rock cliff, Sam wanted to build a pondside home. Even in its dilapidated state, I began to sense the unique beauty that lay beneath the foliage and refuse. Sam's vision became even more persuasive when he led us around the back of the pond to a cave that seemed to act as sentry over the complex. Entering the cave, Sam directed us to stand back against the wall and look out toward the shore. With the bravado of a snake oil salesman, Sam put his hand on my shoulder and proclaimed, "Just think, my boy, someday the pond will be restored, and you'll have a cave with a view."

Sam, knowing that he had a live one on the line, wasted no time tracking down Brad Reid, who co-owned the land with his father. To Sam's dismay, Brad told him that they had decided to keep the property and he was preparing to build a small house. Sam told us not to worry. He would contact the father, who, he was sure, still wanted to sell the land. That snapped me out of my reverie. I told him that *if* I was going to move to Hāna, it wasn't going to involve taking away someone's land. Undaunted, Sam said that he knew of some other exceptional properties, perhaps even more suitable for building a house. Regaining my senses, I was surprised that I had even considered such an outlandish idea. I thanked Sam for his efforts but told him I needed time to think things through before going any further.

Paula and I spent the last day of our vacation at the beach talking about the very real possibility of moving to Hāna. I don't think either of us felt quite ready for such a leap, yet we couldn't help smiling when considering the prospect. Before we could give any serious thought to the idea, we had matters to attend to on the Mainland. Besides moving into the new apartment, I had decided to close the office in Santa Monica altogether. I wanted to think I wasn't permanently closing the door on *Woodpecker*. It was more like hanging out a Gone Fishing sign indefinitely.

On Monday morning, I drove into Santa Monica to start packing up my office. Along the way, I stopped at the little post office complex at the base of the canyon for a cup of coffee. Walking toward the Country Store, I noticed a bronze figure of what I guessed to be a Hindu deity in the window of the stained-glass store. Although I recognized the form, I knew nothing about it and felt compelled to find out more. The store was closed, so I called Paula from the office and asked her to check out the object when she went down the hill later that morning. She called from the store saying that the deity was Shiva, the great Hindu god of change. Serious change, she added. Shiva presided over the ongoing cycle of destruction and creation. Paula was also drawn to the statue and thought it would fit in well at the new apartment. "Do we dare?" I mused. "Why not?" she replied. "Change is already in the air."

Cave behind unrestored fishpond. Stories, historical and legendary, tell of the land having been home to royalty and mythical beings. Hāna, May 1985.

Throwing Caution to the Wind

Shortly after we moved into our new apartment, Marilyn Ferguson called to invite us to the Gathering of Eagles Conference, an event she described as the follow-up to the Mad Scientists and Artists Party. The three-day program was being held in mid-June at the Pecos River Learning Center just north of Santa Fe, New Mexico. We thanked her for thinking of us and told her we would try to work it into our plans. We both had mixed feelings about attending the gathering. I was growing weary of the whole New Age agenda. We had met some very interesting and sincere people, but it seemed that much of the collective thinking was more wishful than substantive. Paula, too, had concerns, yet we both loved New Mexico. We decided to attend the conference but to stay at a hotel near the plaza in Santa Fe.

Sam called a short time later to say that he had come across an exceptional piece of property that was about to go on the market. He described it as three acres of gently sloping land above the Kīpahulu coast near the national park. He said that the natural building site already in place would provide unobstructed views across the channel to the western coast of the Big Island, adding that the location was of perfect vantage to watch migrating humpback whales frolicking off Maui's southernmost shore. Sam concluded by saying that owner of the property had offered us the use of a small cottage he managed at Hāmoa Beach, and if we brought gear, we could camp on the land before making a decision.

Paula and I talked it over and decided that if we were ever going to take a shot at living in Hāna, it was then. Building a house could be just the kind of diversion we needed while working out a plan for the future. After all, even if we built the house and decided we weren't ready to live there, we could always lease it out until we were. I called Sam back and told him that we would make arrangements to come over the last week in June.

The move to the apartment seemed to bring out the best in both of us. Our new location enabled us to resume regular walks on the beach and wander along the creek that ran through the canyon. Paula set up her workstation in the girls' bedroom on the first floor, and I moved my desk and computer to the front of the large loft that also served as our bedroom. We adapted quickly to the new situation and kept out of each other's way on days when Paula wasn't working at school.

One late afternoon Paula came upstairs with a synopsis of a children's story that she had just finished writing. More a fable than a story, *Planet People* encapsulated in just a few paragraphs a whimsical view of reality as a collective "game." *"In time, the game becomes so broken and corrupt that some people decide to give up on it and create a new game based on inclusion and altogether different values, fun being the highest aspiration of all,"* she had written. The story was clever and imaginative, with a playful touch of social criticism. I saw it as a lovely depiction of Paula's vision of planetary, rather than national, identity. I suggested we take a walk down the road to the Sea Lion and continue the conversation over cocktails and dinner. By the end of the evening, we had come up with a crunch plan to promote the *Planet People* story by producing a batch of smiling planet buttons to circulate at the get-together in New Mexico.

The Gathering of Eagles Conference was the complete antithesis of the Mad Scientists and Artists Party. Where the party was spontaneous and playful, the conference was stilted and willful. The party was about the exploration of consciousness; the conference was about saving the world. Marilyn's rationale was that the Cold War was amping up to the point where global annihilation seemed all but inevitable. She thought that by bringing together enough brain power, the group could come up with a plan to avert such a calamity. There was no question that things were touchy in the geopolitical world, but it was hard to take Marilyn's assignment seriously. Despite my reservations as an invited guest, I played along.

Between presentations and general discussions, we worked in small groups to devise survival plans for the planet. Each group presented their peace plan during the closing session. To Marilyn's chagrin the most popular presentation was a fanciful global busing plan from Paula's group, under the leadership of Peter Russell, author of *The Global Brain* and probably the most brilliant mind in attendance. My feeling was that Marilyn had missed the point. The success of the Mad Scientists and Artists Party was its irreverence; some things are too serious to be taken seriously. Paula's Planet People buttons were, however, a big success. Just about everyone was wearing one of the smiling, winking planet pins as the conference came to a close.

We spent our last evening in Santa Fe visiting galleries and admiring the reawakened Native American vision as expressed through art. I found the modern kachina dolls particularly telling. New carvers were taking old traditional images and expressing them in contemporary form. The figure that drew my attention was a sitting black-and-white-banded character eating a watermelon. I was told the image was a Hano or Hopi running clown. The Hano was a trickster or jester who lived apart from the community. The watermelon was commonly associated with the Hano, who was known to sit at the side of the village and spit seeds at society. Paula laughed at the description and said it reminded her of someone she knew. Without further discussion, we asked the shopkeeper to wrap up the clown for the plane ride home.

There were several messages for us upon our return. The most unexpected was from "Pappy" Reid, saying that the Hāna property we had first looked at was, indeed, available and to call him if I was still interested. I called him back and learned that his son Brad had located a larger parcel just outside of town that would be more suitable for a flower farm. Pappy had already been in contact with Sam and knew that we were about to return to Hāna to look at some other land. I told him that was true and suggested we meet somewhere to talk before heading off to Hāna the following week.

Pappy lived in Orange County, so we decided to meet at Hoff's Hut in the Alamitos Bay Marina near Etta's house. I left early to make a call on Etta and fill her in on what was going on. She was concerned that I might be moving so far away but was not surprised. Etta, more than anyone else in my family, took seriously my childhood claim that I was going to one day live in Hawai'i. I assured her that even if I did build a house on Maui, I'd be making regular visits to L.A. and would likely be stopping by just as often.

Pappy and I met for coffee at an umbrella-shaded table in the patio dining area. Resemblance aside, Pappy reminded me of my grandfather, Papa. He was in no hurry to make a deal. We casually discussed how he came to the property, his plan for building a retirement home when his wife was still alive, and what he hoped would become of the land with a new owner. When we got down to terms, he was inflexible with the price but was agreeable to a payment schedule that matched my revenue flow. In my mind, the property was priceless. The sale price was within reach, and I saw no reason to negotiate any further. I told him that we were committed to look at the other property but would make a decision before leaving Hāna. He asked me to inform Brad if we decided to go ahead with the deal. I left feeling good about the way we considered the land as something more than just a commodity. Though the other property sounded tempting, my heart was in the cave looking out across the pond toward the shore on Hāna Bay.

We arrived on Maui in midafternoon, picked up a rental car, and drove on the campground in Wai'ānapanapa State Park a couple miles north of the bay. We pulled in at dusk and barely had time to pitch the tent before nightfall. We took a walk around the grounds and turned in early—there was a lot to do in just a few days. We were awokened at dawn to the sound of Sam's billowing voice hollering our names while looking for our tent. Paula, already somewhat put off by Sam's boisterous nature, was not pleased. I threw some clothes on and crawled out to confront our tormentor. I told him we needed time to get our bearings and would come by his house later. Shortly thereafter we broke camp and went to the hotel for breakfast. Rather than being excited, we were both subdued. Even I was beginning to question the wisdom of our mission.

We met Sam later that morning and drove out to Kīpahulu to inspect the three-acre parcel that had sparked our visit. Right away I knew that the land, located on a gently sloping hill on the mountain side of the road, was not right for us. Nonetheless we got out of the car and walked the substantial distance up to the building site. It was a beautiful location and it was, indeed, isolated and private, but we had just gotten off one hill and I wasn't excited about settling down on another. More importantly, I felt like a fish out of water so far from the shore.

We stayed that night in the Hāmoa cottage that was generously offered by John, the owner of the Kīpahulu property. I felt guilty accepting his hospitality when I already knew we weren't going to buy his land. That evening over dinner Paula and I shared our feelings. I told Paula I was ready to go ahead with the deal with the Reids, but she was noncommittal. Nothing was said, but I sensed that she was having second thoughts about the whole idea of moving to Hāna. The next morning, I stopped by to see John and tell him that his land, lovely as it was, just didn't fit into our plans. He replied that he already had that impression but insisted that we stay the second night in the cottage as his guest.

Brad came by with some fresh local fruit later that afternoon. He invited us to spend our last night camping on his Hāna Bay property. We met him on the land the next morning and pitched our tent at the base of the driveway, near the water faucet. We spent the rest of the day at Hāmoa Beach playing in the surf and trying to get our minds off the big decision that lay ahead. Later, we had an early dinner with Sam and his wife, Patty. Mrs. Eason was the principal of the school and a pillar of the community, quite the opposite of Sam, the town's bon vivant. It had been a wonderful day. We began to feel we were where we belonged.

Back at the tent we lit some candles and snuggled in for the evening. We awoke just before dawn and consummated our decision to go ahead with the property at daybreak. In that moment we had no doubts that we were doing the right thing. Brad stopped by as we were taking down the tent. I told him that his father had said the land was for sale but I wanted his assurance that he felt the same. He said he did and we closed the deal with a handshake.

Paula standing on the cornerstone of property overlooking overgrown fishpond. Hāna, July 1985.

Unforeseen Events

Buckminster Fuller, one of the most innovative thinkers of the twentieth century, believed that the universe and everything within was ever evolving. For him, God was not a noun but a verb. Since the universe is all inclusive, Bucky concluded that every life had meaning and purpose. If things got bumpy along life's journey, it was just the way the universe sometimes works. Others might call the process fate, destiny, or just blind luck. By whatever name, I was about to embark on a year of upheaval, much of it beyond my control.

In early summer, I impulsively purchased a classic 1964 Ford Galaxy that was parked on the side of the road near the Malibu Civic Center with a For Sale sign on the window. Other than the white replacement driver's-side door, the blue beauty looked to be in excellent condition. I had planned to sell the Jeep before moving to Maui anyway, so I figured why not sell it then and have some fun with the Ford. I met the owner and gave him a deposit to hold the car, then paid the balance a week later when I sold the E I Productions Jeep.

The first family excursion in the Ford was dinner at our favorite Italian restaurant near the Malibu pier. The girls took the back seat, Paula rode up front in the middle, and Shooter the dog rode shotgun. We put down the top and took a predinner cruise up the coast before turning around at Point Dune. By the time we reached the restaurant, everyone agreed the Ford was cool.

Over dinner we talked about returning to Hāna in September for a late-summer vacation. The girls were excited to see the land, and Paula and I needed to work out design details with Sam. We also decided to spend a couple of nights on the Lahaina side for some snorkeling and general touristy stuff.

Paula had just made plans to spend a week in early August with her family in Buffalo when I got a call from Laura. Bob Wilson was returning for another speaking tour and she wanted to know if I would be willing to sponsor him as a houseguest during his visit. Curiously, he would be arriving the same day Paula was leaving and would need accommodations for ten nights. Laura also asked if I could provide transportation to radio interviews and appointments while he was my ward. Caught unprepared and without much else on my calendar, I told her that it would be my pleasure to host Mr. Wilson. She added that as promoter she made very little on the tour but would, subject to advance ticket sales, try to reimburse me for meals. I thanked her for the consideration.

The first night was easy. Bob arrived around eight o'clock in the evening. He had eaten on the plane, so we went straight to Malibu. I had made up the girls' room for him, even setting out Paula's computer in case he felt inspired to do some writing. Over a couple of beers, he laid out his agenda for the duration of his stay. He had lectures for the next two nights, a radio interview early Sunday morning, and various other interviews and appointments throughout the remainder of the week. He was very matter of fact, but at the same time was complimentary about the place and thanked me for the hospitality.

At breakfast the next morning, I told Bob I had some errands to run in town and asked if he wanted to join me. He preferred to stay at the apartment, do some reading, and enjoy the tranquil environment. Stationing himself on the living room couch, Bob asked if I had something to use as a side table for his ash tray and coffee cup. The best that I could come up with was to bring my desk chair down from upstairs and set it next to the couch. Once provided, he asked if I could brew a pot of coffee before leaving.

As I was passing my former office near Main Street, I noticed an older pickup truck parked on a side street. It was loaded with furniture that looked to have been made of tree limbs. Intrigued, I pulled over to investigate. The obviously handmade chairs, benches, and tables were beautiful. While I was admiring the craftsmanship, the owner appeared and introduced himself. He lived in Oregon, where he and his family made the furniture out of cherrywood and pussy willow branches. I asked if he happened to have a coffee table buried in the pile. He said he did and, if I could give him a hand, he'd dig it out. After unloading virtually everything else on the truck, he produced exactly what I was looking for. He said he wanted a hundred dollars for the piece. Though short of funds, I bought the table. I helped him reload the truck, put the table in the back seat, and went on with my errands. My last stop was at Laura's bookstore to pick up some papers for Bob. Along with the papers, Laura gave me an envelope with a check for a hundred dollars to help cover hosting expenses. I drove home, revenue neutral for the day, with a handcrafted coffee table in the back seat that wouldn't have been there if it hadn't been for Bob. I liked the mathematics.

Other than a day that Bob spent at Marilyn's, I was with him constantly for the duration of his stay. One day we drove down the coast to San Diego for a radio interview, then stopped on the way back for lunch with an eccentric millionaire in La Costa. Another day we went to Timothy Leary's house for a poolside luncheon with some of Leary's eclectic friends. Even the time spent at a Santa Monica Laundromat was a learning experience. Most evenings we had dinner at the Sea Lion or at the Italian restaurant near the pier. All the while, we engaged in easy discussion about his work and philosophy. I had assimilated much from his writing, but the ongoing dialogue was transformational. The essence of what I learned then and refined over the years was accepting uncertainty as a constant and realizing that reality is, in Bob's words, "always plural and mutable." Unlike a guru who deprograms one set of dogmatic beliefs and reprograms with another, Mr. Wilson, through his writing, lectures, and seminars, broke down attachments to dogma beliefs but left it up to the student to reprogram his or her own "reality tunnel." Without proper preparation it can be a terrifying, even psychotic, experience.

One evening around the midpoint of his visit, Laura brought a small contingent of inner-circle Golden Dawners over for a potluck dinner. They were a playful group and an amusing break from the cerebral intensity of the past few days. Paula called to check in that evening and, hearing the background chatter, asked if she was missing something. When I told her it was some of the Golden Dawn gang that had come over for some socializing and schmoozing with Bob, she quickly lost interest. She said she was having a great time and was glad to be away from all the craziness. Then, in a voice that seemed choked with tears, said she didn't want to come home. Stunned, I asked her what was wrong. She replied only that she felt happy at home and didn't want to leave. After talking things through, she said she would return as scheduled; we could talk further when we had some time alone. Before getting off the phone, I asked her if she would be interested in driving Bob up to San Francisco a couple of days after her return. She said the road trip sounded fun.

I was relieved to find Paula in a cheerful mood when I picked her up at the airport. We caught up on events as we drove home. She asked about the plan for the next couple of days. I told her that Bob had lectures scheduled the next two nights, and we would drive him up north the following morning. She suggested we take Bob to Chez Jay for an early dinner before the lecture that evening. It was a great idea. Chez Jay was Bob's kind of place.

Early Sunday morning, we loaded the Ford's enormous trunk with our overnight bags, Bob's luggage, and Shooter's dog bed. With Bob and me up front and Paula and Shooter in the back, we headed north for a late-morning breakfast in Santa Barbara. Later, while cruising comfortably along Highway 101, we inexplicably ran out of gas (faulty gauge?) on a barren stretch of highway somewhere near Salinas. Trying to make the most out of an awkward situation, I hopped out of the car and caught a ride into town for a can of gas. I was relieved to find Paula and Bob in an animated conversation when I returned, seemingly unbothered by the unscheduled delay.

With late-day traffic at a near standstill, we pulled off the freeway south of the San Francisco airport and found refuge in a cocktail lounge. After sitting out the congestion listening to some of Bob's stories over a glass of wine, we were back on the road and arrived in the city before dark. Locating Bob's new place of residence required another stop for directions. We parked near the wharf, and while I used the phone in a nearby restaurant to call Bob's next host, Bob and Paula had found their way to the lounge and ordered another round of drinks. By the time we delivered Bob to his new handler, the esteemed author was pleasantly tipsy. After saying our goodbyes, Paula and I headed south to Hillsborough for a Sunday-night dinner with my folks.

Early the next morning we drove over to a small café in Half Moon Bay for fresh muffins and coffee. We took the top down and turned onto Highway 1, followed it south to Santa Cruz, then around the bay, passing Moss Landing, Monterey, and Carmel before stopping for gas in Big Sur. We stretched our legs, picked up some lunch fare, and continued on down California's most famous highway. After an exhilarating ride down the switchback, we found an isolated spot near San Simeon for a romantic picnic lunch. Driving to Malibu, Paula mentioned that Bob was returning to L.A. in the spring, this time with his wife, Arlen. She said she had already invited them to stay with us. The rest of the ride was just like old times. No mention was made of our phone conversation. It was like it had never happened.

The Dance of Shiva

We rented the little cottage near Hāmoa for our late-summer visit. Kris Kristofferson and his family were also in Hāna staying at Jim Meeker's house. While the girls had company to hang with on the beach, Paula and I spent time with Sam working out ideas for the house. The more I worked with Sam, the more I came to recognize his creative brilliance. Since our last visit, he had constructed a detailed model of the framing structure he envisioned for the house. Using the model as a starting point, Paula and I made up a list of elements that we wanted to see incorporated into the finished product. The most important features included positioning the structure in alignment with the four directions and having a skylight large enough to watch the moon and stars migrating across the sky each night. Having defined the house, we left Sam alone for the next few days to come up with some designs.

The girls had seen pictures of the land but seeing it for themselves made it real. Surveying the property became an adventure. We climbed the rock cliffs and found overgrown pathways and a hidden lava tube. We walked around the remnants of the old fishpond and out onto the beach. From there, I pointed out how the property might look with a house in place and the fishpond restored. Saving the best for last, we walked back around the pond, cleared our way through some foliage and came upon the cave. The cave, to me, was a childhood fantasy come true. I can only imagine how magical the experience of exploring the cave was for my ten- and twelve-year-old daughters.

A couple days later, Paula took the girls to the beach, and I went to see Sam. He had been busy. Inspired by Lee Oscar's eleven-minute musical opus *Mainland/Island* from the holophonic tape, Sam had been on a design binge. He had sketched out renderings of a two-story-with-loft building where all the floors were connected by an interior spiral stairway. To satisfy the skylight requirement, he had bisected the entire roof with eight-foot-wide panels of tempered glass. I could see immediately that the size and complexity of the house was way beyond my budget. I asked Sam what happened to the simple seven-hundred square foot cottage we had set out to build. He smiled as if expecting the question. He proposed that we have the house built in the Philippines, then disassembled, crated, and shipped to Maui for reassembly in Hāna. By his logic the savings gained by building the house in the Philippines would more than offset the cost of increasing the size of the structure.

Sam's plan certainly caught my attention. I had some reservations about the drawings, most notably the width of the skylight, but I was fascinated with the idea of having the house built elsewhere, then reconstructed as a kit house. Building and customizing models had been a childhood passion of mine. What better way of starting a new life in Hāna than by putting together a model house? The more we talked, the more the idea took hold. Sam, starting with his wife's family contacts, had already begun investigating prospective builders. The leading contender was an architect who worked with the government and built trade pavilions around the world. Sam said he would keep pursuing the prospect and let me know when he had a more definitive plan. Satisfied with his work so far, I wrote out a retainer check with the understanding that the rest of his fee was contingent upon finding a builder in the Philippines and delivering the house to Hāna.

We spent the last day of our visit at the beach. Kris was there with his family along with Jim Meeker. The surf was perfect for bodysurfing, and between catching waves Kris and I chattered about nothing more relevant than swell size and comical wipeouts. When I came ashore, Paula commented about how refreshed I looked. She said Kris and I had the appearance of a couple of kids at play without a care in the world. For the first time in a long time, that was exactly how I felt. After lunch, we returned to the beach, where I gave the girls their first lessons in bodysurfing. Rule number one: Never turn your back on approaching waves. Rule number two: Dive under cresting waves. Rule number three: "Catch a wave, and you're sitting on top of the world."

🔱🔱🔱

Back in Malibu, we started adjusting to the reality of our move to Hāna. I had already made the emotional break from Malibu, but Paula was not so quick to give up her local identity. One of her fellow teachers had announced wedding plans for the summer and Paula was already fretting about how she would be able to attend the event. I wasn't too concerned, figuring things would work out in time, but it did make me realize the move would be fraught with unanticipated consequences.

In mid-December Sam sent us a package of detailed plans and a tentative timetable to have the unassembled house in Hāna by early June. After reviewing the materials, I gave him a call to go over details. Sam had been in regular communication with the architect Jimmy DeGuzman and was convinced that he was the right person for the job. DeGuzman had an impressive list of architectural accomplishments and was enthusiastic about using the house as a showpiece for a potential kit-house business. Sam recommended we schedule a trip to the Philippines right after the holidays. I agreed to the trip but told him that I first had to take care of some matters with my bank. We set mid-January as the target date. My stomach was churning by the time I got off the phone. The abstract plan had all of a sudden become real.

We spent the holidays at home that year. It turned out to be the most memorable of all our holidays together. We hosted an open-house Christmas party one weekend and visited Etta and watched the traditional Naples Boat Parade on another. Paula and Melanie both participated in the acclaimed Carden School Christmas pageant, and we decked out the apartment with homemade decorations. We savored every ounce of holiday cheer as if knowing it would be our last together.

Paula and I decided to use the turn of the year as a time to contemplate the changes that lay ahead. We decorated the room with streamers and carefully placed holiday candles on each side of the statue of Shiva that sat on the mantel over the fireplace. Paula made a special dinner starting with an ahi sashimi appetizer. The Hawaiian tradition is said to bring good fortune in the new year. After finishing our unhurried meal, we lit the candles, turned down the lights, and settled on the couch for a talk. We didn't admit it then, but both of us had feelings of uncertainty about the future, which made our discussion more tenuous than decisive. Still, we were able to come up with enough of a plan to start off the year. Paula decided to take a trip to New York City to spend a couple of days with our friend Kathy, then travel to Buffalo for a post-holiday visit with her family. A few days later I would leave for the Philippines to meet Sam and work out details for the house. We would reconvene at the end of the month and take it from there. That decided, we popped a bottle of champagne, put some change in the remaining jukebox, and danced our way into the New Year.

After the celebration, we snuggled together on the couch and I dozed off into a nap-like sleep. Blinking my eyes open a short time later, I glimpsed the statue of Shiva dancing in the flickering candlelight. Mesmerized, I watched as the great Hindu deity wove his arms and legs in cyclical motions like a spider deftly spinning a web. Paula finally broke the trance by taking my hand and leading me upstairs to bed.

Worlds Apart

Paula was packing for her red-eye flight to New York when a sudden sense of sorrow came over me. I was at my desk watching her lay out her clothes on the bed. I had no idea where the feeling came from, but I told her that I was really going to miss her. She seemed touched but joked that two weeks wasn't that long, and we'd have lots of stories to tell when we returned from our adventures. I let it go at that despite the gnawing feeling inside that something more was unfolding.

The Philippine Airlines flight had a two-hour stopover in Honolulu. Before reboarding, I was upgraded to business class. As we were nearing Manila, I got into a conversation with the passenger sitting next to me. The investment banker was a regular visitor to the archipelago and offered some advice that would serve me well. He said that the people of the Philippines were among the friendliest and most interesting he had ever met, but to keep in mind that family ties mattered most and things were not always what they appeared to be. He pointed out that ethnically the population was Asian, by nature they were tribal, and since the time of Magellan, they had been under Occidental influence, if not domination. He said that most of the population still held favorable feelings about the United States, but as public support was turning against Ferdinand Marcos, distrust of US influence was growing. Moreover, he warned me not to trust anyone until I was sure who they were. He said the city was full of scammers and, as a single traveler, I would be a likely target.

Sam and Jimmy DeGuzman met me at the airport. Jimmy flashed his government credentials and I was whisked through customs and immigration. They dropped me off at a small hotel on a side street not far from the US consulate. Jimmy suggested that I take a nap and freshen up, and he would send a driver to pick me up around noon. I had just fallen asleep when the phone rang. In my groggy state, I assumed that call was from Jimmy but soon realized I was being set up by someone claiming to work for Jimmy. The caller said he had misplaced his wallet and asked if I could meet him in the restaurant next door and lend him some money to be repaid later that day. I told him I would but instead called DeGuzman's office to confirm my suspicions. His assistant assured me that no one on his staff would ask me for cash and to stay in my room until the driver came to pick me up. The wakeup call was an early reminder to watch my step. I was in a very different country.

Jimmy's home was on the other side of town, about a forty-five-minute drive from my hotel. The family lived upstairs and operated a small convenience store on the first floor. Jimmy's architectural office was in a small cottage behind the larger building. His family and staff had laid out a lavish spread for my arrival. After the meal we went to the office to look over the preliminary drawings. To supplement the plans, Jimmy's two young architects had constructed a detailed scale model to help visualize the final product. Seeing the house as a three-dimensional form was far more beautiful than I had expected. The design was postbeam construction, with the roof supported by the frame rather than walls. In a sense, postbeam construction is like building a structural skeleton where the walls wrap around the frame like a skin.

We spent the afternoon going over the plans and making changes and adjustments. The biggest change, which provoked a contentious argument with Sam, involved reducing the width of the bisecting skylight from eight to four feet. After pointing out a few other minor concerns, I gave approval to go ahead with the final blueprints. Sam, who had been bunking at Jimmy's since his arrival a few days ahead of me, stayed on to oversee completion of the drawings, while I returned to my hotel to spend the next few days as a tourist. Once the drawings were complete, Jimmy wanted to take us on a tour around the northern part of the island of Luzon. We would spend the last night in Baguio at the stately manor he had built for his childhood friend. Until then, I was on my own to explore the backstreets and boulevards of downtown Manila.

I had no trouble finding things to do. Manila offered numerous outdoor markets, curious antique stores, and casual cafés. On the negative side, the streets were hot, sticky, and thick with pollution. Most of the problem was caused by jeepneys, which scurried up and down the streets as the primary means of public transportation. Colorful to the extreme, jeepneys were stretched-out Jeep frames, usually made of stainless steel, powered by gas-guzzling, pollution-spewing diesel engines. Each jeepney was named and decked out with an array of mirrors, side horns, gaudy bumpers, and hood ornaments and were often painted in flamboyant colors and design motifs. The longer jeepneys could carry up to thirty passengers packed elbow to elbow like sardines stuffed in a can. My one ride in a jeepney was enough. From then on, I traveled by foot or the occasional taxicab.

By the second day of my wanderings, I began to notice a profusion of the color yellow in the otherwise drab-gray hue that permeated the city. Yellow was most visible in the attire, particularly among women. That evening I stopped by the Hobbit House on Mabini Street, not far from Manila's notorious red-light district. The bistro, as I would soon learn, was established by Jim Turner, an American Peace Corps volunteer who came to the Philippines and never left. Turner, a fan of Tolkien's *Lord of the Rings*, opened the Hobbit House in 1973, staffed the entire operation with little people, and gave them half ownership of the business. I found an empty seat at the back bar and ordered a beer and a bite to eat.

Noticing a yellow "Corazón Aquino for President" banner on the wall, I suddenly made the connection. Yellow was the color of the opposition to the Marcos regime. The bartender confirmed my conclusion and told me that the Hobbit House had become an informal hangout for many of the opposition leaders. When I pressed him for more information, he suggested that I go to the small nondescript bar next door and talk to Jim Turner.

Turner used the side bar as his business office. I introduced myself and told him of my interest in the forthcoming election. Jim was mild mannered but had the enthusiasm of a man on a mission. He was more than happy to talk about what he thought was going to be a great turning point in Philippine history. My first question was, Why yellow? He explained that in 1983 Senator Ninoy Aquino, a leading opponent of the Marcos regime, planned to make a very public return from exile in the United States. He was enormously popular and, taking a cue from the old Tony Orlando song, thousands of yellow ribbons had been tied to trees around Manila to welcome him home. His brutal assassination as he stepped off the plane sparked public outrage, and yellow became the unifying color of the opposition.

Cory Aquino, Ninoy's widow, became the figurehead for the opposition and, by Turner's assessment, would be the next president if the elections were clean. Jim said the Hobbit House had become a gathering place for political dissidents largely due to the regular appearances of folk singer Freddy Aguilar. Aguilar's song *"Bayan Ko,"* banned from radio play, had become the unofficial anthem of the opposition. Turner said he had been harassed by the police, but his American citizenship had thus far kept him from serious persecution. Jim said he knew he was walking a narrow line but felt compelled to play his part in the people's revolution. I returned to my hotel later that evening wearing a yellow "Cory Aquino for President" T-shirt.

I went back to the Hobbit House both remaining nights of my stay. The food was good, the atmosphere was electric, and I felt like I was witnessing history in the making. The last night, Freddy Aguilar, referred to then as the Bob Dylan of the Philippines, made an appearance. Watching his interaction with the audience and feeling the sense of hope that seemed to emanate from his songs left little doubt in my mind that, in the Philippines at least, the times were indeed a-changing.

The morning that we were scheduled to tour the island, the American space shuttle *Challenger* exploded shortly after launch. I was walking along the street after an early breakfast and saw a crowd gathering around a vendor who was laying out the morning newspapers. I made my way through the commotion and picked up a copy of an English-language paper and just stared at the boldface headline: "U.S. Space Shuttle Blows Up." The tragedy had happened half a world away, yet it hit me as hard as if I had been at the launch and seen the event firsthand. I carried the paper back to the hotel and read it in the lobby while waiting for my escorts.

Sam, Jimmy, and the two associate architects pulled up about an hour later. They, too, were shaken by the news and offered condolences as if the event were a personal loss. Despite our dampened moods we stayed with the plan and headed north to the mountain town of Baguio. After a couple hours on the road we pulled into a small fishing village on the eastern coast of the island. We stopped for lunch at a beach house that Jimmy had built entirely out of bamboo.

While his assistants were unpacking the food and setting up the table, I grabbed my snorkel gear and went for a quick swim out to the offshore reef. The equatorial water was so warm it almost felt hot, but the reef was alive with fish. During my brief visit I saw a greater variety of species and overall abundance of fish than I had seen anywhere in Hawai'i. On my way back to the bamboo house I encountered a small group of villagers who had just harvested a net full of fish from the surf. I politely passed on their kind offer to sample the catch. Much as I enjoy sushi, I drew the line at eating fish that were still squirming.

Later that afternoon we headed inland, winding our way up the side of a volcano and deep into the forest, reaching our destination at dusk. Baguio, at an elevation of roughly five thousand feet, was comfortably cool compared with the simmering heat of the lowlands. Jimmy was almost apologetic as he showed us around his friend's house. The home was spectacular, but its owner, who was the minister of information (propaganda in local terms) for the Marcos administration, was an unpopular figure. Jimmy had benefited from his childhood friendship, but he was ambivalent about his association with the government.

Using the huge dining room table as a work site, Jimmy's assistants rolled out the blueprints for inspection. Even at first glance it was apparent that the design was extraordinary. A last-minute decision to put a door at the bottom of the stairway essentially made the building a duplex where the downstairs could be rented out as a separate accommodation. The income potential alone justified the increased size of the building. Pleased as I was with the designs, I was even more relieved when Jimmy announced that the cost of the complete house, including shipping to Maui, was within my budget, assuring that I could get the disassembled house to Hāna. All I had to worry about was putting it back together on my property. How difficult could that be?

We went to the Hyatt Regency Hotel to celebrate our success. Over dinner Jimmy confided that he was planning to use more expensive woods and higher-quality materials than what he had originally proposed. He said he was doing it at his own expense, as he hoped the finished house would lead to additional projects. He knew he would lose his lucrative government contracts if Aquino won the election and wanted to hedge his position by branching out in new directions. After dinner we retreated to the open-air lobby and capped off the night smoking Cuban cigars and sipping cognac. Sam, who had been uncharacteristically quiet that evening, stood up and proposed a toast to "the first all-hardwood house in Hāna." The sly old fox had co-opted my dream to fulfill his. I had no complaints.

We left early the next morning. We had been invited to have lunch with a family that owned a large import/export business. The Fongs were frequent visitors to the West Coast and had become not only valued shipping clients but also good friends with my parents. I introduced Jimmy, Sam, and the associate architects to Mr. and Mrs. Fong and we discussed the ambitious project over lunch. Not that I expected any problems, but the subtle implication that I had an influential family watching out for my interests set my mind at ease. After lunch I signed the contract and gave Jimmy the check to start construction of the wooden masterwork that would soon grace the grounds that were once home to Hawaiian royalty.

When checking in for my flight, I was surprised to find that I had again been upgraded to business class. Then, realizing that I had purchased the tickets through Jimmy's sister, who was a travel agent with close connections to Philippine Airlines, it all made sense. Enthralled with the events of the week, I boarded the plane with a feeling of accomplishment and settled in for the long journey back to Los Angeles.

※ ※ ※

I got in around eight in the evening. Paula picked me up in a rental car, and we stopped by Chez Jay for a late dinner. As usual the place was packed, and we had to wait at the bar for a table. We were both excited but for different reasons. Paula was blunt. She said that since her trip she felt like a changed person. The same could apply to me as well, but I said nothing. By the time we were seated at our table it was clear that more than just time and distance had come between us. As Paula gushed on about how liberated she felt in New York City, I twisted my wedding ring as if it no longer fit. We had come back to each other after our respective travels, but it seemed like we were still worlds apart. I had been down this road before, and the sinking feeling in my stomach warned me that big trouble lay ahead.

Author with architect Jimmy De Guzman & Sam Eason on the way to Bagio. We concluded the deal for the house that evening, late June 1986.

Omens and Endings

I slept in late on Saturday morning—my defense against having to face the day. Paula finally roused me with the reminder that I was to pick up the girls at noon. I showered and made my way downstairs for breakfast. Paula handed me a cup of coffee and asked me how I felt. I took sip and mumbled that I felt confused. She agreed and said we should talk, but with the girls around for the weekend, the discussion would have to wait.

Having sold the Ford just prior to my leaving for the Philippines, we were in immediate need of a replacement vehicle. We had previously decided that a newly introduced Suzuki Samurai would be the ideal vehicle to take with us to Maui, so we gathered up the girls and went shopping for a deal. We made the day an adventure. We drove down to Long Beach and stopped for a quick visit with Etta, then shopped dealerships as we worked our way up the coast. Stopping along the way to walk on piers and pick up snacks, we eventually found a dealer in Manhattan Beach who had the right car at the right price. Paula and the girls drove home in a purplish-blue Samurai with a white fold-down top. I followed behind in the rental.

After dropping the girls off with Denise on Sunday evening, I returned home just in time to answer a call from Steve Wozniak. He had an idea for a film about kids hacking a communication satellite and asked if I would be interested in helping him put a treatment together. I told him I was and agreed to meet him for lunch in San Jose the next day. Paula and I both seemed to be shying away from our impending discussion, so the unexpected diversion was welcome. She dropped me off at the airport and went about her own business before picking me up later that afternoon.

The meeting with Woz went well. After agreeing on a format, he gave me the go-ahead to find a writer and a retainer check to cover my time. Normally such a success would warrant a night on the town, but under the circumstances Paula and I chose to have a quiet dinner at the Sea Lion. After some nervous small talk, Paula said her trip to New York had awakened something inside her and she wasn't sure she was ready to settle down full time in Hāna. At the same time, she said she was still open to helping build the house. I told her that even if I had doubts I was in too deep to turn back. One way or another I was moving to Hāna in the summer. She understood and said that each of us would just have to do what we had to do. At least we were communicating.

After months of fanfare, Haley's Comet made a less-than-triumphant return in the winter of 1986. Dim in comparison to previous appearances, when it had been the brightest object in the night sky, the comet still carried the mystique of being a celestial visitor from beyond the outer reaches of the solar system. Paula, who had been researching the subject for a commemorative flag, found that comets were historically bad news for tyrants and dictators. Julius Caesar's death had been followed by the arrival of a comet so bright it was visible in daylight. More recently, Comet Bennett had heralded the death of Haiti's sadistic dictator Papa Doc Duvalier in late 1970. By Paula's reasoning, the return of Haley's Comet was an omen that the dictator Ferdinand Marcos would be defeated in the election. She was right about the election, but it would take a revolution to get him out of office.

The election that was held on February 7 had two different outcomes. The government's Commission on Elections declared Marcos the winner, while the accredited poll watcher, the National Movement for Free Elections, proclaimed Aquino the winner. Reports of vote tampering and fraud were rampant, culminating in twenty-nine Commission on Elections computer technicians walking out in protest. When the government commission certified Marcos the winner on February 15, masses of Filipinos refused to accept the ruling and took to the streets in protest. Empowered by her growing momentum, Aquino called for strikes and boycotts against the state-run media and businesses operated by Marcos cronies.

Meanwhile, at a base yard on the main boulevard Epifanio de los Santos Avenue (ESDA) near the military bases Camp Aguinaldo and Camp Crame, work was underway on the house. Two shifts of fifteen carpenters each were literally building it by hand, with each piece of wood being carefully prepped and meticulously cut to fit the elaborate structure that was rising in the yard. I had called Jimmy out of concern about the turmoil and was assured the work would continue on schedule regardless of the outcome of the political uprising. At home, Paula and I continued to drift apart. As I became more involved in Woz's project, Paula started spending time with a reacquainted friend from her waitressing days at the Baja Cantina.

A week later, the world's first "people power" revolution was triggered when Marcos' defense minister, Juan Enrile, and the Air Force vice chief of staff, Fidel Ramos, resigned from the government and called on Marcos to do the same. Enrile and Ramos, who was also head of the Philippine National Police, barricaded themselves in Camps Crame and Aguinaldo and enlisted the support of Cardinal Jaime Sin. Cardinal Sin, one of the most influential people in the country, went on Radio Veritas, the only nongovernment media outlet in Manila, and called for people to gather around the bases. Soon, more than a hundred thousand civilians had converged on ESDA and closed off the thoroughfare.

On February 24, with more than a million people occupying ESDA, a squadron of Air Force helicopters defied orders to attack Camp Crame. Instead, they landed inside the camp and joined the opposition. By the end of the day, the majority of the Air Force had switched sides and joined the rebels. The next morning, Corazon Aquino was inaugurated as president in a ceremony at Club Filipino, close to Camp Crame. Cheering crowds sang "*Bayan Ko*" and jubilantly celebrated their liberation from more than a decade of martial law.

An hour later, Marcos conducted his own inauguration ceremony at the presidential palace, but it was all for naught. At the request of the US government, Marcos, his wife, Imelda, and a small contingent of close allies were evacuated from the palace at midnight and taken to Clark Air Force Base. From there they were transported to Hawai'i, where the deposed despot lived out his few remaining years in exile. The next day I received a telegram: THREE DAY WORK STOPPAGE DUE TO REVOLUTION—ADDING ANOTHER SHIFT TO MEET DEADLINE—DO NOT WORRY EVERYTHING BETTER NOW—JIMMY.

A reminder of happier times in our marriage was our weekly "mystery meal." Once a week for more than two years, one of us would deliver to the other a written invitation to dinner. It was up to the host to decide, but not necessarily disclose, the theme of the meal. The invitee was expected to follow whatever instructions were included in the invitation. The meal could be a romantic picnic on the beach where the guest was asked to bring a bottle of champagne, or the invitation might ask the guest to dress in formal attire for dinner at an unnamed location. Afterward, the guest would write a thank-you note to the host. The whole idea of the weekly meal was to distract from the daily routine and reenergize the romance. The correspondence between invitations and thank-you notes was itself a love story.

In early March I got a call from Rebecca. She had just returned from an extended stay in Hawai'i, where she had studied with a highly regarded Hawaiian spiritual teacher. She had brought the woman back with her to conduct a workshop in Santa Monica. Rebecca said she had told her teacher about our plans to move to Maui and was hoping we could all get together. It was my turn to host a mystery meal, so I suggested that they come over the next evening for dinner. I gave Paula a simple invitation: "Dinner at home with surprise guests. Wear a flower in your hair."

Rebecca and Emma Veary arrived just as the golden-red glow of the setting sun flooded the western sky. I took the exceptionally brilliant sunset as some kind of omen. Before entering the apartment, Nana, as she preferred to be called, offered a short blessing and gave us each a long heartfelt hug. Over an island-centric dinner of barbecued fish, rice, and salad, we talked about Hāna. Nana told us that Hāna had always been a special place throughout Hawaiian history, and we were privileged to be able to live there. She seemed pleased when I told her that I had dreams of the property becoming a gathering place for visionaries and others seeking a more peaceful planet. At the end of the evening I was treated to another of Nana's, as I would come to learn, famous hugs. Before breaking the embrace, she looked deep into my eyes with compassion and kindness.

The uncertainty between Paula and I came to a merciful end on Easter eve in late March. Our relationship, which had been in steady decline, finally hit bottom when Paula arrived home late after co-babysitting with her reacquainted friend. When I objected to the intrusion to our marriage, Paula paused, put her hands on her hips, stomped her foot, and declared that "our marriage, as we know it, is over." Without saying another word, Paula opened the pyramid-shaped trinket box that sat on our dresser and pulled out the Camel pack that had been stashed there since the beginning of our relationship. I nodded in agreement as she tore open the pack, pulled out two cigarettes, and handed me one. We lay down on the floor and smoked the stale tobacco side by side. When the ritual was over, I grabbed a blanket and pillow and went downstairs to sleep on the couch. Our marriage was over. Just like that.

Odds and Ends

Easter morning. I awoke before dawn and decided to drive up the coast to watch the sunrise. I should have stayed on the couch. I walked out to the carport and found the Suzuki stripped of its fold-down top and spare tire. In my dark mood I took the violation as a personal assault. Trying to regain my composure, I turned onto the Pacific Coast Highway and headed north. A couple of miles up the road, I stopped at a gas station to get a cup of coffee. Back on the highway, a decrepit old car pulled up beside me as the sky began to lighten. For no apparent reason, the brutish-looking passenger rolled down his window and gave me the finger. Then he and the driver broke out laughing and pulled away, billowing a trail of choking black smoke in their wake. Wanting no more of the morning, I made a U-turn and headed for home. Just before reaching the canyon, George Harrison's poignant tribute to John Lennon, "*All Those Years Ago*," came on the radio. I turned into the empty Sea Lion parking lot, took a spot overlooking the surf, and broke down. I felt empty and very alone.

Paula moved into a cabin at a Topanga beach motel on Easter afternoon. The next day, as if scripted, Bob Wilson and his wife, Arlen, arrived as previously scheduled house guests. Bob was consoling on learning that Paula and I had split up, but it was Arlen who lifted me out of my stupor. She seemed to instinctively know what to do and say to help me refocus my attention on where I was going and on letting go of the past. She also was a wonderful cook who insisted on taking over the kitchen.

During the three days we spent together, I witnessed the dynamics of a relationship that had been seasoned and tempered over years of hardship and joy. Whereas Bob's genius was his intellectual capacity,

Arlen's gift was the innate wisdom of an old soul. It was as if there was a mystical union between them, not unlike the allegorical alchemical wedding referred to in some of Bob's writings.

On the last evening of the Wilsons' stay, Rae Dawn Chong took us to a dinner party in the Hollywood Hills. Bob, who dreamed of seeing one of his novels made into a movie, was enamored to be in the company of filmmakers. While driving home, I mentioned to Bob the project I was working on with Steve Wozniak. Not surprisingly, he found the idea of kids hacking a communications satellite hilarious. He suggested, for example, superimposing Donald Duck talk over a speech by President Reagan. I told him I supposed it could be, but the treatment being prepared by the young screenwriting team we had hired would probably be less subversive.

The next morning, Bob and Arlen shared with me their ambitions for the next year. Bob was about to start another book and was hoping to get enough of an advance to buy a personal computer and a washing machine, both of which were considered luxury items in their Spartan life in Dublin. It struck me as odd that such a remarkable and influential writer had to live so much on the edge. Equally, I was moved by the bond between the two of them that seemed to override their financial shortcomings. Later that day, I drove them down the coast to Palos Verdes and dropped them at the home of another of Bob's sponsors. My spirits lifted, I returned to Malibu to begin the countdown to the move to Maui.

Later that week I met Paula at her latest temporary residence, the home of one of her fellow schoolteachers. We sat and talked in the Suzuki. Although emotions were still charged, in a moment of clarity I told her I felt that what was happening between us was beyond our control, as if we were being pulled apart by forces greater than ourselves. I don't know if she felt the same, but seeing it from that perspective gave me some degree of comfort. I told her I was going back to Maui in a couple of weeks to work out pre-construction details. I asked if she would take care of Shooter while I was away. She said she would take care of the dog but declined the offer to stay in the apartment.

The following week, I flew up to San Jose to deliver to Woz the draft of the film treatment. I told him that I thought the writers accurately portrayed his vision of the story and that I was very satisfied with the result. I also told him that Robert Anton Wilson had expressed interest in the project, and I thought we could get him to do an alternative treatment in exchange for a computer and a token amount of cash. Steve had not personally read anything by Wilson, but he was familiar with his work and readily accepted the proposal. I added that, unlike the PG storyline submitted by the young screenwriters, we could expect Bob's treatment to be closer to an R version of the story. This got Woz thinking about a more adult take on his idea, and he suggested that a meeting with Captain Crunch was in order.

I called Bob, who was still on tour in California, with the good news. I told him that Woz had already ordered an Apple Macintosh computer to be delivered to his home in Dublin, and a check big enough to buy a washing machine with money left over would be forthcoming when he turned in the text. I told him to work within the confines of the original premise of hacking a communications satellite but to make the story his own. He was pleased with the news and said that he would get started as soon as they returned to Ireland that weekend. He promised to deliver a draft within a few weeks.

Meanwhile, I met Woz and John Draper, aka Captain Crunch, in the lounge at the Burbank airport. Draper was infamous in hacking circles, and Woz wanted to tap his brain regarding what it would take to hack a communications satellite. Steve turned on a microcassette recorder, and the two cyber legends began to talk shop. Captain Crunch loved the challenge and said the question was not could it be done, but how. For the next hour or so, I was left in the digital dust as the two of them conversed in a dialect beyond my comprehension. Finally, Woz turned off the recorder and handed me the tape. "It's all in there," he said. "Just don't let it fall into the wrong hands." Meeting over, Steve caught a flight back to San Jose and the Captain retreated to an undisclosed location. I mailed the tape to Bob and never heard anything about it again.

My quick trip to Maui was all business. Besides the mundane tasks of getting a post office box and opening a bank account, I had to find a place to live during the early phases of building the house. As luck would have it, the neighbors across the street from my property had a trailer in their backyard that was available for rent. Although very small, it had a bed, table, camping stove, and compact refrigerator, which was all I needed. I was even able to secure a second, smaller trailer for my brother, Rick, who was coming over for a month to help get things started. Whereas unseen forces seemed to be conspiring to close out my old life, equally implausible factors were apparently opening doors to a new one.

I returned to an apartment that, other than a note on the table, was devoid of any trace of Paula. Her note was brief and to the point. It said that she had taken everything that she came with plus a list of assorted items that she deemed more hers than mine. She closed by saying that she would be staying with her friend until she could find a place on her own. It was a clean break, and I had no problem with her distribution of property; it was one less thing to contend with. At least Shooter was still there to greet me. I picked up his leash and we took a long walk before returning to the apartment, where I grilled a porterhouse steak that we shared for dinner.

Paula and I made one feeble attempt to get a divorce before I left for Maui. We had arranged to meet Dave Anderson, who was also a lawyer, for dinner at a restaurant in Santa Monica. He had said that without kids and with little property to divide, we should be able to come to a quick settlement, file papers, and be free to move on with our lives. Problem was, he didn't show up. As we waited for his arrival, we indulged in a couple rounds of drinks. Eventually, as the alcohol loosened our tongues and as emotion overrode reason, we got into a fight and left the restaurant in a huff. The ride back wasn't much better. Enough went down that evening to preclude any remote chance of reconciliation. Divorce was too much trouble. It was much easier to just abandon each other.

A Round of Farewells

The Chernobyl nuclear meltdown on April 26, 1986, spewed a radioactive cloud that spread across Northern Europe and the upper regions of North America. I flew up to Seattle a few days later as the dissipated but still "hot" cloud covered the region. I went to talk with Tom as both producer and friend. The producer was there to account for the more than four years of trying to get *Woodpecker* into production, and the friend was there looking for guidance. I took the shuttle into town and walked to Tom's apartment a mile or so away. The light drizzle wasn't glowing but was probably best avoided. With barely a month to go before moving, I was emotionally numb and full of self-doubt. Radioactive rain was the least of my concerns.

Tom welcomed me with his usual warmth and charm. We sat in his living room and talked for a while, mostly about where to go with *Woodpecker*. I was relieved that he thought it a good idea to put the project on the shelf for a year or two. The script had been shopped from one end of Tinsel town to the other and had become stale. He thought moving to Maui to build a handcrafted house in the jungle was an exquisite way to bide time while awaiting the next reshuffling of studio executives. I told him my disappointment was more than not getting the film made. In a way, I had seen it as my mission to bring his work to the screen. He brushed my comment aside and told me *Woodpecker* would be just another chapter in my memoir. I laughed then. I'm writing now.

That evening we met a friend of Tom's for dinner at a waterfront restaurant near Pike Place Market. She was collaborating with Tom on an exhibit for one of the local galleries. I admired the intelligent dialogue and playful manner between them. It also added to my doubts about my decision to move to Maui. I enjoyed the intellectual stimulation of being around and working with artistic and creative people. I knew the life I was being drawn to would have its own rewards, but I was unsure of how well I would adjust to a less cerebral environment. All the more reason to envision the house as a gathering place for imaginative and creative minds.

The next morning Tom walked with me to the shuttle stop. I was ambivalent about the parting. With Tom agreeing to put the film project to rest, I could move to Maui unburdened, without second thoughts. Yet I wouldn't even be making the move if I hadn't picked up a copy of *Still Life with Woodpecker* five years earlier. I thanked Tom for his trust and support and told him he would always have a place to hang a hammock anytime he cared to come over for a visit. He threw me a lopsided grin and said he was counting on it. I boarded the bus and headed for the airport as Tom strolled back to his apartment in the radioactive drizzle.

I returned to Malibu to find several urgent messages from Sam. I called him back and found that the engineer, while working out details for the building permit, concluded that the house would not fit on the property as originally planned. The engineer recommended that the house be placed entirely on the flat ground next to the pond, rather than tethering part of it to the lava-rock cliff. I asked Sam what he thought. He said that it would require reworking the entrance, but otherwise should not be a problem. He asked that I come over right away to approve the change so that foundation work could begin. He mentioned that he would also arrange for the blessing of the land during my visit.

A week later I was back in Hāna to meet with Sam and Steve Pitt, the engineer. To my delight, I found that by not having to build support pillars, repositioning the house was actually going to save money. The next day, I met the construction crew Sam had lined up for the job. The man who would figure most prominently in the preparation of the land was Ron Hill. Ron, another California expat, had a backhoe he operated with the delicacy of a surgeon. He had already cleared the ground of overgrowth and leveled out the area where the house would sit, all the while careful not to disturb the natural rock formations. Ron and his wife, Kelly, invited me to their house for dinner that evening. Again, I was moved by the spirit of friendliness and aloha that seemed to be a natural way of life in Hāna.

Hawaiian tradition calls for blessings before and after doing almost anything. This is especially true when building a house. The blessing for my property was held on the last day of my short visit. The event was officiated by Matthew Kalalau, the minister of a nearby neighborhood church. "Uncle Matthew" knew the property well, having grown up in the immediate area. Before the blessing he took me aside to talk. He said that I could not really own the land, as it was there long before me and it would remain there long after me. He added that along with the rights to my tenure came the responsibility to care for the land. He emphasized that the ʻaina was so special that I must say a prayer of gratitude every day. Uncle Matthew then gathered the guests in a circle and invited the ancestral spirits of the land to join the ceremony. He blessed the land twice, first in English, then, for the benefit of the ancestors, in Hawaiian.

Sam and Patty hosted a small reception at their home after the blessing. Among the attendees was a young man from Tonga. Their guest, who was about to start college in Utah, had come across an ʻawa plant while exploring the hills above the Easons' home and harvested a batch of its roots to take with him to Utah. ʻAwa root, or kava, as it is more widely known, is ground into a powder-like substance, mixed with water, strained, and served as a ceremonial drink throughout Polynesia. Sam, aware of my apprehension about the move, gave me a small bag of the cuttings and told me to take it home and pulverize it in a coffee grinder and squeeze it through a paint strainer. He said the beverage was relaxing and would help ease my anxieties. It sounded like good medicine, so I took Doctor Sam's advice and packed it in my bag.

While browsing through the airport bookstore, I came across *Maui the Demigod*, by Steven Goldsberry. I picked up the book, subtitled *An Epic Novel of Mythical Hawai'i*, and discovered that the storyline took place in Hāna. Finding the book when I did seemed to be another affirmation that, despite my misgivings and trepidations, I was on the right path. During the flight back to Los Angeles, I jotted down a list of things that needed to be done in advance of making the move. I had two weeks to vacate the apartment before catching my one-way flight back to Maui. I was grateful for the 'awa.

One of my first priorities was to meet with my accountant. Bob Eddy was a friend and former neighbor from when I lived on the beach. He was also one of the few people who didn't think I was crazy throwing everything away and moving to Maui. As my accountant, he knew my delicate financial position and saw the move a matter of having little left to lose. Bob wished me well and said he looked forward to coming over for a visit when the house was standing. On the way back to Malibu, I stopped by Chez Jay for lunch. Jay was surprised to see me there without Paula and asked if everything was all right. I told him that the marriage was over and that I would be building a house on my own; otherwise everything was fine. He was sorry to hear the news but noted that I was a survivor and he had no doubt that everything would work out for the best. He thought building a house in the Philippines during a revolution, then reassembling it near a cave in Hāna, was a wonderful caper.

Next on my list was a quick trip up the coast to see Woz. I had mailed him a copy of Wilson's film treatment, and we needed to discuss where he wanted to go with the project. We met at a restaurant near the San Jose airport. Steve was amused by Bob's rather unconventional take on his story idea, but his attention had shifted to other priorities and he had decided to shelve the project altogether. I told him that Bob really liked the concept and wanted to develop the treatment into a script. Woz, perhaps flattered by Wilson's interest in his idea, asked me to relay his gratitude to Bob and to tell him that he was free to develop the treatment any way he wanted. After lunch, as he drove me to the airport, Woz mentioned that he loved Maui and he would look me up the next time he visited the island. Pulling up to the curb, he handed me two checks, one for Bob and the other for my efforts. I told him I liked his style and that I'd follow up with contact information when I got settled.

That evening I blended a cup of 'awa and started reading *Maui the Demigod* while sitting on the front deck. I had a lot on my mind but knew I needed a moment to relax. The 'awa did the trick. With Shooter by my side, I drifted off to a time when Hāna was home to gods and legendary mortals. The more I read, the more I became excited about the move. I wasn't just moving to another place; I was starting anew in a land with mythical origins. The uncertainty that had been holding me back suddenly gave way to the realization that what I was about to do was privileged. Rather than fret, I should be living in gratitude. Inspired, I went upstairs and started discarding relics from the past to make way for the future.

I didn't flinch when a collector came by to pick up my record collection. I didn't even blink when a buyer rolled away my jukebox. I was so intent on letting go of everything, I gave most of it away. The one thing I should have let go of, but didn't, was Shooter. I couldn't bear the thought of making the transition alone, so I signed Shooter up for the four-month quarantine at the state-run kennel in Honolulu. I took him to the airport a few days before my departure and checked him in at the freight counter. Shooter, who normally loved adventure, looked dismayed as the attendants lifted his crate onto the conveyer belt that carried him away to a pressurized cargo hold.

The girls came over the night before I moved out of the apartment. We went out for dinner and talked about Hāna. I couldn't tell if the girls were really happy that we were going to have a house there or if they were just trying to mimic my enthusiasm. In any case, we had a fun evening. After dinner, we went to a movie and stopped by the Rose Café for dessert on the way home. We talked more over breakfast at the Colony Coffee Shop the next morning. We made plans for them to come over toward the end of summer, and I told them I would likely be back in about a month to ship the last of my belongings to Hāna. We decided that it would be fun to write letters back and forth and, as soon as I could get a line installed, talk regularly on the phone. Since they were already spending most of their time with Denise, we agreed that the move was a good thing. We could still be close, though living far apart, and have a home in Hāna as well.

After dropping off the girls, I met Margot at the apartment to sort out what was left of E I Productions. I took the corporate documents and books to leave with Bob Eddy. Margot took the computer, printer, and file cabinet to store at her house. I rented a van and shuttled everything else to Etta's house for temporary storage. It was late afternoon when I returned the van and picked up the Suzuki. Margot had offered me a room at her house that evening. It was Friday night and I had promised her a night on the town. I was about to go home and clean up when suddenly it struck me that I no longer had a place of my own to shower and shave. It was the first of many nomadic nights to come.

I spent the next day with Chuck Alton at his apartment in the valley. I had met Chuck at the Mad Scientists and Artists Party, and over time he had become a good friend. Chuck was a radio guy, his passion being the production of inspirational stories. He used his second bedroom as a studio but had a wide and comfortable couch that I would get to know well in the times ahead. I tried my best to lure him to Hāna to help build the house, but he wasn't buying the pitch. He said he would rather visit when he knew he would have a roof over his head.

I had one more stop to make before leaving for Maui in the morning. I excused myself that evening and made a pilgrimage out to the Old Place. It was a busy night, but I was able to squeeze into a seat at the bar. Barbara, who knew I wouldn't be alone unless there was a problem, was discreet and didn't ask questions. Cowboy did. The first thing he said when he saw me was, "Where's the missus?" I told him that the marriage was over and I was heading off to Maui alone. Over dinner I shared with him that I was coming to see our parting as inevitable; I was just sorry it didn't end on a higher note. I paid the check and was about to leave when Cowboy said he had something to show me.

He took me out back and told me he thought there might be a message for me in the women's bathroom. He recalled that on our first date, after showing Paula the way to the restroom, she came back laughing and asked him for a pen. He didn't know what she wrote, only that she seemed very pleased with herself. I took Tom's flashlight and, while he stood guard, ventured into the women's room. After a few minutes of reading some very clever and inspired graffiti, I found it. There, just below the mirror, to the left of the sink, she had scrawled:

The Woodpecker Lives!
Paula 3/25/82

I rose early the next morning and, with a single suitcase and a toolbox, drove the Suzuki to the airport. I parked the car, left the keys under the seat, and put a tape that I'd made for Paula in the tape deck. It closed with Leon Russell's *"Back to the Island,"* which seemed to say it all.

I boarded the flight and took my seat by the window. It had been a long road, but I was finally on my way home. I closed my eyes and sighed. It was time for a new life to begin.

Part Three

The Journey

"*I say, follow your bliss and don't be afraid, and doors will open where you didn't know they were going to be.*"

—Joseph Campbell

Picking Up the Pieces

My brother, Rick, who was taking a four-week leave of absence from his life in Northern California to help me get started building my house, was at the gate to meet me when I arrived in Honolulu. Our first order of business was to take a cab to the animal quarantine station near Aloha Stadium to check on Shooter. The kennel was clean and as humane as could be expected of an animal incarceration facility. Shooter, no doubt believing that I had come to liberate him from captivity, looked betrayed when Rick and I left without him a short time later. I knew that subjecting Shooter to a four-month quarantine was a foolish mistake, but it was too late to do anything about it.

We flew to Maui later that afternoon, picked up a rental car, and spent the night at the Pioneer Inn. The next morning, we drove over to the Kahului harbor to meet Ron Hill, who had made the arrangements to get the disassembled house to Hāna. After signing the shipping and customs documents and paying the fees, the forty-foot container, which was too long to make the tight turns on the Hāna Highway, was trucked to a base yard a few miles inland. There, for the next three days, Ron, Rick, and I unloaded the container and stacked the contents onto two twenty-foot-long flatbed trucks. Central Maui was blistering hot and walking in and out of the long steel box was like taking a sauna in the desert. Exhausted, we crashed each night on the floor of a nearby house Ron used when working on that side of the island.

We finished loading the trucks late Friday afternoon, and Rick and I drove to Hāna to get some sleep before their arrival early the next morning. My trailer was smaller than I had remembered, and Rick's was barely larger than a tool shed, but we were happy to have mattresses. Even the comfort of a bed could not calm my restlessness that night. The cold reality of what I was doing was setting in, and I was feeling apprehensive about the whole venture. Building the house had become a bigger project than I had imagined. Worst of all, I was questioning my capacity to follow it through.

Rick, Ron, and I were waiting on the side of the road when the trucks pulled in just after dawn. Ron directed one driver to back partially down my tenuous dirt driveway and sent the other to a staging area down the road. I was mentally preparing for the daunting task of again unloading twenty-six-hundred square feet of my unassembled house when Sam and three stout young men pulled up in a pickup truck. Sam, who had been heralding the arrival of the "most beautiful house in Hāna" for weeks, had rounded up a welcoming committee to offer their kōkua (assistance). With their generous help, we unloaded the trucks and had neatly restacked the lumber in piles on the plateau at the base of the driveway by midafternoon. The pieces would be moved and sorted numerous times before being used in construction, but even in its fragmented state, my house was home.

We had just finished covering the wood with tarps when Ron's wife, Kelly, and a couple of her friends came by to start setting up for a party. As I was quickly learning, local-style parties are often as much about gratitude as celebration. In my case, it was both. Rick and I took Kelly's empty cooler into town and returned it filled to the brim with ice and beverages. Ron fired up a portable barbecue, and soon we had set out a table full of food on one of the woodpiles. Neighbors, friends, and friends of friends started arriving just before dusk and lingered well into the evening. Most brought food to contribute to the ever-changing smorgasbord of offerings. The outpouring of kindness and goodwill from the community was overwhelming. I could only hope to live up to everyone's expectations.

Ron came by early Monday morning with local builder Jerry Smallwood. Jerry's job was to lay out string lines and mark the spot for each of the eighteen concrete footings on which the house would stand. The normally routine task was complicated by two factors: placement of the house had to be just right to fit into the horseshoe-shaped lava cleft and, since the foundation pieces were already cut, the location of the mounting brackets had to be a hundred percent accurate. Jerry artfully fit the footings into the tight quarters while skillfully aligning the foundation to face due north. I later learned that Smallwood was also an acupuncturist.

The next day we started digging holes. Even with the help of a couple of Hāna High wrestling team graduates, it took a week of digging and building the forms before we were ready to pour the concrete. While Jerry directed the foundation work, Ron built a sixty-four-foot-long plywood shoot to move lumber down from the staging area as needed. When completed, we slid the heavy support posts and first-floor framing materials down to the job site and stacked them in place next to the footings.

By mid-June the site was set and ready. Construction, however, could not begin, as master carpenter Roger Albea, who had been contracted to lead our construction team, had been detained in the Philippines due to visa problems. With little left to do, Rick brought his girlfriend over from the Mainland and spent his remaining time touring the island. Two weeks later, word came that Roger was on the way. I flew over to Honolulu early the next morning and, after visiting the quarantine station to see Shooter, returned to the airport only to find that Roger's flight had been delayed. With time to kill, I found a comfortable spot in the lobby overlooking the airport garden and got out the journal that I'd picked up on Maui. I took a pen from my pocket and, on the first page of the blank book, began a dialogue with myself.

June 28 – Honolulu Airport

Awaiting the arrival of a stranger who holds my fate in his hands. Roger, I'm told, is the wizard who will put my disassembled house back together. Could use some reconstruction myself. Like Humpty Dumpty after the fall, the old pieces no longer seem to fit. Too much to worry about now, the challenge at hand is to get the house off the ground.

On eve of brother Rick's return to California. Footings he helped form in background prepped and ready for master carpenter Roger at house site. Hāna, July 1986.

House Raising

Roger brought with him a handsaw, chisel, hammer, and hand planer—everything he needed to build a house. I recognized him from the photo Jimmy had sent and introduced myself as he cleared immigration. We caught the next flight to Maui, then drove to Hāna, talking story along the way. Roger lived with his wife and two children in a small village just outside Manila. He had worked with Jimmy for several years building trade pavilions around the world, but this was his first visit to Hawai'i. He was looking forward to working in Hāna and excited to be rebuilding the house that he first built in Manila. He said it was the most beautiful house he had ever worked on. After a quick inspection of the job site, I took Roger over to Ron and Kelly's home, his temporary residence until the new house became habitable.

We started work with a crew of five men and a backhoe on the day after Roger's arrival. The plan was to build the frame up to the roof, then fill in the walls and floors working down from the top. The heavy hardwood posts and beams that formed the house were notched to interlock and be bolted in place. The largest pieces were tied to the backhoe and lifted into position for assembly. Slowly, piece by piece, the skeletal frame took shape. Within a couple of weeks, the structure had risen to its full thirty-foot height above the jungle floor. For an exquisite moment, the house, without walls, floors or roof, stood naked on the 'aina, transparent to its surroundings. Its geometrical shape conformed to the angular rock cliffs with the symmetry of a Zen garden.

Building the frame went fast, but it would take more than a year to complete the house. The carpentry team consisted of Roger, framing crew carryover Danny Baker, and myself. Roger ran the show, Danny was his apprentice, and I filled in as needed. As Roger and Danny began placing the rafters, I took temporary leave of my on-site duties for a quick trip to Los Angeles. I still had to collect, crate, and ship the remainder of my personal effects and, more importantly, to liquidate whatever I could.

A light fog dimmed the usually sparkling Los Angeles city lights as my flight touched down at the airport. I picked up a van and drove down to Long Beach to see Etta. Her house had been a sanctuary since childhood, and it was the only place left that still felt like home. I spent most of the next day sorting through everything I had packed up in Malibu. I found I had kept more stuff than I had need of, or space for, on the island. Setting aside a couple of fine art pieces and some antique oriental rugs that I had collected in better times, I culled out the essentials to be shipped to Maui. With the art, rugs, and discards loaded into the van, I drove over to Santa Monica to distribute the goods. I dropped the unneeded clothing and personal items off at a thrift shop on Main Street, consigned the carpets to a nearby rug merchant, and left the art with Dave and Barbara Levene for future divestiture.

After spending time with my daughters the next morning, I drove back down the coast to pick up the computer and office supplies that I had left with Margot. Finally, with my belongings pared down to a bare minimum, I took everything over to an expeditor in San Pedro, who packed the goods and delivered the crate to the dock for shipment to Maui. That evening over dinner, I shared with Etta my second thoughts about building the house in Hāna. I told her that I had underestimated the construction costs, and it was questionable that I had enough funds to complete the project. She candidly reminded me that once begun, a job must be completed, then offered her modest portfolio of Craig Corporation stock as a contribution to my new home. When I started to object, she remarked that she had bought the stock in the first place because of my enthusiasm for the company, so by her reasoning, she was just reinvesting in me. I was humbled and in no position to refuse her generosity.

Flying home, I sketched out the expenses and concluded that with Etta's stock I would be able to keep Roger and Danny on the payroll and at least get the plumbing and electrical system installed.

Depending on what the rugs and art sold for, I might even have enough to buy appliances and furnishings. It was going to be tight, especially if construction took longer than expected. I had already adjusted to a humbler life; with a little luck, I thought I just might be able to go the distance.

🔺🔺🔺

I moved out of the trailer and into the house in early September. It was still more job site than home, but the roof was on and the floors were mostly down. The site had electricity courtesy of neighbors across the overgrown pond, who kindly let us string a power line into their electrical box. On-site plumbing was limited to a hose out front that doubled as a shower on the deck; public restroom facilities were available at the ballpark just down the street. It wasn't an ideal situation, but it beat paying rent.

It didn't take long before the place began to feel like home. I started off sleeping under a mosquito net on a small futon mattress on the floor of the master bedroom closet. My kitchen needs were met with a large ice cooler for food and drink and a grill on the deck for cooking. A phone line was connected to the site and cable hookup was forthcoming. Other than once or twice weekly supply runs to the other side of the island, I was living and working in the house twenty-four hours a day. Over time, as the walls went up and the rooms took shape, I felt like I was growing into the house as it was being built around me.

September 16 – Home

Took a serious fall last evening, lucky to have survived. Was looking at the night sky and walking across the living room for a better view when I stepped off the open stairwell and tumbled to the bottom floor. Hit my butt hard on a protruding floor board on the way down. Hurt so bad I couldn't move, only moan. Took a while to get the strength to drag myself out and climb back upstairs. Don't know why the stairwell was left uncovered, but I should have been watching my step. My head has been in the clouds since I got here and last night I got my ass kicked because of it.

House raising from jungle floor, wooden chute for delivering lumber on bottom left at job site. Late July 1986.

Roger Albea guiding ceiling rafter to helpers on peak thirty feet above ground at job site. August 1986.

Settling In

The next step in economizing was replacing the rental car with a vehicle of my own. The car of choice was another Suzuki, but a new one was out of reach and second-hand models were hard to come by. I'd about given up the thought and was looking into other options when I came across an ad for a Suzuki very much like the one I had left behind. I called the owner and found she was leaving the island and wanted a quick sale. We arrived at a price over the phone, and Danny Baker and I drove out to Lahaina and picked it up that weekend. I had to take out a loan, but the monthly payments were less than half what I was paying for the rental. In time, the car would more than pay for itself, but that's another story.

Shooter was released from quarantine in early October. Packed in his traveling crate, he flew into the Hāna airport on a commuter flight from Honolulu. I picked him up in the Suzuki and after a rousing round of wags, hugs, and licks, Shooter hopped on board and we drove off as if our separation had just been a bad dream best forgotten.

Shooter quickly explored his surroundings and adapted to the camp-like environment. He especially liked traversing the plank that ran from the corner of the deck to the midway point on the rock stairway that connected the two levels of the property. While just walking across the plank was a tightrope act that I never got used to, my four-legged friend ran across the narrow board like it was sport. With Shooter riding shotgun, my frequent supply runs to Kahului became less a burden and more a chance to spend quality time with my canine companion. He and the replacement Suzuki provided at least a small sense of continuity with a past that was rapidly slipping away.

🌴🌴🌴

Around the middle of October, Roger expressed concern that we were going to be short of materials to complete the job. The woods needed for on-the-job modifications and additions were not available on the island, so we called Jimmy DeGuzman and found that procuring the lumber wouldn't be a problem, but shipping would be. Since the shipment would be too big for standard delivery service and too small for a container, Jimmy suggested that I make a quick trip to the Philippines to purchase house furnishings to combine with the lumber to fill a small container. He pointed out that by buying directly from the factories with a favorable exchange rate would make the trip worthwhile.

A week later I was back in Manila, this time staying at a less secluded hotel on the main boulevard near the US embassy. On the surface the city looked the same, but a post-revolution vibrancy made it feel almost like another country. As Jimmy drove me across urban Manila that first afternoon, I noticed a different look about the population. Everywhere, even in the poverty-stricken areas where kids played basketball on crumbling roads, people were out and about, sporting smiles and moving with a sense of confidence. When asked about the revolution, Jimmy, apart from his likely loss of government contracts, felt confident that Aquino's administration would stimulate a more inclusive economy, which at the very least would benefit his family store and eventually boost his architectural business as well.

After a welcoming family meal, Jimmy and I went over my shopping lists. I told him that I wanted the furnishings to be tropical, preferably rattan and bamboo, yet elegant. The next day, Jimmy and Rose, a designer on his staff, took me on a tour of furniture showrooms from one end of Manila to the other. The following day, we drove out of town to visit a couple of factories that specialized in bamboo furnishings. Over dinner that evening, we discussed the options and decided to go with a combination of bamboo and traditional furniture. Upon agreeing on a room-by-room furnishings list, Jimmy arranged for his driver to take me on an overnight tour of the southern side of the island while he negotiated prices and worked out shipping details. Two days later I was on my way home. Jimmy was right: I had saved enough on furnishings, shipping included, to more than cover the cost of the adventure. By happenstance more than intention, I was becoming versed in the intricacies of International trade.

🌴🌴🌴

I returned to Hāna just in time to join Roger and Danny on the roof. The three of us painstakingly nailed each of the mahogany shakes in place. The job was hot and tedious. There were a couple of roofers in town who could have completed the job in much less time using nail guns, but Roger assured me that by using copper nails as protection against the corrosive salt air, the roof would last twenty-five years. It took us more than a week to nail the shakes onto the massive roof and it was still not complete. The real challenge would be installing the fourteen tempered-glass skylight panels that were being fabricated in California and wouldn't be on-site until after the first of the year. Until then, we kept the rain out with plastic-wrapped plywood.

With the roof secured, we shored up the frame by filling in the exterior walls and wrapping the entire house with tongue-and-groove hardwood siding. The job took longer than it should have, as all the pieces were precut and numbered, and we spent more time sorting and locating than nailing. When the exterior walls were complete, we framed the interior walls, then called for the plumber and electrician. Both contractors, based on the other side of the island, ended up camping on the job site to avoid the commute. It saved me money, and they enjoyed the chance to surf and fish on the beach.

I spent my first Thanksgiving in Hāna alone at home sweeping up and clearing the house of the heaps of sawdust left behind by the "rats and termites," Roger's term for plumbers and electricians. That simple, most basic task brought about an unexpected sense of gratitude to be tending to the magnificent structure that was soon to be my home. The Hawaiian word *mālama*, I would eventually learn, means "to take care of" and applies not just physically but in a spiritual context as well. Even without knowledge of the word, it was then in the act of cleaning the house that I recognized the interconnectedness between myself and the land over which I presided. In a subtle way it was a transcendental moment not unlike that experienced at the birth of a child. After phone calls to family on the Mainland and sharing a Thanksgiving dinner platter (courtesy of the Hill family) with Shooter, I retired to my futon in the loft and fell asleep content and grateful for the privilege of being where I was and doing what I was doing.

🌲🌲🌲

The plumbing inspector approved the rough-in on the following week, and we had a working toilet and sink in the upstairs bathroom by the beginning of December. Having reached that welcome milestone, Roger, Danny, and I spent most of December preparing the master bedroom for my daughters, who were coming over for Christmas. They had made a short visit in late summer when I was living in the trailer, but this was the first time they would be staying in the house, and I wanted it to feel like home. We installed the doors, windows, and screens, finished off the walls with paneling, and had the room ready for temporary occupancy with days to spare.

After dismissing my crew for the holidays, I placed a potted Norfolk pine, known locally as the Hawaiian Christmas tree, in the bedroom and decorated it with tinsel and garlands from the Hasegawa General Store. On Christmas Eve, I laid out the girls' futons with the comforters that Paula had made for them and hung stockings filled with trinkets and treats on the wall next to the tree. At dawn Shooter and I, both wearing Cowboy's festive holiday ties, drove over to Kahului to pick up the rest of our family. It was hard to tell who was happier to see whom. Shooter was all tail, wagging so hard I thought he might knock down the girls, who were climbing all over him. After a quick stop in Pāʻia for a snack at Hats, our reunited clan drove to Hāna for our first Christmas in our new home.

Matters of the Heart

Climbing on to the roof was easy when all it took was a ladder from inside the loft to the open skylight. It became a different story when installing the four-by-four-foot tempered-glass panels that were too large to maneuver up through the spiral stairway and too heavy to haul twenty feet up an outside ladder. Roger's solution was to bridge a plank from the edge of the cliff to the entry-area roof. He reinforced the twelve-foot span with a makeshift scaffold of scrap framing lumber and ropes tied to rocks and trees. The bridge was secure, but the twelve-inch-wide plank left no room for error when carrying the glass panels over the jagged lava-rock garden two stories below.

I liked the openness and simplicity of the angular loft and had slept snugly in a darkened corner since the holidays. Once the skylights went in, my nighttime retreat became a window to the universe. I would fall asleep each night watching the moon, planets, and stars come into and out of view. There was a new look to the sky every time I awoke. The rhythmic dance of celestial bodies combined with the whims of weather made each night a unique event. When it rained, it was like sleeping under a waterfall.

By early spring, I felt like I had finally progressed from camping on the job site to living in my house. We still had several more months of sanding, painting, and finishing details ahead of us, but the doors, windows, and screens were in, the electricity was on, and the major appliances were operational if not formally installed. Roger had moved into the downstairs bedroom, and a new acquaintance was becoming a frequent after-hours visitor. Annmarie, another Southern California renegade going through a divorce and starting anew in the jungle, was a welcome complement to our male crew. Shooter seemed especially happy to have some female companionship.

The longest, most boring part of the job was sanding every square inch of the massive structure. The pickets and deck railings alone took Danny and me weeks to finish, the whole job lasting months. While we toiled with our vibrating sanders, Roger built the cabinets and attended to carpentry details. We took a break from our routines just before Easter, when I received notification that the furniture was on its way. With no place to store the furnishings, we had to jump ahead and paint the inside walls and finish the floors before the container arrived. My temporary relief from sanding duties was replaced with frequent round-trips to Kahului for equipment rentals and finishing supplies.

A month later, the twenty-foot container landed in Kahului and was trucked out to Hāna. Most of the furniture was too big to carry over the ramp, so we had to haul it up and down the unimproved natural path through the lava-rock garden to reach the upstairs entrance. After a long day of lifting and lugging, the container was empty and the house had the makings of a home. Annmarie came over that evening to help prepare and share our first meal at the large circular dining table. She brought with her a gallon jar of lilikoʻi juice made from fruit in her garden. The honey-sweetened passion fruit beverage became even more intoxicating when Roger, Danny, and I discovered that it mixed well with tequila.

Annmarie and I had arrived in Hāna under similar circumstances, but our histories and life trajectories were very different. She was born into a devout Christian family and married her high school sweetheart shortly after graduation. Through a succession of unlikely events, she had come to possess a modest off-the-grid house next to a running creek in the middle of a meadow surrounded by lush vegetation and an assortment of fruit-bearing trees. She had purchased the Eden-like property with the intention of one day establishing it as a sanctuary for traveling missionaries.

I was attracted to Annmarie the moment we met at a lūʻau in November just as her marriage was ending. A few months later, I saw her at the pay phone in town and stopped to ask how she was. "Divorced, free as a bird," she replied. Technically, I wasn't, but we were both in the same boat and glad to have found each other.

Annmarie would often join Shooter and me on our weekly supply runs. The two-hour drive on the Hāna Highway gave us plenty of time to talk and share personal stories. We had very different cosmologies but found we had very similar attitudes about life and purpose. Whereas she would quote an inspirational biblical passage, I would illustrate the point with a line or lyric from the gospel of John, Paul, George, and Ringo. In the end we came to agree that, be it from the Bible or the Beatles, *love is the answer.* Finding humor in our respective predicaments, we early on began referring to each other by title rather than name. She, with the lavish spread in a magical garden, was the Contessa, and I, because of the similarity of my house to a fine wooden ship, was the Captain.

I marked my first-year anniversary in Hāna by driving across the island to pick up Shooter after his three-day stay at the vets. He had been listless for a couple of weeks, and when he started coughing up blood, I made an emergency run to the veterinary clinic in Kahului. The doctor called that morning to say that Shooter's condition had stabilized enough to bring him home, but the diagnosis was not promising. He said that an x-ray exam detected an enlarged heart, but he suspected there was another underlying condition that caused the hemorrhaging. He said it could be a virus that would pass or something more serious. In either case, there wasn't much more that he could do. My heart was heavy with guilt and regret for bringing him to Hawai'i to begin with. No matter what the cause, I was sure it traced back to his quarantine in Honolulu.

Shooter never recovered. He died on a Sunday evening, the first day of summer. Annmarie, Roger, and I had just finished dinner and were sitting on the front deck enjoying the twilight when Shooter, uncharacteristically, came up to each of us for a moment of affection. A short while later, I heard him whimpering and rushed around the deck to find him attempting to cross the plank from the stairway to the porch. In his weakened state, he seemed unsure of his footing. Desperate, I called to him in a lowered voice as commanding as I could, "Shooter, come!" With a momentary burst of energy, my loyal companion crawled the rest of the way across and continued to my bedroom door. There he started shivering and collapsed, laying his head on Annmarie's lap. I held him the best I could, petting his head and telling him he was a good dog and that I loved him—over and over until his trembling body stilled and he slipped away.

Cooler heads than mine prevailed that evening. Annmarie counseled that I wrap my departed friend in his blanket and find a special place in the garden to lay him to rest, while Roger rounded up the tools to dig his grave. We buried him that night under the royal palm on the bank of the dormant fishpond.

June 22, 1987 – Home

It was a tough day today for everyone. Roger lost his patience and actually swore while working on the "son of a bitch" stairway railing. Danny had to hang from the deck rafters while sanding the underside of the roof, and I spent my time robotically sanding the siding, trying to get my mind off of last night. My grief is mixed with anger, mostly at myself for embarking on this fool's journey in the first place. Shooter's death was a costly price to pay for the folly that has led me here. To make matters worse, I see no alternative but to sell the house upon completion, rendering the whole endeavor one big mistake. My daring escape to another life has morphed into being trapped in a dream that has seemingly gone bad. With bridges to the past burnt to a crisp, and the way forward shrouded in uncertainty, whatever the future holds I must now face alone.

Home Stretch

Shortly after Shooter's death, Annmarie and I were driving over to Kahului when our discussion turned to my dire financial situation. She questioned why I planned to sell the house before even having a chance to enjoy the fruits of my labor. I explained I had run out of options; overloaded with debt and lacking credentials for a bank loan, I saw no other way out. She replied that she thought I was being hasty and questioned the wisdom of selling the property when in time it could be providing an income. She was right about the house; when finished, it had the capacity to cover the mortgage by being rented out to overnight guests. Yet despite Annmarie's assurance that something would come up, I was at a loss as to where I was going to find the funds.

A week later Annmarie and I met with her father and her financial adviser to work out the terms of a short-term mortgage. Her advisers made it clear, however, that the loan was only temporary, and in the event of default, my property would be foreclosed on just as forcibly as if the loan was with a bank. It was a roll of the dice, and I had no idea how I was going to repay the loan, but like teacher in the Sufi story who buys time from a death sentence by promising to teach the king's horse to talk, I had been graced with three years to find a way.

By the end of July, the upstairs was finished enough to host a pre-completion gathering featuring none other than Robert Anton Wilson. The event was the result of a phone call I had received few months earlier. The caller, who identified himself only as K.C., had attended a Wilson lecture in Vancouver and approached Bob about doing some events on Maui. Bob was game and gave K.C. my phone number, suggesting that he give me a call. We met for coffee a few days later at the Artful Dodger bookstore in Kahului.

K.C. was also newly arrived on Maui and, like myself, had felt drawn to the island as if following a primordial dream. Besides being a fan of Wilson's writing, K.C. was interested in esoteric philosophy and wanted to bring a series of great thinkers and visionary writers to the island for lectures and workshops. I wasn't sure I wanted to make that my calling but offered to work with him in setting up a couple of events for Bob. The owner of the Artful Dodger readily agreed to host a lecture, and I offered my home as the venue for an intimate one-day workshop. I didn't expect to make much on the venture, but at the very least, it was an opportunity to spend some quality time with Bob.

It was fitting that Bob was my first house guest. He was with me when my life in Malibu was falling apart, and he was with me as the pieces were coming back together in Hāna. The workshop, attended by only the most ardent Wilson fans willing to drive all of the way out to Hāna, was so engrossing that several of the participants stayed on beyond the potluck dinner that was to conclude the program. Having long thought of the house as being a gathering place for artists and visionaries, Bob's event, and the lavish comments from the colorful and intelligent attendees, seemed to consummate that vision. After the workshop, I took Bob on a grand tour of the island, ending up at the Pioneer Inn for a parting night in Lahaina. Driving back to Hāna the next day, I couldn't help but laugh at the thought of Bob, like a mischievous child, leaving a trail of Bob Dobbs (patron saint of the Church of the Sub Genius) stickers affixed to signs and landmarks at the various places we visited. As Tom Robbins aptly concluded in *Still Life with Woodpecker*, "It's never too late to have a happy childhood."

I had no sooner dropped Bob off at the airport when I met a teacher of a different kind. I was talking with Patty Eason at the post office when she introduced me to Parley Kanaka'ole, a vice principal and faculty member at Hāna High School. Parley had a humble, kind presence, but his stature and bearing gave the impression of a mighty Hawaiian chief. Patty noted that we had something in common, as Sam had also designed Parley's house. Parley joked that he hoped we had more than just houses in common and asked me what I did before moving to Hāna. Awkwardly, I told him that I had taken time off from film producing to build the house, but as it neared completion, I was uncertain about returning to that business. He responded by saying that maybe Hāna was trying to tell me something about taking a new direction in life. I was taken by how well he read my situation and agreed that he might be right. Before leaving, I invited Parley to the completion lū'au that was scheduled for the Labor Day weekend. He said he would like to attend and asked me if I had selected a name for the house. When I told him that I hadn't yet given the idea much thought, he said he'd see if he could come up with some suggestions.

A week before the lū'au, I still hadn't come up with a name for the house. House names never mattered when I lived in places where homes were identified by street address or descriptive location, but they did matter in Hawai'i. Polynesian culture identifies not just people but also inanimate objects like homes, places, and even canoes with names that are reflective of who or what carries them. Names are not chosen arbitrarily; they often appear in dreams or in messages from ancestors. Sam had offered several suggestions, but none felt right. The massive open skylight and golden hue of the finished hardwoods gave the house a spacious, luminous ambience that I felt should be considered in the name. I had a feeling but couldn't yet find the words.

Finding the name wasn't my only problem. With only days to go before the lū'au, I had been unable to arrange for someone to do the blessing. Uncle Matthew, who sanctified the land before construction, was going to be out of town, and the other local minister was already committed to the island-wide softball tournament that same weekend.

Sam assured me that the person conducting the blessing didn't matter as much as the intention with which the prayer was given. He told me not to worry, that someone would be there to do the honors when the time came. I was uncomfortable with the uncertainty but didn't seem to have any option other than to trust the process.

Tiffany and Melanie arrived on the Sunday night before the party, and my folks flew in from the Bay Area a few days later. Annmarie, who had been considering starting a tour guide service, stepped in to keep everyone amused while I frantically tended to last-minute details. Roger, Danny, and I finally put down our tools early Friday afternoon. There was still some trim and detailing to be done after the lū'au, but for all intents and purposes, the house was ready for its coming-out party. That evening, we cooked up a dinner for family and crew that resembled a rehearsal dinner before a wedding: lots of toasts, lots of jokes, and lots of love.

Robert Anton Wilson during his Maui lecture tour and workshop at mostly completed house. Hāna, June 1987.

Finishing Line

I awoke before dawn the next morning and quietly slipped out to the beach to watch the sunrise. The day marked the official completion of the venture that had set my course to Hāna, and I wanted to savor the milestone from daybreak to sunset. As the eastern sky lightened and the stars began to fade, I recalled the incongruous sequence of events that had brought me to that moment. Was it fate, destiny, or just dumb luck that lifted me out of my old life and deposited me on this distant shore? Was the move a conscious escape from the past in search of a brighter future, or had I just grasped a lifeline when my world was disintegrating? It really didn't matter. I was where I felt I belonged. Humbled and grateful, I sat in wait as the sun slowly rose from the sea and the new day began.

First order of business after breakfast with the family was to drive out to Sam's to use his Hawaiian-English dictionary. I had more precise feelings about the name for the house and wanted to see if I could find a Hawaiian word to match the expression. While I glanced through the book, Sam asked what kind of meaning I wanted the name to imply. In my highest aspirations, I wanted the house to be a place where people would gather to exchange ideas and learn from each other. Sam thought for a moment then, with a knowing grin, suggested I look up (he pronounced the word slowly) *ma-lama-lama*. I read the definition aloud, *"light of knowledge, clarity of thought, enlightenment, radiant-clear."* Hale Mālamalama—house of light and knowledge—so it should be.

I returned to the house to find it abuzz with activity. Roger and Danny were cleaning up the last of the building debris that littered the yard, while my parents and daughters were inside washing windows and vacuuming the floors. Ron came by a short time later and took charge of setting up serving tables and stringing decorative lights about the area. By midafternoon my mother had taken over the kitchen, cooking up an assortment of pūpū (appetizers) and side dishes to complement the traditional lū'au offerings that were being prepared elsewhere.

The kālua pig arrived just as we started laying the food out on the table. Henry, one of the young men who had helped in the early days of construction, and his father, Milton, had cooked the ti-leaf-wrapped hog in an *imu* (underground oven) all day and delivered the carved delicacy in two huge serving warmers. Other friends dropped off a commercial-size pot of rice, and Annmarie and her neighbor stocked the refrigerator with platters of iced lomi salmon. All that was left was the poi. A taro farmer from nearby Ke'anae had delivered a quantity of the purple staple but left no instructions on how to prepare it for serving. Knowing at least that it had to be thinned with water, I was about to open the first package and start mixing when Parley Kanaka'ole came up behind me and asked if he could give me a hand.

How he knew to show up early I'll never know, but his timing was impeccable. Poi, which is pounded from taro root, is the most sacred of all Hawaiian foods, and preparation has its own protocol. Parley asked for a large bowl, preferably wooden, and told us that kneading poi is traditionally done by men and that it would be his pleasure to prepare it for us. While Parley was readying the poi, I tended to the last detail by lighting the welcoming tiki torches to illuminate the crooked path that led to the house.

As guests began parading down the hill, Parley inquired if I had selected a name for the house. I told him that Hale Mālamalama seemed to best express my vision of the house as a place of peace and learning. He paused a moment and said that, though he had come up with a couple of other suggestions, he agreed that Hale Mālamalama was the right choice. Then, without forethought, I asked if he would offer the blessing. He replied that he would be honored to do so.

At dusk I called for the guests to gather around the food table and started the evening by thanking everyone for their support and generosity in helping to make the day possible. I gave special thanks to

Roger and Danny for their hard work and dedication, and to Sam, who led me to the 'aina, designed my home, and mentored my freshman year in Hāna. Parley took it from there and asked that we join hands and form a circle. He began by inviting the ancestors of the land to join us as he offered a pule (prayer) in Hawaiian. He told us that the 'aina was once the provenance of royalty and praised the work that we had done to restore its luster. He then offered another pule in Hawaiian that concluded by announcing that the house was to be known as Hale Mālamalama. Lastly, he removed the ti leaves that had been protecting the food and offered a prayer of gratitude for the meal that we were about to share.

After feasting, the party kicked into gear as streams of guests filed in and out of the house, dancing and singing well into the night. At one point so many people were stomping on the living room floor, I feared it might collapse. Roger, somewhat tipsy from a night of nipping on his special reserve bottle of Chivas Regal, told me not to worry, *"Hale Mālamalama,"* he said, "was built to last."

From left Annmarie, Melanie, Roger, Author with Parley Kanaka'ole offering blessing. Hāna, Labor Day weekend, 1987.

Roger returned to the Philippines shortly after the completion party. It took Danny and me another month to finish up the last of the details. When done, I signed on with a local overnight rental service and, on November 13, welcomed the first overnight guests to visit Hale Mālamalama. Initially I rented out just the downstairs unit while I kept residence in the much larger upstairs quarters. Soon finding that I needed the additional income, I moved my meager belongings into the supply room behind the laundry facilities and made the upstairs available for overnight rentals as well. The idea was that I would use the storage room as a base and reside in whichever suite wasn't occupied by guests. Paradoxically, as occupancy rose, I ended up spending more nights in a hammock in the supply room than in the finer quarters that were being enjoyed by strangers. I had created a castle and was living like a servant.

December 21, 1987 (Winter Solstice) - Home

Much to be grateful for this passing year; house is finished and I'm marginally keeping afloat. Appearances aside, however, the box I've built myself into is unsustainable—priced out of my home and lacking capital to make another run on "Woodpecker" or anything else for that matter. Rather than despair, been keeping busy pulling weeds and dressing the garden, writing letters to friends and family, catching up on reading and, since amicable parting with Annmarie, finding contentment taking long walks and daily swims with just my own company. Learning to live more in the moment and trusting in a process beyond my ambitions. As my first full year in Hāna comes to an end, I must trust it won't be my last.

Author with Annmarie and Danny Baker toasting Roger Albea on eve of his departure to the Philippines. Hāna, October 1987.

Old Haunts and New Prospects

In late January I packed my sparse winter wardrobe in a carry-on bag, turned the house keys over to Stan, the rental agent, and caught a flight to Los Angeles. The purpose of the trip was to put some new life into *Woodpecker,* but it also afforded me time to spend time with my daughters. I didn't know it then, but the visit would be but the first in a succession of tours of duty to Los Angeles and other Mainland destinations that would keep me on the road for the better part of the next two years.

The Mainland junket began where I had left off a year and a half earlier, sleeping on the couch in Chuck Alton's apartment in the San Fernando Valley. Dennis, a Maui-based producer and newly acquired production partner, was staying with friends in the Hollywood Hills. Dennis and I met a couple weeks earlier when he approached me with interest in producing a film version of another of Tom's novels. After a lengthy discussion and learning of Dennis' close personal ties with a wealthy Swiss investor as well as his considerable industry contacts, we decided to combine our resources and coproduce *Still Life with Woodpecker.* I was uncomfortable forming a partnership with someone I hardly knew and whose personality was distinctively different from mine, yet expediency overrode caution and I went for the deal.

I had already filled Phoebe in on our plan to meet with Dennis' Swiss investor in San Francisco at the end of the week and had asked for an option agreement for film rights in order to move forward. By the time Dennis and I met with her in L.A., she had already spoken to Tom and offered us a conditional thirty-day option that could be extended only if we could put together a development deal within that time. The time frame was fine, as Anders, our prospective investor, would be returning to Switzerland on Saturday morning. Our only chance to make a deal would be over dinner Friday night.

I spent the next couple of days with my daughters and making the rounds of old haunts and hangouts. One evening I stopped by the Central Park Café in Brentwood and ran into a table full of old advertising cronies. They invited me to pull up a chair and join them. As the evening wore on, I started sharing stories of my island adventure while circulating photos of the house. I told Paul Decker, creative director of the agency handling Suzuki's automotive advertising, about how my Suzuki had become a trusted companion during my ongoing runs across the notorious Hāna Highway to pick up building materials and supplies. I went on to boast about how it never let me down, no matter what I put it through. Paul paused for a moment, then commented that he had always wanted to do a commercial on the Hāna Highway.

Dennis and I took to the road early Friday morning. The seven-hour drive gave us the time to prepare our pitch, which had to be subtle enough for dinner conversation, yet straightforward enough to get the deal. Dennis, a gifted schmoozer, had wined and dined Anders and his wife at his modest cottage in Kīpahulu during their recent visit to Maui. In that enchanted setting, Dennis had warmed his guest to the idea of investing in a film version of a Tom Robbins best-selling novel. My job was to provide enough substance and detail to close the deal. We decided to ask for a $200,000 initial investment to set up a small pre-production office, develop a new script, find a director, and secure legal presentation. We also felt entitled to a small producers' fee for our efforts to put a package together.

We checked into the hotel with barely enough time to dress and prepare for dinner. At the appointed hour we caught the elevator and arrived in the lobby just as Anders and his lovely bride stepped out of an adjacent car. Anders greeted Dennis with the warmth and enthusiasm of an old friend.

Though the meeting had been at our request, Anders took over and acted as our host. Over a relaxed meal, Anders inquired about my background and involvement with the project. I shared with him my belief that the unique nature and popularity of Tom Robbins' bestselling book had the potential to make the film both a commercial and artistic success. I handed him photographs of my newly completed Hāna home and commented that what Hale Mālamalama was as a house was comparable to what I envisioned *Still Life with Woodpecker* could be as a film. Anders was amused by the analogy and offered that his interest in filmmaking was more than financial. His nephew Jonathan was putting together a film production company and he thought our project might fit well into his portfolio. We saw no problem with a joint production agreement as long as we retained creative control.

We got down to details over brandies and coffee, telling Anders that we needed $200,000 in development funding and that we were projecting a production budget of eight million. Anders thought our proposal reasonable but deferred committing funds until consulting with his nephew. When Dennis pointed out we were working within a narrow window of opportunity to secure film rights and needed some earnest money up front, Anders offered to write a personal check for $25,000 as a good faith deposit if we could provide a letter of understanding stating what the money was to be used for and what rights would be granted to the investors. We told him he would have the letter in the morning.

Without legal advice, we kept the memo simple, stating only essential information and deferring the details until later. We finished the letter just before midnight and dropped it off at the front desk to be typed up overnight. Noticing that the hotel's bar was still open, we stopped by for a nightcap. It had been a good evening, but it was only a step forward. We needed a plan to close the deal.

We presented the letter to Anders over breakfast the next morning and asked if he had any objections to Dennis accompanying him back to Switzerland to help make the presentation to his nephew. Anders smiled agreeably as he reached for his pen and wrote out the check.

Fortunately, Dennis always carried his passport when traveling. Unfortunately, neither of us had the funds to cover the airfare. My credit cards were maxed out and Dennis was late on his American Express payment. Refusing to let the opportunity pass, Dennis called Amex and talked his way into a temporary lifting of the credit hold on condition the overdue amount be paid within five days. I took Anders' check and Dennis' card number and promised to post payment immediately after opening Alchemy Entertainment's bank account on Monday morning. With that understood, we packed our bags, checked out of the room, and went our separate ways.

"Woodpecker" Rising

February 13, 1988 – Pioneer Inn

Finishing up all-too-short break from Mainland business at the PI after two weeks in Hāna tending the land and recharging my spiritual battery. Back to Los Angeles tomorrow to meet our Swiss investors. If all goes well, the balance of initial funding will come through and the "Woodpecker" saga begins once again. Mixed feelings about L.A. Been away not even two years and feel like a phantom. I'm there and not there. Too soon to know if this "Woodpecker" incarnation is actually going to take flight, but at least for now someone else is paying the bills.

Although Dennis had managed to get a letter of conditional commitment while in Zurich, the release of the balance of funds was subject to Andres' nephew Jonathan and his lawyer, Richard, approving our development plan. Dennis and I met with Phoebe a couple days prior to the arrival of our prospective investors to finalize our presentation package. Phoebe, with Tom's blessing, recommended that we hire their mutual friend John Binder to write the second draft of Tom's script. The hitch was that John would accept the job only if he was also attached to the film as director. Binder's credentials as a writer were stellar, but with only one low-budget (though delightful) film to his directing credit, Phoebe was concerned that this might be a problem with the backers. Dennis felt they were mostly concerned about the bottom line, and experience directing a successful low-budget film could be seen as a positive. Figuring we were in a stronger position with a writer-director on board, we decided to go with Binder and let the cards fall where they may.

Dennis and I greeted our prospective investors at the airport and escorted them to their hotel in Santa Monica. I picked them up a few hours later and took them to a dinner reception that Dennis was hosting at his guest residence in the foothills above the city. The visually stunning house could have been on the cover of *Architectural Digest*. The sleek steel-and-glass structure protruded over a bluff, affording an unobstructed view of open sky and a million sparkling lights in the basin below. Dennis and his friend/host had invited a few of their film industry associates, mostly female, to add to the ambience. In a bizarre way the setting looked like a set out of a movie about making a movie. After a mellow evening of eating, drinking, and mingling, I drove our contented but jet-lagged guests back to their hotel and reminded them that we had a meeting at Phoebe's office at eleven in the morning.

🌲🌲🌲

In the midst of the comings and goings with the investors, I got a call from Paul Decker informing me that Suzuki wanted to make a commercial of me driving the Hāna Highway while building my house. I was flattered but more intrigued about how a casual barroom boast could become cause for an actual commercial. I told Paul I would come by his office to go over the details on Friday morning after dropping Jonathan and Richard off at the airport.

Phoebe, Dennis, and I were in sync and put on a persuasive presentation. More importantly, Jonathan and Richard accepted our assessment that John Binder's first film was well crafted and demonstrated that he had the wit and skill to translate Robbins' quirky novel to the screen. With that settled, we reached a quick agreement and sealed the deal over lunch at Chez Jay.

A week later Dennis and I signed a short-term lease for a small apartment in Malibu, inked a contract with John Binder, and retained the services of a highly regarded entertainment lawyer. Kathy, friend and former secretary, was moving back from New York and would come to work for us as an executive assistant on the first of the month. Like a phoenix, *Woodpecker* was again rising from the ashes.

Dramatic Conclusions

April 7, 1988 – Hale Mālamalama

Just finished three days of shooting the Suzuki commercial on the Hāna Highway. What a trip! The most resolute "I'll never" declarations in my adult life came back to slap me in the face like I was an insolent child: "I'll never drive the Hāna Highway again"; "I'm done with advertising, I'll never make another commercial." My arrogance fated me to driving the Hāna Highway so many times I became a commercial. I am humbled and greatly amused.

⚜⚜⚜

After shooting the commercial in Hāna, I returned to Los Angeles to do the voiceover. A few days later John Binder and I flew up to Seattle for a story session with Tom and Phoebe. John had scoured both the novel and Tom's original screenplay and sketched out a skeletal script. Tom was pleased with Binder's synopsis and, after clarifying a few areas of concern, gave John his blessing. With Jonathan and Richard coming to town in mid-June for a progress report, we had little time to lose. At the very least, they would expect to see a script.

⚜⚜⚜

During the time John was writing the script, a sequence of events transpired that ultimately led to the undoing of Alchemy Entertainment's relationship with the Swiss investors. In a nutshell, the first sign of trouble was when Jonathan hired Michael, an independent producer, to act as his adviser during the development process. Shortly thereafter, Dennis took Jonathan to a Hollywood gala along with his date, Jeanine, a producer from New York. Jonathan fell for Jeanie and courted her in New York, and a month later she became president of Jonathan's production company. All the while the consultant Michael was preparing an independent analysis of our project. Initially everyone was cordial and cooperative. The unraveling began once the script was delivered.

I was having dinner at the bar at Chez Jay in late April when one of the waitresses came by to compliment me on the Suzuki commercial. She said she recognized my voice and had a big laugh when she realized it was me. I hadn't yet seen the spot and didn't even know it had started to air. In a short while, the spot was running on heavy rotation and I was getting calls from old friends and even strangers who would look up my Maui phone number to see if I was a real person.

Meanwhile, Dennis and I were having our own troubles within the partnership. Problems started to arise as the development funds dwindled and Dennis and I started squabbling about how the remaining funds should be allotted between entertainment and operational expenses. Most of our funds were already spent or committed, and the amounts in question were relatively small, but it was a tug-of-war down to the last dollar.

Had Binder's script arrived under different conditions the movie might well have been made. John did a superb job, offering a fresh take on the novel while retaining the essence of Tom's writing, but it got caught up in a deal going bad. By the time we presented it to our investors in mid-June, Jonathan was hardly speaking to Dennis and seemed averse to our involvement with the project altogether. Richard accepted the screenplay as fulfillment of the terms of our agreement but withheld further comment until reviewing Michael's accounting of our expenditures. We were told they would evaluate the material and notify us within sixty days whether they wished further involvement and under what conditions.

As our relationship with the Swiss cooled, my career as a commercial spokesperson came to an abrupt end. My downfall was the result of the July issue of *Consumer Reports*, which rated the Suzuki Samurai as being unfit to be on the road. The cover story claimed that the Samurai was prone to rolling over and gave the product a rare "Not Acceptable" rating. The scandal became headline news and made a mockery of my commercial (even more than two decades after the fact, Seth MacFarlane spoofed the spot on an episode of *Family Guy*). Had it been my call, I would have stood by the commercial as a testimony to the road worthiness of the car. Suzuki, however, was shaken by the attack (rumored to have been instigated by Lee Iacocca of Chrysler, whose Jeep sales had suffered since the introduction of the Samurai two years earlier) and chose not to publicly challenge the findings, pulled all advertising, and phased the Samurai out of its lineup altogether. Whereas being taken off the air prematurely was a blow to my ego (I was getting used to the attention), the loss of residuals, anticipated to last through the end of the year, was a serious blow to my already meager pocketbook.

I ran out the lease and closed down the office at the beginning of July. With little to be done until hearing back from the Swiss, I returned to my land and readjusted to a simpler lifestyle. An actress I had recently met before leaving Los Angeles came over for a couple of weeks to hang out and island-hop when Stan booked us out of the house. Even if I had only a temporary residence on a space-available basis, it felt good to be home.

Our estranged investors contacted us through Michael, requesting we meet in Los Angeles in mid-August. Dennis and I made our own respective arrangements and met with Phoebe and our lawyer just before the meeting. Jonathan and Richard arrived a short time later, accompanied by Jeanine and Michael. The staging was clear: They were running the show and we were there to listen. After a brief summary of their evaluation of the project, they offered to finance a budget of three million dollars contingent upon our attaching at least one marquee actor, such as Tom Cruise, to the film. They further insisted that they would control the budget. When we responded that the budget was untenable for below-the-line production alone, they offered to take it off our hands and produce it themselves. In return for the script and film rights they offered us executive producer credits and minimal fees upon completion of the film. Our attorney asked for their position if we chose not to accept either option. We were told that we were free to pursue alternative financing as long it was understood that their investment be returned out of any future funding. We conferred for a moment, then answered that we found both offers unacceptable and would seek funding elsewhere.

One of the perks of doing the Suzuki ad was that I was given the use of a car whenever I was in Los Angeles. They kindly extended the privilege through the end of the year even though the spot was off the air. The day after the meltdown with our backers, I dropped Tiffany and Melanie off at their mother's house in Serra Retreat and ran head-on into Paula. Approaching the narrow Malibu Creek crossing from opposite directions we met face-to-face in the middle. I got out of my Suzuki and walked over to hers. We eyeballed each other for a moment and broke out laughing at the incongruity of our chance encounter. Paula chided me about the commercial and said she was thinking about approaching Suzuki to do a sequel of her driving the Pacific Coast Highway over five hundred times while her husband built his house in Hāna. We chatted briefly and decided to "do dinner" some time to discuss our divorce. After exchanging contact information, we shared a friendly kiss goodbye.

Two days later I packed my bags and was preparing to take my Suzuki back to the corporate office parking lot when I discovered it gone. It had been stolen off the street in front of Chuck's apartment. I called the police and filed a report, then caught a cab to the airport. It was Sunday morning; I would call Suzuki from Maui. All I could think of was getting out of town. I'd had enough drama in the City of Angels.

A Year of Service

October 11, 1988 – Hāmoa Beach

Faced a moment of truth last week when a guest made an offer to purchase Hale Mālamalama. First impulse was to accept the offer and make a fresh start. Then it hit me that I really don't have anywhere else to go and the offered price wouldn't net enough to do much with it in any case. Seems I have little choice but to stay with the land and somehow make it work. Maybe it's time to let go of seeing Hale Mālamalama as my home and develop the property into an actual inn. By adding a couple of cottages on the bluff I could live in one and use the other as an additional rental. When the fishpond is restored (as I trust it will be some day), the setting could become one of the most beautiful sites in Hāna. Something to think about.

※ ※ ※

While my daughters were visiting over the holidays, I acted on an idea that I had been chewing on since hiking in the Malibu foothills with Melanie in early August. We had been following a rutted dirt trail when we came to a sizable pile of rubbish that someone had gone great lengths to dump in a dry creek bed. On the way down the hill we talked about how much of the assault on the natural world was, in the case of litter at least, just plain bad manners. We speculated about how cool it would be to have a designated day when everyone took time out from what they were doing to join together to pick up trash and clean up their respective neighborhoods. We calculated that if only 1 percent of the five billion people living on the planet participated, the event would still generate a workforce of over fifty million volunteers.

Whimsical though it may have been, the thought stuck in my head like a tune that wouldn't go away. I started imagining how a global cleanup campaign could actually become a reality. I was playing with two ideas: how to communicate the message and how to motivate participation. Advertising was obviously the key to communicating the event, and promoting community after-work parties seemed a good way to attract participants. In the grandest of all plans, key local parties with celebrity performers would be linked together in a global broadcast.

By the time my daughters arrived, I had convinced myself that the cleanup event could happen. While sitting on the beach with Tiffany and Melanie, I began the pursuit by writing "A call for a worldwide cleanup day," a one-page document that defined the event. Since I'd be returning to Los Angeles after the first of the year for some unfinished *Woodpecker* business, my thought was to circulate the manifesto and spread the idea of a cleanup party to anyone who would listen.

Our *Woodpecker* team reassembled in the middle of January at the Rose Café in Venice. We had a script and a director and not much else. John Binder had garnered tentative commitments from a couple of well-regarded actors but neither had the star power to get the film made. We weren't getting any traction with the big studios, and the independents we had approached found the material too big a risk. Nonetheless, Dennis had a new lead in New York that he wanted to pursue, and Phoebe still had a couple of contacts she wanted to approach. We all agreed to keep a low profile while "chumming the waters" and reconvene should something rise to the surface.

The first person I called on for the cleanup project was a former advertising cohort and longtime friend, Sam Morgan. Over dinner I gave Sam the rundown. I told him how the idea of a universal day of community cleanups came about and why I felt it important to make the effort to see it happen. I added that the event was also an opportunity to demonstrate a constructive use of advertising, explaining that information about the cleanup effort could be piggybacked on existing ad schedules. Coca-Cola, for example, could produce a spot showing a group of people cleaning up litter in a park with a voiceover inviting viewers to *"Do your part and join Coke in celebration of the Global Cleanup Party."* The ad closes with the group loading their litter-filled bags into the back of a truck while popping Coke cans to toast their achievement.

Sam listened intently and asked how I planned to raise the money to get things started. I naively answered that launching the event was more about spreading an idea than selling a product. Rather than solicit corporate financial sponsorship, we would encourage advertisers to promote the cleanup as they sell their products. Sam said he got that part but wanted to know how I was going to run an organization without any money. I told him I was counting on lots of volunteers. He shook his head, picked up the check, and told me to count him in.

A few days later, Chuck Alton suggested I get in touch with Dr. Noel Brown of the United Nations Environment Programme. He had recently seen Dr. Brown on a panel discussion and said he was very supportive of grassroots environmental projects. I contacted Dr. Brown's New York office and was told to send a letter outlining the event and how the Environment Programme might be involved. A week later, Dr. Brown contacted me to say he was intrigued with the use of advertising to promote environmental awareness and action. He said he was going to be in Los Angeles in early March and asked if I could arrange a meeting to discuss the idea with some of my advertising associates. I told him I would set something up and get back to him with details.

Sam and I presented the cleanup day plan to Dr. Brown over dinner at a popular boutique hotel in Westwood. We invited a few of the key players in the Los Angeles advertising community to join us in the discussion. The guests had only been told the nature of the get-together; they learned the details firsthand with Dr. Brown. The concept took hold as the conversation morphed into a brainstorming session. One idea inspired the next as a collective vision formed. The idea that most personified the "We are all in it together" spirit of the cleanup party was an imagined spot featuring the CEOs of both Coke and Pepsi toasting each other with their respective products while saying something to the effect of "Though we are spirited competitors, we all win when we come together to clean up the planet." Dr. Brown thought the event would be a natural tie-in with the United Nations Environment Day on June 5, so we selected Saturday, June 2, 1990, as the working date for the cleanup party. The advertising wizards offered to conjure up an official name and logo, and Dr. Brown offered to host a follow-up conference in New York.

While preparations were underway for the New York conference, I had a personal matter to attend to. In late February, Etta had unexpectedly passed away. I had been entrusted by the family to lay her ashes to rest with her husband in Red Lodge, Montana. With her urn stowed safely in my carry-on bag, Etta and I boarded a flight from Los Angeles to New Mexico for an overnight stop in Albuquerque. The next morning, we flew to Billings, Montana. During the flight I discovered that the pair of young women sharing my row were ballroom dancing instructors. I couldn't resist telling them of my conscripted ballroom dancing classes in my youth, adding that the reason for my trip was to deliver my benefactor's ashes for interment in Red Lodge. Learning that Red Lodge was their destination as well, I offered them a ride.

The two-hour drive gave me a chance to reminisce about Etta with my traveling companions. Etta, the youngest and most beautiful of three sisters, was born on a farm in Iowa. In childhood, her family migrated to Pomona, California, to start an orange orchard. As a young woman, Etta ventured to Long Beach, where she met and married William Meyer, owner of the Strand Theater, the premier movie house in the city. "Billy" was from a wealthy Montana family known for its refined hospitality. Together they traveled around the world, where Etta assimilated the social graces of European society. She became an accomplished Viennese dancer and a formidable bridge player. Billy died prematurely when Etta was in her forties, and though she remained socially active over the years, she never remarried.

I told them how Etta had always been an angel on my shoulder and speculated about how different my life would have been without her generosity and unconditional support. The girls, both of whom lived in Orange County just a few miles south of Alamitos Bay, were drawn into the story and joined me when I delivered Etta's ashes to her husband's crypt. An angelic pair of ballroom dancers escorted Etta on the last leg of her journey. Her final waltz couldn't have been more exquisite.

I stopped by Sam's office shortly after returning to Los Angeles to review the ad hoc committee's recommendations. The committee's name for the event, "The Great Global Cleanup Party," was self-explanatory; the logo of a stylized stick figure sweeping a broom was right on the mark. The humble yet energetic image was clean, simple, and friendly. Fraternity brother Bill Rakow contributed a stock of The Great Global Cleanup Party stationery and business cards, and our mark became official.

A few days later I met Dave Anderson for lunch. Dave had moved on from holophonic sound and was producing *Voice of the Planet*, an environmental miniseries for Turner Broadcasting. He signed on to the cleanup event and offered to help in any way he could. Knowing he liked to dabble with recording equipment, I asked if I could borrow a video camera. He had a VHS model in his car and said it was mine to use as long as needed. After running me through operational details, I pointed the camera at Dave and asked him for a short statement of support for the Great Global Cleanup Party. Dave's testimonial was the first on a long list of tributes that would eventually include (among others) a doctor, a lawyer, and an Indian chief. Armed with a name, date, logo, and a video camera, I took the cleanup campaign on the road, first stop New York City.

🔺🔺🔺

The associates Dr. Brown assembled for the New York conference were quite different from the advertising practitioners gathered for the dinner in Los Angeles. The invitees included environmentally conscious business executives (the term green had yet to come into common usage), representatives of environmental nonprofits, and advisers and members of Dr. Brown's staff. The concept of the Great Global Cleanup Party was presented to the attendees in the form of a United Nations Environment Programme press release, most of which was lifted from the document I had written on the beach. Everyone approved of the idea and event, though opinions differed about how to bring it about. Whereas the advertising executives understood the power of commercial persuasion to spread the message, the pragmatists in the New York meeting were more interested in how to structure and fund the organization.

Dr. Brown and I followed up the next day in his suite. He provided me with consultant credentials and offered the full backing of his office. He said he could cover some of my transportation expenses out of his budget and would try to secure additional funding through UNEP support groups. I thanked him for his support and reaffirmed the commitment I had made at the Los Angeles dinner to devote a year of service to the cleanup campaign. After setting the date for our next meeting, I pulled out the camera and asked Dr. Brown for a statement. Ever the diplomat, he delivered a sound bite that was short, sweet, and eloquent.

I moved into Etta's house after returning from New York. Most of her estate had gone to my parents, so I took temporary residence to help ready the house for sale. Over the next few weeks I cleaned out drawers, closets, and files, in the process reconstructing Etta's long and colorful life. Looking at old photos, letters, even artifacts left over from college days, brought back memories of my earlier life as well. I wasn't just closing out Etta's house; I was closing out an era.

While I was taking care of business in Long Beach, Dave Anderson lined up Cleanup Party office space in the postproduction studio where he was finishing up *Voice of the Planet*. The commute from Long Beach to Burbank would be long, but it beat sleeping on couches and working out of my accountant's office.

After a quick trip home to tend to my property and personal matters, I traveled to Washington, D.C., to attend the American Association of Advertising Agencies conference. From there it was back to New York for the next meeting. By the time I returned to Los Angeles, Dave had raised enough cash to put Dr. Brown's daughter on staff as my assistant. With Noelle running the office, I spent most of the summer dashing around the country spreading the word and recording sound bites.

One of the stipulations governing the Cleanup Party was that it was a day of "no blame." The cleanup campaign did not promote or support any political ideology or agenda. Perhaps because of this, doors seemed to open everywhere I went. During the first of several visits to Washington, D.C., I was introduced to Tia Nelson of the Nature

Conservatory. Tia networked me into a circle of environmentally conscious congressional representatives and diplomats and escorted me to a charity dinner where I talked up the Great Global Cleanup Party to members of President George H.W. Bush's administration.

In Atlanta I met with a senior executive in charge of environmental affairs at Coca-Cola who arranged a follow-up meeting with the company's ranking brand managers. On the West Coast, *Body Glove*, a company already committed to environmental responsibility, offered to participate by sponsoring beach cleanups. Back in Burbank, Noelle and I sent out announcements of the cleanup day to a long list of environmental organizations and institutions such as the Boy Scouts and Girl Scouts of America. We formed an alliance with the Keep America Beautiful campaign and opened discussions with the Earth Day 1990 organizing committee. By the end of summer, we were corresponding with service organizations outside the United States.

Etta's house sold over the summer. I helped my dad clear out the last of the furniture, then moved into a small bungalow on a canal in Venice in early September. The location was near the airport and much closer to the Burbank office, but the six- month rental agreement only added to my financial burden. At that point I was so personally and emotionally invested in the project, I neglected to fully consider the economic consequences of my year of service. Sometimes, I suppose, that's for the best.

October 9, 1988 – Venice

Met Paula for lunch at Chez Jay yesterday. Less festive than our sake-fueled reunion dinner earlier in the year, but more open and honest. Said she was done with Malibu and moving to Boston. I told her I felt like I was caught on a treadmill I couldn't get off. We laughed a lot and for a brief moment I felt I was back in time conversing with the beguiling young woman I had fallen in love with. Feelings aside, we are just too far down our respective paths to turn back the clock. If that be our final farewell, the parting was sweet. I wish her love and happiness.

Etta's house on the shore of Treasure Island in Alamitos Bay.

Matters of Time

The January 2, 1989, "Planet of the Year" special issue of *Time Magazine* kicked off a year of environmental consciousness not seen since the early 1970s. The special edition featured eighteen articles. Some voiced alarm, others championed solutions, all acknowledged the physical impact of our species on the planet. One article, "Global Warming, Feeling the Heat," was among the first mass-media stories to give serious attention to an issue that scientists had been warning of for more than a decade. A few months later the *Valdez* oil spill, the biggest man-made environmental disaster in history, put a spotlight on the fragility of the natural world. The entertainment industry, led by Lyn and Norman Lear, formed the Environmental Media Association to promote environmental awareness through television and film productions. The times favored a worldwide cleanup party; timing for the event, however, proved to be inauspicious.

The next GGCP planning meeting in New York was expanded to include representatives from Ted Turner's Better World Society, the Foundation for Global Broadcasting, The U.N. Department of Public Information, Anheuser-Busch recycling, the Greenhouse Network, Ad-Net, the Peace Awareness Council, and House and Garden Magazine. Most of those who participated in the first meeting were also in attendance. Dr. Brown conducted the meeting as an open conversation focused on ways to make GGCP a major event. Ideas were exchanged and discussed, and by the end of the afternoon, a collective vision of the Cleanup Party began to form. The one area of concern was timing. With barely nine months until the event, some questioned if we had enough time to properly prepare.

Most of the next five months were spent traveling between Los Angeles, New York, Atlanta, and Washington, D.C. My job, beyond pitching the vision of the GGCP, was gathering commitments, then building on those commitments to get more commitments. It was a circular process, going from one place to another, then returning again and again, momentum building with each visit. Individuals caught on and were quick to agree to participate. Corporations, governments, and institutions, while warm to the idea, were burdened by bureaucracy and slower to commit. The most empowering attribute of the GGCP was that it encouraged everyone to pick their own place to clean up. With or without organizational structure, the event grew with each new volunteer.

Nothing can match the magic of the Big Apple during the holiday season. The brisk air, twinkling lights, and bustle of busy shoppers conspire to cast a spell over the entire city. Dr. Brown conveniently scheduled a GGCP meeting to coincide with the annual United Nations Christmas gala. After the black-tie affair, I moved on to Washington, D.C., for a series of meetings and gatherings. Perhaps most important was a meeting with Hal Uplinger, producer of the *Live Aid* global satellite broadcast, and Ann Boren of the Environmental Protection Agency. Uplinger was encouraging about the feasibility of a multisite global broadcast but cautioned that sites would be limited to cities with uplink capabilities, and variations of international broadcast protocols may need to be worked out. Ms. Boren, already the EPA's liaison for the forthcoming twentieth anniversary Earth Day festivities, saw the GGCP as a great follow-up event. The critical pieces were falling into place; it was only the political and corporate will that was lumbering.

The highlight of the Washington visit on a personal level was the night Tia took me to her parents' house for holiday cocktails and dinner at a nearby Chinese restaurant. Her father, Gaylord, founded Earth Day in 1970 when he was a US senator from Wisconsin. Over the meal the senator lauded the spirit and vision of The Great Global Cleanup Party. He felt it was truer to his original vision of Earth Day being about volunteerism and personal responsibility than the more tightly organized Earth Day being planned for 1990. He concurred with Dr. Brown's idea to publicly launch the GGCP by "riding in on Earth Day." He offered his complete support, even a place to stay if I tired of sleeping on his daughter's couch. His vote of confidence and encouragement helped keep my spirits high when confronting the problems that would soon arise.

Reckonings and Relief

December 26, 1998 – Pioneer Inn

Shared Christmas dinner with Woz and his entourage last night. Preferring not to spend the holiday alone in the supply room, drove over to Lahaina on a whim. Checked the answering machine and found Steve was on the island and had invited me to dinner. Turned out to be a jolly good Christmas after all. Absorbing as much island aloha as I can, a week from now heading back to New York. As Dr. Brown has reminded me, the long-distance runner knows it's all about pacing.

New York City, after the holiday spell has broken, is still a winter wonderland but with more slush and a lot less joy. The January 5 GGCP meeting opened on a cautious note, with Dr. Brown questioning whether we had time to get our organizational structure in place for the public launch on Earth Day. I advocated that the Earth Day announcement was a media opportunity that we could not afford to miss and pointed out that the Cleanup Party was as much about locally organized events as it was about institutional direction. After much discussion, it was decided to pare down the scope of the June 2, 1990, Cleanup Party to a manageable five or six official media sites, while continuing to encourage self-organizing efforts at the community level.

From New York I flew to Washington, D.C., for more discussions with the Better World Society and to spend some time with Tia's new recruits. A couple days later, I returned to Atlanta for a fourth meeting with Coca-Cola and to confer with J.J. Ebaugh, producer of *Earth*

Beat, a weekly environmental news show on Turner Broadcasting. I had met J.J. at a Marilyn Ferguson gathering some years earlier and was reacquainted with her at the reception for the launch of Earth Beat in October. We were like-minded on the importance of promoting environmental consciousness through the mass media and discussed ways that *Earth Beat* could support the GGCP. J.J. understood the deeper, more subliminal message of peace and cooperation underlying the cleanup campaign.

The meeting at Coca-Cola concluded with mixed results. The company was not ready to commit to a full-scale media campaign on the corporate level, preferring instead to support local cleanup events arranged by regional bottlers. They, too, felt it better to concentrate on a few well-organized sites in preparation for a bigger rollout in 1991. I was told that they were "opening doors" in Spain and England where they had strong government connections and solid interest from the local bottlers. They said they hoped to have a couple more sites on board in time for the Earth Day announcement. I was disappointed but not discouraged. Even without Coke's media support, one of the biggest consumer product companies on the planet was taking the GGCP seriously enough to at least get their feet wet.

Later in the month Phoebe asked Dennis and me to meet her for cocktails at the Westwood Marquis. The place where the dinner with Dr. Brown kicked off the GGCP campaign also earned the distinction of being the place where the *Woodpecker* adventure came to an end. With our option expired and an extension not forthcoming, the game was over. We parted on good terms, and I was relieved to let it go. Though I never quite found the fabled "golden ball," the journey had led me to Hāna. Returning to Maui to live a simpler life as an innkeeper was looking better all the time.

THE ROAD TO EDEN • 271

🌲🌲🌲

In mid-February, Dr. Brown hosted a luncheon for eighty guests in the United Nations formal dining room. I knew many of the attendees from previous meetings; the rest were ranking representatives of industry, media, and governmental agencies. The purpose of the luncheon was to announce a United Nations-sponsored ten-year campaign to reduce solid waste. By the time the lunch was over, Dr. Brown, in a brilliant act of diplomatic expediency, transmuted the GGCP one-day cleanup project into a decade-long commitment to solid-waste reduction. In doing so, the GGCP was relegated to being a lesser element in a much bigger project. At the same time, the pressure was off the June 2 cleanup party being an all-or-nothing event. I could live with that.

Dr. Brown and I met later that afternoon to discuss the future of the GGCP. He said he still very much believed in the project but was afraid the frenzy of activities already scheduled for Earth Day would drown out our message. He recommended we postpone public announcement of the GGCP until 1991. Grassroots efforts could still go on as planned but he felt we should officially launch the GGCP when there was less competition for media attention. I had to concur even though I knew that someone else would have to pick up the ball. My year of service was about to expire, and renewal was not an option.

After the day of reckoning in New York, I swung back through Atlanta and Washington to inform the troops of the scaled-down plans for the June 2 event. I encouraged integrating the community-based cleanup campaigns already in the works into the Earth Day 1990 campaign.

With time on my hands while winding down the Burbank office, I spent long hours exploring the Venice canals and mentally processing events of the past two years. I knew that *Woodpecker* had to have been ridden through to conclusion, and I had no regrets about my one-year commitment to the GGCP. However, I also knew that the time for battling windmills and chasing rainbows was over. I had property that needed my attention and a personal life that needed reconstruction. For better or worse it was time to tie up loose ends to go home.

The weekend before returning to Maui, I flew up to Seattle to spend the weekend with Tom Robbins and Alexa, the new woman in his life. With the *Woodpecker* quest essentially over, the visit had the easy feeling of just hanging out with an old friend. Sunday afternoon Alexa offered to give me a tarot reading. I generally try to avoid psychic or astrological guidance, preferring that my inner compass not be swayed by external stimuli. This time was different. I was vulnerable and in need of direction. The reading, suggesting that the challenges lying ahead would be overcome, was encouraging and intuitively rang true.

Later that evening, Tom and I sat next to the fountain in the courtyard of the Inn at the Market Hotel and talked about the environment. I told him that the most alarming of UNEP's reports and studies were those concerning the warming of the planet. Some projections even suggested that the line had already been crossed and cataclysmic climate change was inevitable. Tom asked if overpopulation wasn't the core of the problem. He was right, but ignorance and a collective unwillingness (or inability) to comprehend the consequences of our impact on the planet compounded the problem. Even more than population control, we needed a massive global wakeup call to snap us out of our apathy toward the natural world with which we are inextricably connected. Tom said he, too, feared we might be heading to a doom of our own creation, yet was still optimistic we would come to our senses before it was too late. "Well, I hope so anyway," he hedged.

I was back on Maui in late February determined to find a way forward. Although I would have to return to L.A. one more time to clear out the Venice bungalow and wrap up some business matters, I was home for the long run. The first order of business was to refinance the property. Annmarie's loan was coming due, and an extension had not been offered. My loan broker recommended applying for a non-income-verifiable mortgage that would require only that I provide documentation that I had the means to make the payments. Without a savings account or stock portfolio, I had little to offer that might be considered bankable. Then I recalled that my previous monthly bank statement had mistakenly shown a $90,000 overage on a recent deposit. How it happened I'll never know, but that one errant statement, backed with references from Dr. Brown and Tom Robbins, was enough to eventually secure a loan large enough to pay off Annmarie and cover some overdue maintenance expenses.

Rites of Passage

I loaded my remaining winter clothes and leave-behinds worth keeping in the rental car and turned in the bungalow key on April Fool's Day. It was supposed to be a quick trip, just time to close out the partnership, see my daughters, have dinner with Bob and Arlen Wilson, who had recently moved into the area, then drive north to drop off my belongings at my folks' house in San Mateo. I had planned to fly home on a one-way ticket out of San Francisco the following day. Things changed along the road.

I left early and was in no hurry, so I took a leisurely drive up Highway 101 through Malibu along the coast until it turned inland north of Santa Barbara. Looking out at the Channel Islands reminded me of a story told by Grandfather Semu, a Chumash medicine man I had met a year earlier. The story told of the first Chumash people who inhabited the Channel Islands and, being without trees to build canoes, were unable to cross the water to reach the coast. They called on the Great Spirit, who helped them by casting a rainbow bridge across the channel. The people who crossed the bridge were warned not to look down or they would fall into the ocean. Some couldn't resist, but it wasn't that bad, as those that fell turned into dolphins. That, he said, is why the Chumash are known as the dolphin people. The dolphin people's territory extended from Malibu all the way up coast to Pismo Beach.

Of all of the exceptional people I met during my year of service, it was the Native Americans with whom I felt the most affinity. Although I had been a professional marketer for a dozen years, I related less to the product managers at Coke who saw the cleanup campaign as an opportunity for a short-term gain over Pepsi (they had no interest whatsoever in a cooperative ad with their archrival), than to the Native Americans who viewed environmental stewardship as a long-term commitment to the future.

My introduction to the Native American community began with a phone call from my sister Kathy when I was living in Etta's house. She called to suggest I contact her friend Debra, a film producer who was interested in getting the Native American community involved in the cleanup party.

The following Saturday Debra picked me up at the San Jose airport and drove us south to spend the weekend with her friend Tom Nason, aka Little Bear, and his family at their ranch in the mountains above Carmel Valley. During the two-hour drive Debra told me of meeting Little Bear while working on a project and soon becoming friends with his family. Little Bear, besides running the ranch, was an Esselen spiritual leader and cultural practitioner. Debra added that our visit was very timely as an old medicine man and his wife were also staying on Little Bear's property.

Little Bear was fixing a fence with a weathered old ranch hand when we came to the gate that led to his property. After warmly greeting Debra and offering me a welcoming handshake, Little Bear gave us a quick tour of the land, pointing out the sweat lodge that was under construction, the meeting house, and a traditional bison skin tepee while leading us to his house, where his wife was preparing lunch. During the meal Little Bear and I discussed his vision of the cleanup event as a ritualistic healing ceremony for both the earth and the participants. I agreed with him that on a deeper level the event could be seen as a healing ritual, but on the physical level the cleanup party was about working together for a common cause and having fun in the process. Little Bear smiled in agreement. We shared the same vision, just viewed it from different perspectives.

That afternoon I took my turn at repairing the broken fence. My fence-mending partner was Jay, a retired rodeo cowboy, who taught me how to lift, hold, and hammer in one easy motion. After finishing the job, Little Bear took me over to his guest cottage to meet Grandfather Semu. I had been under the impression that very few pure-blooded Chumash were still living. Meeting a medicine man who was born at a time when the tradition was still practiced was a rare privilege. Little Bear led me into the cottage and introduced me to the elderly man sitting in an overstuffed chair at the far end of the room. Grandfather was impeccably dressed in pressed blue jeans, cowboy boots, a long-sleeve shirt, and a red vest matching the headband that crowned his silver-white mane of neatly braided hair.

During our conversation, Grandfather told me of his childhood, having been born in a cave in Ojai and moving from place to place to avoid living on a reservation. His father was a medicine man, and through him, Grandfather met and was taught by medicine men from other tribes throughout Central and Southern California. When taking leave, I thanked him for his time and he thanked me for what I was doing for Mother Earth. We both expressed hope to meet again.

That evening after dinner, Little Bear took Debra and me out to the tepee for a smoke ceremony. We were accompanied by Jay and Michael, a young man of Japanese-Philippine descent who was born and raised on Kauaʻi. Debra and I sat aside while Michael helped Little Bear prepare his sage and dried herbs, and Jay worked the fire in the middle of the tepee. When everything was ready, we formed a circle and Little Bear passed a pipe, asking each of us to take a puff to unite our spirits. He then pulled out a second pipe, instructing Debra and me to draw a breath of smoke and close our eyes while he hypnotically led us down a deep, dark tunnel to meet our animal spirit guides.

After our encounters with our respective animal guides, we were given blankets and logs for the fire and told to enjoy the night. Finding it too cold to sleep without a fire and too smoky to sleep with one, I spent most of the night alternately stoking the fire and huddling under my blanket.

Debra called me a couple of months later to say she had arranged, through Little Bear, for me to meet Archie Fire Lame Deer, a respected Lakota chief and medicine man. He was finishing up his work in Santa Barbara and was about to head north for the summer. He offered to meet at his home on Sunday afternoon. Realizing it was Father's Day (and Melanie's birthday), I asked if I could bring my daughters. She thought it would be very appropriate, especially since Chief Lame Deer was considered the spiritual father to his people.

Archie Fire Lame Deer was a big man with a commanding presence. Judging from the crated boxes stacked around the living room, he was taking precious time from other duties to meet with us that afternoon. Nevertheless, he was very attentive and wanted to talk of the deep spiritual obligation we have to take care of the planet. He commented that even among his people many had lost the way and no longer felt the attachment to Mother Earth. He said that our planet belongs to our children and we must do everything we can to protect it for them. His video endorsement was so beautiful and impassioned it could have, in itself, been the flagship commercial for the Great Global Cleanup Party.

Learning that it was Melanie's fourteenth birthday, Lame Deer told her that, in his tradition, it was the age a girl became a woman. Before leaving, Archie Fire took me aside and advised that now, with two daughters on their moon cycles, the role of the father became even more important. As children, they are under the protection and guidance of the clan mothers; as young women, they are influenced by their fathers when selecting a mate. It was my job, he said, to inspire them to choose wisely.

As I approached Salinas I decided to take the Monterey turnoff and follow Highway 1 along the coastline to San Mateo. Just before reaching the peninsula, I opted to take a detour and make an unscheduled call on Little Bear.

Little Bear was grinning when he saw me at his door, saying he had recently been on the phone with Debra asking how to reach me. We sat down at his kitchen table. After a short exchange of pleasantries, Little Bear invited me to join him and ten other participants on a three-day expedition to a sacred cave site in the wilderness area behind Big Sur. The purpose, he said, was to perform a ceremonial reopening of the ventana, or window to the west, as it is known to native people. Little Bear told me that opening the ventana came to Grandfather Semu in a dream, and though too old to make the trip, Grandfather would be giving us instructions and offering a prayer to start our journey. The trek wouldn't begin for another couple of days, which meant postponing my return home. I thought about it a moment, then told Little Bear to count me in. It was an opportunity I wasn't going to miss even if it meant a few more days in California with little left to do.

On the morning before the excursion, I left my folks' home early and slowly worked my way down the coast to Big Sur. Around noon I pulled off the road near Santa Cruz to watch a pod of gray whales working their way north for the summer. Closer to shore a cadre of dolphins frolicked in the calm, smooth waters just beyond the surf line. I got out of the car for a better look. By the time I reached the shore, the aquatic mammals had moved on. Gazing out over the empty sea, I felt sadness in knowing that I was in a place that I loved but no longer belonged. I got back in the car and continued up the road for another night in Little Bear's tepee.

After breakfast with Little Bear and his family, I was taken over to the guest cottage to visit again with Grandfather Semu. This time his wife, Eneke-Alish, joined us in the conversation. Grandfather told more stories about his life, saying that his people all belonged to the clan of their mother; he was born into the Owl Clan; his father was Roadrunner. I told him that it sounded much like the family ʻaumākua in Hawaiian culture. ʻAumākua are considered to be deified ancestors expressed in the form of sharks, turtles, owls, moʻo (lizards), or other animal embodiments. Hawaiians look to their ʻaumākua for protection and guidance. Grandfather was interested in the comparison and said he hoped to travel to Hawai'i one day and meet with Hawaiian elders. I told him he had a place to stay whenever he cared to come visit. He thanked me for the offer, clasped my hands in his, and said he had a feeling we would meet again.

Once the rest of the group (including Debra and J.J. Ebaugh, who unbeknownst to me was also a friend of Little Bear) had assembled, Grandfather told us the reason for our mission and why we were invited to make the journey. The ventana, he said, was known as the western passage to the spirit realm. The gateway had closed long ago when native people stopped tending it. In his dream, Grandfather was told to gather twelve people to perform a reopening ceremony in a cave at the foot of the ventana. Little Bear would lead the ritual, and each of us would be asked to join him in prayer for restoration of the portal. He closed with an invocation that, with peace in our hearts, we would be protected in our travels.

We left midday. Little Bear's mother, who was in charge of meals, and another woman rode on the pack horses; the rest of us walked. The mostly downhill trek took about four hours to reach the base camp. Michael and Jay went to work setting up the tents while the rest of us were free to explore the surroundings. I followed Little Bear as he climbed up a nearby cliff to a shallow cave about twenty feet off the ground. Quite suddenly I felt nauseous and retreated to the base camp, where I began a bout of spasmodic vomiting that lasted into the evening. By nightfall I was so weak and parched that I had to surrender to the assistance of my companions just to get into my tent. I felt humiliated at being so helpless but was too sick to put up any resistance.

I woke up at dawn worn and weary, but the illness had passed. The day's agenda called for a long hike to the sacred cave and back. Knowing I was still out of sorts and determined that we would all reach the cave site together, Little Bear insisted that I saddle up on one of the horses. We followed a trail that wound through forests and across shallow creeks and reached our destination around noon. By then my strength was returning with an appetite to match. We sat around the clearing beneath the cave and ate our provisions while Little Bear told stories about the land and histories of his people.

After lunch Little Bear led us up a path on the side of the cliff to the cavernous chamber that sat on a plateau overlooking the valley below. The vaulted walls inside the cavern were covered with carved and painted hands, many with spirals covering the palms. Little Bear told us that the reason for the carved hands had been lost, though one Esselen legend tells that the hands hold memory of the history of the site. Once we all had a chance to examine the great chamber, we were directed to sit in a line in front of the cave. Little Bear sat in the middle and started a slow, rhythmic beat on his drum as he offered a prayer to restore balance and clarity to the ventana. He then called for us to join with him in silent prayer that Grandfather's plea be heard. He closed the ceremony by passing a pipe and asking us to each partake in the offering.

The next morning, I awoke feeling fresh and invigorated. Whatever had stricken me had passed completely and left me with a sense of extraordinary well-being. We broke camp after breakfast and were trekking back up the hill before noon. Michael and I fell into a pace that quickened into a trot that took us up to the road a full hour ahead of the others, who were taking their time navigating the steep and winding trail. I don't know quite what happened to me during that excursion, but I charged up the mountain feeling like a new man. I was fit and ready to return home to Maui—this time for good.

🌲🌲🌲

J.J. called me the day I got home and asked if I had heard the good news. I didn't have a clue and asked for a hint. She said StarKist had just announced the adoption of a "dolphin safe" policy: It would not purchase any tuna caught in nets with dolphins or taken with gill or drift nets. I told her it was great news, but I missed the point. She reminded me that the Chumash are known as the dolphin people and the dolphin-safe announcement was made the day after we opened the ventana with Grandfather's prayers. My rational thought was that it was just coincidence. All the same, I had to admit I was beginning to wonder if the old medicine man had something to do with the sudden illness that purged me back into good health. I told J.J. that it really was exciting news and I was looking forward to her upcoming visit. She replied she couldn't think of a better way to spend Earth Day than by being in Hāna. Me, too, I said, me too.

Building a Business

My career as an innkeeper formally began in April 1990, when I took back the keys from the rental service and began tending to my own business. I first turned to Sam Eason for help in designing a logo and font. The image we settled on was simple stylized line rendering the Philippine hardwood structure. While the business cards and handouts were being printed, I placed a small ad in the Yellow Pages and sent announcement letters to the various travel guides and magazines. I rehired Danny Baker to help take care of some overdue maintenance and repairs. When the "inn" was deemed guest-ready, I posted a small sign at the top of the driveway and officially opened Hale Mālamalama for business on May 1, Lei Day in Hawai'i.

During my weekly supply runs I would stop by the resort areas and distribute brochures to concierges and talk story with activities directors. As word spread, we started attracting a small but steady stream of adventurous travelers preferring small lodges to resorts, as well as staycation guests from the other side of the island. Reservations picked up when the new phone directory came out in July, and by summer's end I was spending most of my nights sleeping in the supply room.

As growth in overnight rentals approached sustainable levels and my living conditions became less sustainable, expansion went from being a consideration to becoming a necessity. For several months I had been toying with plans for a small residential cottage for myself and another cottage for rental use on the bluff around the parking area. In early autumn I worked out a deal with my folks for a construction loan. Once again it meant putting everything on the line in order to move forward. The money that my parents were using to make the loan was from their retirement account and would have to be repaid within three years. Although foreclosure was not an issue, it was understood that anything short of full repayment would necessitate the sale of the property.

Sam Eason did me a big favor by refusing to draw up plans for the additions. He instead deferred the task to me, suggesting that I was most suited to do the job. He encouraged me to start by walking about the area and letting the land dictate where and how each cottage should sit. Once the footprint of each building was established, he said it would just be a matter of designing the roof structures and laying out the floor plans. Beyond that, Steve Pitt could prepare a code-compliant set of plans for the building department. I felt like I had been tossed into the pool when I wasn't quite ready to swim. At the same time the thought of designing the cottages from the ground up was refreshingly buoyant.

I followed Sam's advice and practically camped on the bluff for a week pounding spikes in the ground and laying out string lines to determine the best placement and shape of each cottage. The first cottage fit neatly on the narrow strip of land to the right of the parking area where Paula and I had pitched our tent five years earlier. The second cottage, which was to be positioned at the base of the driveway, presented a problem. Finally, after concluding that a five-hundred-square-foot building could not fit on the bluff without removing at least one of the four parking spaces, I pulled up the spikes and walked away. The entire concept had to be rethought.

I took a break and walked along the shore. As I was returning from the beach, I noticed how the roofline of the neighboring house across the pond was steeped in three modules that conformed to the slope of their land. That triggered a thought of designing the cottage as a two-story split-roof structure built atop a carport with the sleeping area cantilevered out over the trees on the side of the cliff. The effect would be like being in a treehouse, only anchored to the ground. I rushed back up the steps and started taking measurements and laying out string lines. The new design fit perfectly. A week later I dropped the drawings and elevations off with Steve Pitt. A month later I took the plans to the building department and applied for building permits.

I ran into a snag when I found that I could add only one new residential structure without upgrading the existing septic system. Upgrading the system was financially out of the question, so I designated the one-story cottage as an office/storage facility and had to forgo indoor plumbing. To remedy the situation I added a toilet and sink to the laundry room that was attached to the back of the other cottage. For bathing I could use the bamboo-walled outdoor shower that was adjacent to its entrance. It was a compromise I could live with—I was just glad to be getting out of storage room purgatory.

December 16 – Paniolo Bar, Hotel Hāna Maui

Ending a year full of endings. "Woodpecker" is over, the partnership dissolved, and the GGCP is out of my hands. Retired the Contessa's loan and took care of repairs and caught up on maintenance. And as of last Thursday, no longer married—granted uncontested divorce after unsuccessful attempt to find Paula.

Looking ahead, thinking of ways to build business beyond new additions. Can envision putting some cottages on the adjacent property, maybe even involve the neighboring Heavenly Hāna Inn beach cottage as well. More than enough to deal with already, just playing with ideas.

Old Door, New Perceptions

Most of the embellishments that characterized the "Indo-Pacific" motif of what would be known as the Tree House Cottage were sourced through the *Maui Bulletin*, a weekly classified handout. A batch of one-inch-diameter bamboo poles left over from a hotel remodel was used to build the outdoor shower and kitchen cabinets, and a large roll of decorative tapa cloth procured in Tonga by a local sailor was cut into strips and used to adorn the upper walls of the cottage. The paper-like tapa cloth, or kapa, as it is known in Hawaiʻi, is made primarily from the mulberry tree and was worn as clothing and used in ceremonial practices by native cultures throughout Oceania. The labor intensiveness of its production has made tapa a more rarified commodity in contemporary Polynesia.

The most fortuitous find from the *Bulletin* was an object that I had no idea I was looking for. An ad that had been running for several weeks announcing the arrival of a container full of Buddhas from Bali included an aside listing of a Balinese temple door. I had been intrigued with the door, yet the only place where I could employ such an item would be as the entrance door to the rental cottage bathroom. It seemed to be an odd consideration, yet I felt compelled to call the seller. Sonny, importer of the artifacts, hinted that the one-thousand-dollar price was negotiable and urged me to take a look and see what the door might be worth to me.

Sonny lived in the guest house on an estate above Makawao town on the northern slope of Haleakalā volcano. The path from the parking area to his cottage was marked with stone and concrete Buddhas discreetly pointing the way. His abode was cluttered and colorful, the furnishings looking transitory like that of a circus. Sonny had a hipster's way about him that suited his eclectic surroundings. Before showing me the temple door, he told me that he had neglected to point out a small problem. The door, which had been propped against his patio wall, blew over in a rainstorm, and one of the panels became warped. He assured me it could be fixed, and he would make an adjustment in the price to make it worth my while.

Other than the warp the door was exotically beautiful. It consisted of two full-length saloon-style panels encased in an intricately carved matching frame. The serpent and floral motif was detailed in vibrant colors and highlighted in gold leaf against a glossy black background. We settled on a price of five hundred dollars, two hundred in cash and the balance as credit at Hale Mālamalama. Despite the considerable work required to smooth out the warp, the purchase of the deformed door may well have been the best investment I've ever made.

My construction crew, Tim and Dan, two young but competent carpenters newly arrived from Idaho, were not impressed with the temple door. It meant reframing the bathroom wall and, from their provincial perspective, the ornate door was a bit over the top for a bathroom. Nonetheless, they saw the job as a challenge and reengineered the wall to accommodate the oversized frame. I took on the task of mending the bent door panel myself. I laid the door out between two sawhorses and as a daily routine, soaked the backside with damp towels, then heated it from underneath with a hairdryer while tightening the clamps to slowly muscle it back into shape. After a month on the rack, we took the door panel downstairs and installed it in the frame with the other panel. A small bow remained, but the panel worked. Even Tim and Dan had to admit the temple door assembly made for an impressive entrance to the throne room.

Supervising construction of the new cottages while running the inn left little time for recreational pursuits. The one exception was Parley Kanaka'ole's Monday-night ethnobotany class at Hāna School. Since the blessing lū'au for Hale Mālamalama, Parley and I had formed a friendship based on my interest in and his knowledge of Hawaiian culture and history. His class was a onetime, one-semester offering as part of the Maui Community College outreach program. In some ways, taking the class was as life changing as reading *Still Life with Woodpecker*. What made his class so engaging was Parley's ability to draw us into an entirely different world of perception. He began by telling us that to understand the Hawaiian relationship with plants you have to start first by learning about the gods.

Parley presented the four great akua in a living context. One of the creation stories tells of Kāne, known for mirth and merriment, who created—with the assistance of Kū, akua of war and fishing, and Lono, akua of fertility and games—the first man and, from him, the first woman. Kanaloa was presented as a mysterious akua associated with deep waters and the underworld.

Most interesting were Parley's accounts of local lore. One story in particular that would have a bearing on my future endeavors told of the god Kūʻulakai (Kū of abundance in the sea) coming to live on earth as a man named Kūʻula. Kūʻula and his wife, Hina, resided at Lehoula, a small cove about two miles south of Hāna Bay. There he built the first Hawaiian fishpond, traces of which can still be seen today. Before he died, Kūʻula gave his son ʻAiʻai four magical objects to control fish and taught him how to address the gods in prayer. Following his father's instructions, ʻAiʻai traveled the island building fishing shrines. At each shrine two fish from the first catch were offered, one to Kūʻula and one to Hina.

Legend tells of ʻAiʻai placing the stone, Makakiloiʻa (eyes of the fisherman) on the top of Kaʻuiki hill. From this location the fishing watchmen could look out over Hāna Bay for schools of akule, then bark out directions to the canoes circling below. The Makakiloiʻa stone now resides in the nearby Hāna Cultural Center, yet the fishing practice taught by ʻAiʻai continues. Now, however, as Parley pointed out, the fishing watchman calls out directions over a walkie-talkie, and canoes have been replaced with small motorized fishing boats. And true to tradition, the catch is always shared with the community.

Beyond the gods, Parley gave us a brief overview of Hawaiian history from precontact through Kaʻahumanuʻs time as regent queen. We eventually got around to plants later in the semester, but in Parley's class it was context that mattered most.

The eight or so of us participating in the Monday-night gatherings were treated to a course in Hawaiian cosmology taught by a man whose family was considered a fountainhead of traditional cultural and spiritual knowledge and practices. I suspected before the semester ended that Parley was much more than just a humble schoolteacher.

I moved into my office/cottage in early May. It wasn't complete, but it was walled, roofed, and electrified. I put Tim and Dan full time on the Tree House Cottage, and I took over finishing up my own space. At barely 400 square feet there wasn't much to do beyond building a closet for my belongings and a countertop desk for the computer and office supplies. I initially slept on a futon that folded into a couch by day and, though without an actual kitchen, I had an undercounter refrigerator, toaster oven, coffee maker, and a small outdoor Weber grill that met my needs. After nearly three years of bunking on friends' couches and being a gypsy in my own palace, I finally felt I had a home. I was still sleeping on a couch, but it was my couch, and that made all the difference in the world.

Inaugural Cruise

May 13 – Home

Feel like a gatekeeper in my new quarters. All comings and goings have to pass my roost. I'm a bit exposed but can't deny the appropriateness of the location. Spent part of the afternoon sitting on the flat rock in the back of the cave just absorbing the wonderment of this magical land. Peered out over the remains of the old fishpond and envisioned what it looked like in its prime. Would so like to see it brought back to life.

⁂

Tim, Dan, and I scrambled to make the Tree House Cottage habitable for the first guests scheduled to check in on July 8. Inaugural guests Tom Robbins and his soon-to-be bride, Alexa, were coming over to experience the early-morning solar eclipse on July 11. Other than a few minor details, notably installation of the cliffside Jacuzzi tub in the temple-gated bathroom, the cottage was functionally complete by the time of their arrival. Daughter Tiffany and friend Nel, fresh out of high school, also came over for the solar event and moved into the Hale Mālamalama first-floor suite. The upstairs, known as the Royal Suite, had been reserved by an Italian couple for the entire month. Three more unexpected guests rounded out the roster for a party that lasted nearly a week.

The last-minute arrivals were Suki, a gregarious redheaded actress that I had met in Los Angeles while winding down *Woodpecker*, her friend and fellow actress, Carrie, and Fred the pataphysician, who happened to be passing through Maui on his way home from New

Zealand. Fred took over my old quarters in the storage room, and Carrie and Suki moved into the first-floor girls' dorm with Tiffany and Nel. I felt like a cruise ship captain with my first full charter.

Hale Mālamalama was just the staging point for our adventure. Due to the dynamics of the celestial mechanics, Hāna would experience only a 99 percent blackout during the eclipse. To get the whole effect, we had to journey over to the Big Island and stay with friends in Hawi, where the eclipse would be total. I made arrangements with Scott, a part-time Hāna resident and part owner of a five-passenger Cessna, to shuttle our eight-person party across the thirty-eight-mile ʻAlenuihāhā Channel to the landing strip near Hawi. On the afternoon before the big event, Scott delivered the first set of guests to awaiting hosts Jim and Joan Channon, then flew back to Hāna to pick up the rest of us. Half an hour later our reconvened entourage was driven up the road to the Channons' hillside retreat on the northernmost point of the island.

In a way I already felt akin to the Channons' chateau. Two years prior, I had met Jim and Joan in the Philippines when they were on the first leg of their honeymoon. I was there to introduce them to Jimmy DeGuzman and help them work out a kit-house package to be reconstructed on their property on the hill above Hawi. Jim had prepared remarkably detailed sketches of an elegant, environmentally sensitive small house designed to fit unobtrusively on their gently sloping land. DeGuzman and his staff took it from there and put together a package that included employment of Roger Albea to lead the project, including reconstructing the Channons' house in Hawaiʻi. Visiting Jim and Joan in their new home was a homecoming of sorts. Our houses differed in design, but they shared a common origin in the Philippines and the distinction of having been crafted in place by the same master carpenter.

The Channons' home seemed to have been designed with slumber parties in mind. The accordion-style doors that encompassed most of the living room wall folded back to merge the living space with the lanai. There were enough Balinese daybeds and large throw pillows about the place to assure each of us a comfortable, if not exactly private, sleeping space. Before turning in for the night, however, Joan had prepared an elegant feast to kick off the countdown to the post-sunrise spectacle. Toasts and jokes were the order of the evening. Tom, romancing the eclipse as an alchemical union of the sun and moon, anointed the women in our party as bridesmaids to the moon and the men as attendants to the sun. Jim led us in a rousing "Gooooo Planet!" cheer as we departed from the table to settle in for the night. The sky was still and starless; the obvious and unspoken concern to everyone was the weather.

Dawn broke with no sign of the sun. The clouds were thick and widespread. We still had an hour and a half before the full eclipse, and the clouds could burn off, but the prognosis was not promising. A half hour before showtime, we abandoned our base, hopped into the Channons' cars and went searching for the missing groom. The cloud cover was less dense down the hill, but sun sightings were fleeting at best. Finally, at the appointed moment we had to stop in place, get out of the cars, and gaze into the sky. Our drop-dead spot was on an isolated road next to a cow pasture. We caught only glimpses of the ring of fire as the moon engulfed the sun but experienced the totality of the eclipse when the day suddenly turned into night. The three minutes of darkness was like being caught under a crashing wave, knowing it's going to pass yet ever so slightly afraid it might not. Then in an instant, the sky lightened, and the spell was broken. Our roadside ensemble exhaled and broke out in giddy laughter while the nearby cows began mooing as if a new day had just dawned.

Finding that we had ended up near the north Kohala coast, our hosts decided to top off the eventful morning with a visit to the nearby Puʻukoholā heiau (temple). The heiau, completed two hundred years (practically to the day) prior to our visit, was the site where Kamehameha sacrificed his rival chief Keōua to his war god Kūkaʻilimoku. The sacrifice of Keōua was accepted by many as a necessity in Kamehameha's quest to unify the Hawaiian Islands, but the moral justification was not resolved until a reconciliation and healing ceremony that would take place just a month after our visit. Of course, I knew none of that then, only that I sensed a powerful energy about the place that I attributed to post-eclipse elation.

Later that afternoon we returned to Hāna and carried on with activities and events for the next several days. Carpenter Dan came by with a twenty-pound ahi that he claimed to have caught precisely at the moment of daytime darkness. It was a good story and it fetched him a good price for the sanctified tuna that kept us fed for the duration of the party. Fred left first, then Tiffany and Nel. Tom, Alexa, Suki, Carrie, and I finished up the week by driving to Lahaina and spending the night at the Pioneer Inn.

A few days later I got a fax from Tom offering a short blurb for our new brochures: "Somewhere between Eden and Paradise is Hale Mālamalama: a resting place with soul, with heart, with integrity and magik, as well as beauty."

Capping off the magical mystical eclipse party at the Pioneer Inn with Tom and Alexa Robbins. Lahaina, July 1991.

Sidetracks

As I became accustomed to the ins and outs of innkeeping, I found that while an on-site presence was mandatory, I had ample time for other pursuits while on duty. Videography, as both hobby and income supplement, became a secondary occupation. The event that triggered my interest in recording local events and activities happened a year earlier after returning from a visit to Australia with Melanie. While driving home from the airport I learned from a hitchhiker that Hasegawa's store had burned down while I was away. The arsonist(s), who hit in the middle of the night, torched the gas station as well, although damage was slight. My passenger said rumors were rampant, but no one had been arrested. I dropped her off at Waiʻānapanapa Park and drove straight over to Hasegawa's to find Harry, whose father had cofounded the store in 1910, standing amid a burnt pile of rubble, looking dazed. I walked over to him, took hold of his hand and expressed my sorrow. He just shook his head in bewilderment and mumbled, "Why? Why would anyone do this?" Sadly, the question remains unanswered to this day.

Deeming that the rebuilding of the beloved Hasegawa's General Store would be a worthy venture into documentary filmmaking, if only as a local historical document, I invested in a video camera and suitable editing equipment. My plan fizzled, however, when Harry and his staff found refuge in the old Hāna movie house. Less than two months after the fire, Harry's employees had transformed the theater into a store so functionally complete that the need to rebuild was no longer a necessity. The real story, about how every employee was kept on the payroll during the transition, was better told than recorded. Nonetheless, the equipment purchased for the project set me up as a videographer. Weddings were plentiful in Hāna, and recording the blessed events became my specialty.

I was finishing up a video of a couple exchanging vows in front of the cave (a popular wedding location) when I got a call from Tiffany. She wanted to tell me of her plans to trek through Thailand with her boyfriend, Jules. I knew of and supported her decision to postpone her first semester at college for some traveling, but starting with Southeast Asia caught me by surprise. We talked at length and came up with a tentative plan to rendezvous in Tokyo for a couple of days, then fly to Bangkok to meet up with Jules. From there we would spend a few days together before going our separate ways. As if the trip was destined, I was able to book passage with my accumulated GGCP travel miles and entice my sister, Kathy, to take a working vacation and run the business in my absence.

Tiffany and I connected at the Tokyo airport and caught a train into the city. After getting lost trying to find our way on foot, we gave up, hailed a cab, and reached our destination just before dusk. We were staying with Todd and Miko, Hale Mālamalama guests who had become friends. Their apartment was typically small but well appointed. Our gracious hosts, proud parents of a three-month-old daughter, had moved the baby in with them and laid out mats for us in the nursery. After a sashimi dinner delivered room-service-style from the restaurant downstairs, we hit the mats early. Todd, a commodities broker whose workday began at seven in the morning, insisted on taking us on a predawn tour of the Tokyo Fish Market.

By the time of our five-thirty arrival the market was in full swing. Some of the smaller vendors had already begun closing up for the day. Much larger than the Los Angeles produce market that I had visited with Constantine, the fish market was a cornucopia of aquatic life gathered from the seven seas. The sheer abundance of fish, crustaceans, sea grasses, and even whale meat was staggering. Todd reminded us that this was an everyday event, not just a one-day phenomenon. Granted, Tokyo was a wealthy city with perhaps the highest per capita fish consumption on the planet, but by any measure the size of the daily bounty was astounding. Todd pointed out that the Tokyo market, considered the largest in the world, was but the tip of the iceberg. Fish harvesting worldwide was beyond sustainable levels. Without proper management of declining resources, the depletion of many fish stocks was inevitable. Commodities broker Todd had a knack for seeing things in the context of supply and demand.

My flight to Bangkok was in the morning, Tiffany's not until the afternoon. I flew on ahead, took a taxi into the city, and checked into a modest hotel near the center of town. While waiting for Tiffany's arrival, I wandered the nearby streets, visiting shops and snacking on offerings from the numerous vendors. In all my travels I had never been to a place so alien. Colorful and vibrant, the city was alive with activity and chatter. To my unaccustomed ears the native Siamese language had a musical cadence that made it as delightful to hear as it was difficult to comprehend. Later I returned to the airport to meet Tiffany. Her plane was late, and the road back to Bangkok was jammed with cars, motorbikes, and practically anything else with wheels. Night had fallen by the time we reached the hotel. Lanterns lit the temple yards, and swarms of vehicle lights streaked the streets like neon ribbons. Tiffany jokingly commented that we certainly weren't in Kansas anymore.

We met Jules at the appointed café for breakfast the next morning. He had arrived a day earlier and spent the night at a nearby youth hostel. Over the meal, Tiffany and Jules laid out their plan to start their trek in Mai Sai, the northernmost town in Thailand, and work their way south until they ran out of time or money. Without an agenda of my own, I tagged along and we caught the train to Chang Mai early the next morning. After a night in the mountain resort town, we took a crowded bus to Chang Rai, and from there an even more crowded bus to the border town of Mai Sai. Across the Nam Ruak River from Myanmar, Mai Sai was one of the few crossing points from Thailand into the then military-controlled country formerly known as Burma. Lodging being limited, we settled for a couple of barren shacks at a small guest house near the center of town.

We rented motor bikes the next morning and set out for the Golden Triangle, a serene and beautiful place, notoriously known as the opiate capital of the world during the Vietnam War era. We rode on dirt roads through small villages and farmlands, wild poppies evermore present the closer we got to our destination. The triangle is the convergence of three countries and two rivers. We took lunch at a restaurant on the intersection of the Mekong and Nam Ruak Rivers. Our table faced Myanmar, and off to our right was Laos. Both countries looked peaceful, mysterious, and inviting. The geopolitics of the time, however, prohibited our entry. After our meal we toured along the Mekong River for a few miles, then turned onto a paved highway that led us back to Mai Sai.

I left my daughter and her friend early the next morning. We had stayed up late the night before participating in the Buddhist festival taking place on the street that ran through town and crossed into Myanmar. Local villagers were joined by their counterparts from the other side of the river as authorities opened the crossing for the special event. Late in the evening at my instigation, we tried sneaking across the bridge with a crowd of Burmese who were returning home for the night. We made it as far as the checkpoint on the Myanmar side before being chased back by an irate armed soldier who saw no humor in our prank. I knew then it was time to leave. The kids would be safer on their own

I'd been home a couple of weeks when I got a collect call from Tiffany. She was back in Bangkok and called to say that they were finishing their trip in Vietnam. They had met some American backpackers in Phuket who told them Vietnam was beautiful, unspoiled, and cheap. I asked how she was going to get around the US travel ban. She said the Vietnamese government stamps slips of paper that are collected upon departure. Nothing is shown on the passport. The situation was darkly comical. Many in my generation went underground to avoid going to Vietnam. Now my daughter and her friend were going underground to gain entry. Admiring Tiffany's sense of adventure, I wished her safe travels.

November 9 – Home

Been bothered thinking about the blanket of brown polluted air that covered the entire Southeast Asian peninsula sky when flying back from Bangkok. Same concern about stagnant, trashed waterways visible when approaching stopovers in Taiwan, Japan and Seoul. Region being touted for economic prosperity, yet environment taking a hit. Must environmental degradation be a by-product of economic progress? Brings to mind words of Medicine Man Rolling Thunder speaking at an engagement in Ojai. When asked to agree that spiritually our concepts of God and the Great Spirit are essentially the same, he pointed his finger at the audience and emphatically replied, "Absolutely not, your god is the almighty dollar!" Took it as a metaphor then, rings true in literal sense today.

Guardians

The more familiar I became with the 'aina of which I was a steward, the more accepting I became of the mythological beings and stories embedded in its history. I was particularly drawn to stories relating to *mo'o*, shape-shifting giant lizards, or dragons, that reside in streams and fishponds. Stories tell of mo'o taking the shape of a beautiful woman and seducing young men away from their families as well as accounts of mo'o being fierce protectors and guardians of freshwater sources. On a deeper level, the Hawaiian historian and cultural authority Sam Ka'ai tells of mo'o allegorically being identified with storytelling, the dragon being a life force: its head looking to the future, its front feet being youthful curiosity, and the hind legs being the strength and stability of parenthood. The tail and spine embody the wisdom of elders and ancestors, acting as reservoirs of knowledge of all that has gone before.

Kihawahine, the most powerful of all mo'o, emerged in the sixteenth century and is still considered a vital force by many. The once-mortal Kihawahine was born as Kalā'aiheana, daughter of the high chief Pi'ilani. When the revered chieftess died, she was transmuted through a sacred ritual into the mo'o Kihawahine. So powerful was the goddess that Kamehameha came to her shrine in Hāna and made offerings and prayers that she would come with him to O'ahu as he began his quest to unify the islands.

Kihawahine has been associated with fishponds throughout Hawai'i, most notably Moku'ula in Lahaina, the once spiritual and political power center of the Kingdom of Hawai'i. Hāna, however, is her home. The Hawaiian spiritual practitioner Danny Akaka, while researching the history of the area, came across an ancient chant that mentions Kihawahine residing in a cave next to a fishpond in the Hāna district.

Restorations

The dream of restoring the fishpond began to actuate when the pondside neighbors, the Buck family, gathered in Hāna for the holidays in late 1991. Mims, Doug, and I had been discussing the idea for some time. We had even gone so far as inviting archaeologists and geologists from the University of Hawai'i and the State Department of Land and Natural Resources out for weekend visits and informal surveys. Buddy, a cave specialist from the university, hypothesized that the cave was formed by an underwater lava flow, then pushed upward by subterranean volcanic forces. The freshwater springs that fed the pond were likely created by the same upheaval. Anne, an archaeologist with the state using information off old surveyor maps, helped us outline the perimeter of the fishpond, some of which ran under the Buck's lanai. Over time, as we learned more about the history of the land and the importance of fishponds to Hawaiian culture, we began to see restoration of the pond as being as much a service to the community as it was enhancement of our properties.

I had just returned from a holiday visit with my daughters when I got a call from Doug inviting me over for dinner and to talk about the pond with his family. We talked into the evening, discussing not only the benefits of restoring the pond but also the risks involved in rebuilding and operating the pond. We didn't know for certain if the springs would still be active once unclogged nor did we know if it was even possible to remove all the accumulated muck and junk that buried the pond. Doug, a retired insurance entrepreneur, expressed concern about liability once the pond was completed and put into use. All in all, we agreed that restoring the pond would be of benefit to everyone yet understood that the potential problems had to be mitigated before we could proceed. The next step was to call upon Ron Hill to make a presentation.

Ron had had his eye on the pond ever since he started groundwork on Hale Mālamalama six years earlier. When the time came to put forth a restoration plan, Ron was ready. He wanted to start by filling in parts of the marshy basin with enough rock and gravel to allow heavy equipment access into and across the pond. He planned to quarry the fill from the nearby Kawaipapa riverbed and use his backhoe and rented dump truck to deliver it to the site. Once the base was compacted, he intended to bring in a sixty-five-foot boom crane with a clamshell attachment to clear the surface of overgrown vegetation and accumulated discards. At that point we could see what the surface and broken walls looked like and assess the viability of going forward. Ron's plan was less ambitious than I had hoped for but cautious enough to get the Bucks to commit. The next day I set out early for Wailuku to get a permit.

What could have been a complicated permit process proceeded smoothly largely due to our established relationship with the State Department of Land and Natural Resources. The inland location of the pond was out of the jurisdiction of the Army Corps of Engineers, and the fishpond's designation as a historic site shifted authority from county to state officials. The permit, granted in early February, included stipulations that DLNR archaeologists conduct an official survey of the site before work began and that the entirety of the restoration be videotaped and submitted as an edited documentation of the project upon completion.

Restoration officially commenced on a crisp sunny morning in mid-March, when Anne and a fellow archaeologist arrived on-site and started taking core samples. The unceremonious discovery of a decayed layer of pig poop just below the surface confirmed previous use as a hog farm. Deeper samples contained bits of charcoal likely washed into the pond from fires set along the banks. The deepest cores contained red cinder, consistent with the premise that the pond and surrounding lava-rock cliffs were the remnants of a collapsed cinder cone volcano. After carefully measuring and recording the terrain, the archaeologists completed their benchmark study and gave us a green light to proceed.

The stars initially seemed to be aligned in our favor that winter. The grace of an unseasonable drought enabled Ron to build a road into the dry riverbed and quarry enough material to compact a ramp into the marsh and repair the rock walls. A sudden storm could have washed out the road and set the project back by weeks. The rains continued to hold back while he cut and cleared the overgrown kamani trees behind the pond to make way for the boom crane. When the site was ready, Ron brought in the big rig, and that's when the trouble began. Despite Ron's diligence, the dirt banks and gravel-filled ramp were too soft to support the outriggers that stabilized the truck housing the crane. I watched Ron's pained expression as he tried to nurse each scoop out of the pond. The consequences of the crane falling into the pond were unthinkable. After a few near disasters Ron literally threw in the clamshell.

We had come to an impasse that we had not anticipated. The scope of the job had proven to be beyond the reach of Ron's backhoe. He was able to dig out enough mud around the base of the old walls to reset the rocks, but his equipment was inadequate to dredge the entire pond. On top of everything else, the initial budget was almost spent and the Bucks were about to return to Colorado. On an overcast afternoon in late May, Ron and I sat down with Doug and Mims on their lanai overlooking the mucky mess to consider our options. Abandoning the project altogether would leave the site in worse condition than before we started. Removing the gravel ramp and clearing the marsh of junk and debris by hand would be costly, messy, and difficult. The third option was to double down and contract an excavator to finish the job. As it was the Bucks who were fronting the project, it was their call. Doug and Mims consulted with each other a minute but seemed to have already made their decision. As Doug aptly put it, we were in too deep to turn back. Their willingness to put up additional funding, however, was contingent on finding a bonded and licensed contractor willing to truck his excavator across the narrow, winding Hāna Highway. "No problem," Ron replied—he knew some folks who would love the challenge.

It took a month, but Ron came through. Contractor Bruce's excavator was the answer, but its reach was shorter than the boom crane, so material dredged out of one place often had to be used to fill another. The procedure was not unlike a giant game of checkers with some scoops of mud jumping several times across the pond before finally being loaded onto a dump truck and carted off to a landfill on the other side of the riverbed. Even with two trucks constantly carting mud to the fill site, the work was slow and tedious. The loud, muddy, messy process pushed the patience of many in our quiet community as well as Hale Mālamalama guests who had come to Hāna for rest, relaxation, and romance. Even my own nervous system was on overload. I felt like I was tiptoeing through a mine field—one broken-down piece of equipment, a sudden storm, or an irate neighbor could bring down the show.

By the end of the second week, Bruce had removed enough mud that, in places, water began to appear. It was a relief finding that the springs were functional, but the water was a hindrance to scooping up the mud. Bruce drove back to Kihei that weekend and retrieved an industrial-size gas-generated pump to extract the water as it entered the pond. We put it to use on Monday morning and it worked wondrously, sucking up the spring-fed water as quickly as it appeared. Unfortunately, it too, was loud and the steady stream of water being pumped across the road was enough to warrant a visit from the police. Although our permit was in order and we hadn't broken any laws, the officers informed us that they were receiving complaints, especially about the muddy trails being left by the dump trucks. We agreed to start reducing the size of each load and assured them that we would scrape the road clean on completion of the job. They took no action other than warning that the sooner we finish the job the better. No argument there.

Another visitor that week was Parley Kanakaʻole. Officially, he came by at the request of the Hawaiian Burial Commission to make sure we weren't disturbing any grave sites; unofficially, he just wanted to talk. As we walked around the pond identifying the springs bubbling up through the mud, mostly in the back of the pond near the cave, he shared with me that he had been invited to preside over a three-day healing ceremony for the Island of Kahoʻolawe. The unoccupied Island, which had been a United States military bombing site for a half century, was being prepared to be turned over to the state of Hawaiʻi to be held in trust until the time when a sovereign Hawaiian entity could take over stewardship. The connection was intriguing: The long-neglected and misused fishpond was being restored in concert with the healing and restoration of a bombed-out island. I found the association to be both fitting and humbling.

Finally, after five weeks of constant dredging, nearly a thousand dump truck runs to the landfill, and nineteen nervous breakdowns, the job was done. Water had returned to the pond and life was restored to the ʻaina.

Removing last of the road into pond. Springs fill pond to sea level. July 1992.

Regenerations

The Hawaiian way of learning is through observation. I spent the next couple of months watching in amazement as a primitive ecosystem took hold of the pond. Frogs, dragonflies, and small mosquito fish appeared on their own and settled into territorial jurisdictions. Each day the water turned a slightly different color as it stabilized into cycles of algae blooms and die-offs. The most inspiring sight of all was watching the pond rise and fall with the tide table, breathing like a living being. I saw it as a microcosmic rendering of life before humankind, governed only by the natural rhythms of nature.

The window in front of my desk framed the pond like a kinetic watercolor painting. Wind and rain textured the surface with complex patterns of waves and ripples, and passing clouds shaded and heightened its many hues. On windless nights its silvery-smooth surface reflected a world turned upside down. Specks of light sparkled on the water like stardust fallen from the heavens above. Sometimes I'd get up before dawn, fix a cup of coffee, and sit on the cornerstone rock above the pond just to watch the day begin. The sight of the rising sun streaking the pond in a golden glow never failed to inspire a sense of awe.

The Bucks returned to their now-waterfront home in early September. We convened the next afternoon over tea and cookies on their lanai to discuss our duties and responsibilities as stewards of the reborn pond. A newly formed nonprofit, the Hawaiian Fishpond Restoration Foundation, had approached us about putting the pond to use as part of their statewide aquaculture program. We declined their invitation to manage the pond but agreed to participate in their program as independent operators. We put Ron on a retainer to maintain the rock walls and keep them clear of encroaching vegetation. Most importantly we agreed on two criteria to govern our operation of the fishpond. First, whenever possible the use of the pond was to be for the benefit of the community; and second, whatever was put into or taken out of the pond was to be for the good of the pond. Our charge was the care of the pond—the size of the crop was secondary.

The first batch of mullet and awa (the Hawaiian name for milkfish, not to be confused with the plant of the same name) was introduced into the pond in early October. The stock was provided by the Hawaiian Fishpond Restoration Foundation in association with the Oceanic Institute on Oʻahu. The fry were released into a floating holding tank made out of PVC piping lined with fine mesh netting. The holding tank was placed alongside the bank of the pond nearest to the Philippine house. Eventually, when the fish were large enough to eat the pea-size commercial pellets, they would be released from the tank. Until that time my first job as a fish farmer was to pulverize a batch of pellets in a coffee grinder late each afternoon and feed the fry by scattering the powdered protein across the surface of the tank.

As the fishpond regenerated so, too, did the Island of Kahoʻolawe. After the healing ceremonies, various programs were put in place to rid the island of spent and unspent ordnance and to clear the beaches of tons of cargo nets and bulky jetsam that had accumulated over decades of inattention. Through my association with the Maui County Community Work Day Program I had been invited to participate in a beach cleanup near the end of October. Access to Kahoʻolawe was restricted; participating in the cleanup was a privilege.

It was still dark when we assembled in Māʻalaea harbor and started loading the boat with cleanup supplies and provisions. There were about twenty of us, four organizers and the rest volunteers. As we crossed the channel we were told that we would have about four hours to collect as much sea trash as possible. It was pointed out that some of the cargo nets and ropes would have to be dug out and some of the bulkier items might have to be broken up. Small items were to be bagged and everything was to be piled near the back of the beach where it would be picked up by a pair of Navy cargo helicopters later in the day. Our boat approached a small cove on the northern side of the Island just in time to catch the sun popping up like a fireball over the top of Haleakalā.

Without pier or landing, we anchored outside the surf line and waded the rest of the way ashore. Some of us formed a relay line and passed supplies and equipment overhead hand-to-hand from boat to beach. What started out as a group of strangers quickly began to function as a seasoned team. Together we managed to dig out and remove even the most deeply embedded flotsam and piled up so much rubble that the Navy had to call in a third helicopter.

Our group parted at the dock in Māʻalaea just past noon. Strangers no more, we shared in the experience of contributing even in a small way to the recovery and restoration of Kahoʻolawe. Two years later I, along with eight hundred other witnesses, sat on La Perouse beach and watched as the undersecretary of the Navy signed the island of Kahoʻolawe over to John Waihee III, governor of Hawaiʻi and trustee for a sovereign Hawaiian entity. The deed, written in Hawaiian, along with a four-hundred- million-dollar cleanup commitment, was a remarkable accomplishment for what started as a small but determined grassroots movement challenging the moral and legal authority of the United States military to continue bombardment of a sacred island.

🌺🌺🌺

Thanksgiving weekend had long been targeted as the time to bless the pond. The Bucks were staying on the island, and my daughters were coming over for the holiday. At first we discussed hosting a community-wide lūʻau, but as the date approached, we took no action. The idea of a big celebration just didn't feel right. In early November Parley called saying that he had family coming to Hāna Thanksgiving week and was inquiring about accommodations. I offered him one of the cottages and mentioned that the Bucks and I were thinking of having the pond blessed that weekend. He noted that the timing was interesting but made no other comment.

Thanksgiving Day arrived, and we were still without plans for a blessing. There was an ominous feeling about the day. The weather was unsettled, winds were shifting and turning, and there was a general heaviness in the air. That night Tiffany, Melanie, and I had just finished Thanksgiving dinner at the Hāna Ranch Restaurant when it started to rain. By the time Melanie, who had just acquired a learner's permit, fetched the car, the rain had become a downpour. As we turned off the Hāna Highway toward home, the downpour became blinding. Melanie, rising to the occasion, clenched the steering wheel, leaned into the windshield, and determinedly held course. We pulled into the carport under the Tree House just as a thunderous lightning bolt struck near the fishpond. I followed the girls upstairs rather than try to forge through the torrent of water to reach my cottage. We dried off and rode out the deluge playing cards and drinking herbal tea.

The eleven inches of rain that fell in less than four hours destroyed three roads, swept four cars into the bay, and took one life. I still shudder to think that we were just minutes ahead of the wall of water that carried the cars out to sea. The elevated Hale Mālamalama structures survived the storm without apparent harm; the pond, however, was in disarray. Ron and I walked the grounds early the next morning and surveyed the damage. The road on the other side of the Bucks' house had washed out and formed a trench that channeled a river of water into the pond. The back bank had overflowed, and the surface was covered with a thick carpet of kamani nuts, leaves, and tree branches. Ron recruited a couple of helpers, and we spent the rest of the day cleaning up the mess.

By Saturday morning the floodwater had started to subside, and the fickle winds had corralled the remaining surface debris into the shallow corner on the backside of the pond. Sensing that it was now or never, I called Parley to ask if it was possible to conduct a blessing while our families were still in town. He agreed that it would be a good time to do so but had to first check with his own family, who were in Hāna to confer about Kanakaʻole Foundation matters. Without further ado Parley and his two sisters and brother-in-law arrived without notice a short time later. I put in a quick call to the Bucks, rounded up my daughters, and led the procession down the steps to the pond.

Positioned in front of the cave and standing behind a protective maile lei, Doug, Mims, Tiffany, Melanie, and I watched in silence as chants and prayers were offered in words we didn't know but somehow understood. A light, steady rain fell on the pond like a crystal curtain, and gusts of wind swept the surface as if in accompaniment to the offerings. After a closing prayer honoring the cave as guardian of the pond, Parley turned to us and announced that with the healing and blessing the pond had been given a name. He explained that before the ceremony they had discussed stories attributed to the area and noted surrounding conditions such as the direction of the winds, the cycle of the moon, and the feel of the air. Lastly, they had considered the efforts we had made to bring life back to the pond. The name loko Waihua, meaning heavy waters ready to bear fruit, was what they had decided on. Parley then looked at me and with a slight smile cautioned, "Just because the fruit is ready to bear, do not think that there is nothing left to do." And with a nod he directed our attention to the water still in shock from the flood: "This is where the real work begins."

New Year's Eve Day, 1992 – Home

Don't know quite what to make of this remarkable year. Restoration of the fishpond became a reality not so much by plan as by circumstance. The fact that the Bucks and I came to agreement after years of discussions, the ease with which we were given the permit, even the exceptional weather was perfect, as if it were destined to happen. On the other hand, when the moment arrived, I was ready.

On a deeper level it feels like something is changing within me. Ever since making the move I've been plagued with bouts of self-doubt and second-guessing my motivations. Restoring the pond has provided a sense of purpose beyond self. Still questionable how long I can financially maintain the property but know now the effort has not been for naught. Loko Waihua will sustain regardless of my tenure with the land.

Last detail to finish up the year is to complete the overdue essay I promised to send to guest Tim Gable of Clark City Press for possible inclusion in a book about stewardship. Narrative is done—just need an afterthought.

As the water settled, the pond became a mirror reflecting the surrounding flora and sky above. Hāna, September 1992.

Auspicious Visitors

Restoring the fishpond led to further involvement in Hawaiian cultural activities and practices. In a short time I was invited to join the board of a Native Hawaiian land trust and became an active member of the Hāna Canoe Club. Paradoxically, as I was finding a place and acceptance in the community, economic realities necessitated that I put the property up for sale. It wasn't crisis time yet, but the writing was on the wall. The property was listed with Carl Lindquist, a longtime Hāna resident sensitive to the historical importance of the 'aina. In accepting the listing Carl pointed out that prospective buyers for Hāna property are a rare breed, especially for something as unique as Hale Mālamalama and cautioned that finding the right one might take some time. And that it did. For the next three years I lived out a dream tending the land, running the business, and integrating with the community while simultaneously struggling to unburden myself of the debt that had enabled the dream to manifest.

In late January 1993, Tim Gable called, informing me that my submission had been accepted for inclusion in Michael Katakis' book *Sacred Trusts: Essays in Stewardship and Responsibility*. The essay, though focused on the restoration of the fishpond, concluded with a call for a rethinking of our relationship with the natural world and put forth a vision of applying indigenous wisdom with progressive technology for environmental restoration. The image of ancient knowledge combined with cutting-edge science had sparked my imagination since seeing Primitive Future imprinted on a bumper sticker in a Malibu surf shop shortly before moving to Maui. In a peculiar way the unexpected arrivals of a couple of personal guests just weeks after completing the essay seemed to exemplify the vision.

It began with a call from a friend of a friend on the Big Island who was bringing a Native American medicine man over to Hāna to meet with local kapuna (elders) and to perform a ceremony on the Pi'ilani Hale, the largest heiau in Hawai'i, built in the fifteenth century by the high chief Pi'ilani. Our mutual friend had suggested that I might be able to provide accommodations for their visit. As he provided details I realized that the medicine man in question was Grandfather Semu.

A few days later I was walking Grandfather around the grounds and telling him about how everything seemed to just fall into place when we decided to restore the pond. He responded that it was because the ancestors who once lived on the land were helping to make it happen. He explained that Mother Earth is the root of our being, not only in the physical world but in the spirit world as well. As we paused by the cave to feed the fish, Grandfather elaborated, "Treat Mother Earth well, and the spirits will always be at your side."

Incongruous as it was for the old Chumash medicine man to suddenly appear, it was equally astounding when Steve Wozniak dropped by a week or so later. Woz was vacationing on the other side of the Island with his (new) wife when they decided to venture out to Hāna on a whim. He called me from the Hāna Hotel to ask if it was convenient to stop by for a visit. I gave him directions and a few minutes later was giving him the same tour of the land I had just given Grandfather. I shared with the Wozniaks some of the history of the area and told them how I saw the fishpond serving as a model of a grassroots environmental restoration. Woz agreed and said that with the growing capabilities of the Internet it was the kind of story that could be shared and compared with other stories from around the world. Whereas Grandfather had spoken of looking to ancestors for guidance, Woz spoke of technology enabling us to learn from each other. I see the future as the best of both worlds.

Friends from California make unexpected visits shortly after restoration of pond. With Woz after feeding fish. Hāna, 1993.

With Grandfather Semu and his clan. Fom left: Author, Red Sun, (Grandfather's son), unknown, Grandfather Semu and wife Eneke-Alish. Hāna, 1993.

The visitor who would have a most profound effect on my future, however, had arrived few months earlier. Sonny, the Buddha broker, redeemed his temple door credit for a stay at the inn and brought with him his landlord, Patricia Steele, and her friend, Joann from Newport Beach. As I escorted them to their upstairs quarters in the Philippine house, Sonny invited me to join them for a glass of wine later that afternoon.

After feeding the fish, I prepared a platter of sashimi and gathered with my guests on the Royal Suite deck overlooking the fishpond. The visit, I learned, was part of a recovery journey for Joann following the unexpected passing of her husband. Still, Trisha and Joann, friends for many years, were quick to laugh at Sonny's stories of adventure (and misadventure) collecting Buddhas in Bali. My guests were fascinated with the pond and enjoyed hearing stories about the history of the land. Trisha, an avid sailor, admired the nautical influence on the architecture—it reminded her of a finely crafted ship. As the evening set in, we decided to carry on our conversation over dinner at the Hāna Hotel.

We got together again the next morning for breakfast, a strange but amusing juxtaposition of being treated as a guest in what was my home. Prior to their departure later that afternoon, Joann asked if she could come back for visit over the holidays. She said she needed some time alone and felt Hāna would be a nurturing environment. I told her that was fine with me, as I would be working on a writing assignment and likely wouldn't be much of a host.

Joann returned again in mid-February. Despite our separate agendas we had had some good times during her visit in December. By day, I tended to the inn and worked on the essay while Joann went about on her own, exploring the area and working through her thoughts. We would convene in the late afternoon, when I would read to her my musings of the day and she would tell me of her wanderings and insights. Later we would fix dinner and often carry on conversation into the evening. At my invitation she returned for Valentine's Day.

It seemed almost destined that Joann should be there when I picked up the huge mailing tube that contained a Russell Chatham lithograph, payment for my contribution to *Sacred Trusts* (Chatham owned Clark City Press, original publisher of the book). As I set the hefty tube in the middle of my already cramped office/cottage, Joann asked where I was going to display the picture. I told her that besides not having a space big enough for it, I wasn't sure how well a Montana landscape would fit in a tropical environment, adding that what I really needed was a new computer, specifically one of Apple's new laptops. Joann suggested that she buy a computer through her late husband's company and trade it for the print. She thought a Russell Chatham landscape would fit nicely in her home, and it would also serve as a reminder of her time in Hāna. Sight unseen, Joann took the Chatham print with her when she returned to California, and I was sitting at my desk with a brand-new computer the following week.

I was paid with art for my first published story and was able to redirect the art to a loving home in exchange for a tool of my trade. The integrity of the transaction could be described as *pono*, a Hawaiian word so rich with meaning that it has a multitude of definitions, not the least being "a state of harmony or balance."

Deep Taro

The first East Maui Taro Festival was held at the Hāna Ballpark in March of 1993. It came about as a grassroots community effort led by local resident and anthropologist Maria Orr. Following the example of a similar event that had taken place on Oʻahu, Maria thought that holding a taro festival in Hāna would not only shine a light on the importance of taro farming to Hawaiian culture but could also be an economic boost to the community. On a deeper level Maria saw the festival as an opportunity to bring a divided and torn community together.

The cause of the rift was an attempt by the new owners of the Hotel Hāna Maui to build a golf course on Hāna ranch land, which they also owned. The Japanese-led investment group, known as Keola Hāna Maui (KHM), had purchased the hotel and ranch in 1989 and claimed that the development of a golf course was essential to making their venture profitable. Closure of the hotel, the largest employer in Hāna, would cause economic havoc to the community. Employees feared for their jobs while others, often even members of the same family, feared for the loss of Hāna being "the last Hawaiian place."

Maria began her quest by consulting with Mitsue Cook-Carlson, one of the organizers of the Oʻahu festival. Mitsue, whose vision was that locally produced taro festivals would become annual events on each island, offered her total support and told Maria to just select a date and move forward. The Oʻahu festival was in summer; Maria decided that late March around the time of spring break would be the ideal time to stage the inaugural East Maui Taro Festival.

Maria's next step was to call on longtime Hāna resident and grande dame of the Hāna Cultural Center, Coila Eade. Coila offered to talk up the idea among her friends and suggested that Maria talk to J. Kalani English, a locally born and raised young man with a passion for the practice and protection of Hawaiian culture. Maria described to Kalani her premise: Since at the core of Hawaiian mythology kanaka (native Hawaiians) and taro share the same common root, taro represents Hawaiian culture at its deepest level. Publicly, Maria envisioned the festival as an opportunity to build cultural pride and showcase the uniqueness of our community for the rest of the world. Kalani, who would soon embark on a political career of his own, saw the wisdom of Maria's vision and offered his full support along with a list of names and contacts who he thought might be interested in participating in or sponsoring the festival.

Maria then met with Parley and Ipo Kanaka'ole and presented the festival as being an opportunity to reunite the community by honoring the food that has been a staple to Hawaiians since the beginning of history. Parley gave her his blessings and offered to act as liaison with Hāna School. From then on, the festival seemed to take on a life of its own. By the end of summer an ad hoc committee had been formed, and the first public meeting was held in early October. Monthly meetings continued for the rest of the year. By January the meetings had become weekly events, and the structure and agenda for the festival had been firmly established. About that time, I signed on and offered to accommodate some of the musicians that would be performing at the event.

Pre-festival festivities began the evening of March 26 at Helene Hall on Hāna Bay with a panel discussion by prominent University of Hawai'i taro researchers and a video presentation of taro-farming techniques throughout the Pacific. The next morning the festival opened at the Hāna Ballpark with a chant by cultural icon Keali'i Reichel, followed with a prayer by Parley Kanaka'ole. It is estimated that a crowd of three thousand guests visited Hāna that day and, for the weekend at least, Hāna was at peace and true to its roots as "the last Hawaiian place."

Whereas the taro festival was a step in bringing the Hāna community back together, the battle for and against the golf course continued to play out at city hall. The nearly two-year drama came to a head when the issue went before the Maui County Council for the final reading of a motion to approve the zoning change to allow for construction of the golf course. The majority of those who testified at the daylong hearing were in opposition to the golf course. Additionally, a League of Women Voters straw poll found Hāna residents 58 to 42 percent opposed to the golf course, and an informal survey taken at Hāna School found students opposed to the golf course by a margin of 3 to 1, yet inexplicably, the council voted 8-1 to approve the zoning change. The lone holdout was Hāna district councilman Tom Marrow, former owner of Tom's Rental Cars.

The case was not closed, however, as the council's resolution stipulated a three-hundred-foot rather than the customary two-hundred-foot setback for fairway development. KHM strongly objected to the restriction and filed for reconsideration. When the general manager let slip in an off-the-cuff comment that the setback really wasn't an issue, the council, already feeling heat from their initial approval, had had enough. They reconsidered KHM's application and reissued the zoning change ordinance, this time requiring a setback of fifteen hundred feet, all but killing the project. The other shoe dropped when the Japanese government disallowed KHM's plan to finance the golf course by pre-selling golf club memberships to Japanese corporations and executives.

Though rumors of an imminent shutdown were rampant, KHM managed to keep the hotel open until new owners took over in July 2000. By then old wounds had healed and the taro festival had become an annual event. As is often the case, the path to peace was the middle road that found common ground apart from issues of division. From its humble beginnings as an exercise to reunite the community, the East Maui Taro Festival has risen to become one of most celebrated festivals in all of Hawai'i and a perennial reminder of how a small community looked to its roots to find peace and place in an ever-changing world.

Filling the Void

A week or so after the pond blessing Parley stopped by to talk story. While discussing the ceremony he asked if any of us had felt ill or troubled after the event. I didn't know what to make of his question until he explained that, along with the blessing, he and his sisters had performed a healing to release negative energy that had accumulated in the 'aina. He said that when the energy was released it could have been harmful to anyone not properly prepared or protected as we were behind a maile lei. His brother-in-law, who had assisted in the ritual, suffered fevered dreams that night, and Parley was concerned that any of us might have also been affected. I told him that my daughters and I, if anything, felt elated after the event and as far as I knew the Bucks had felt the same.

Our discussion that evening led to an ongoing series of conversations about everything from local issues to speculations about the future. We were both dreamers and liked to envision history taking a turn for the better. We half-jokingly decided that infusing Hawaiian cultural understanding into the greater worldview could be just the tonic for an ailing planet. We discussed more immediate issues as well. One of Parley's biggest concerns was how to make traditional culture relevant in contemporary life, particularly for young Hawaiian men.

In a similar vein, the Native Hawaiian sovereignty movement was a topic of frequent discussion. The sovereignty movement had been simmering ever since the overthrow of Queen Lili'uokalani in 1893; the Hawaiian cultural renaissance nearly a century later gave it momentum. The movement intensified in the early 1990s as American involvement in the overthrow of the Hawaiian monarchy was under renewed scrutiny and the legitimacy of the United States congressional joint resolution annexing the Islands to the United States in 1898 was being called into question.

Parley and I did not discuss politics as much as vision and it was an intriguing notion to imagine how a sovereign Hawaiian government might take shape. With so much of world governance rooted in stagnant ideologies from earlier times, it was refreshing to consider the opportunity to create a new form of government that valued the well-being of its land and its people above all else.

One afternoon in early spring Parley dropped off a box of VHS tapes, eighteen hours of unedited footage of the Kahoʻolawe healing ceremony that took place the previous summer. He said the tapes documented the three-day gathering of more than two hundred individuals, old and young, Hawaiian and non-Hawaiian, living and working together, preparing the long-abused island for healing and rejuvenation. Parley modestly proposed that maybe the basis for a new constitution began with what happened on Kahoʻolawe.

A couple of months later, I stopped by Parley's house to give him a gift. As he had just returned from attending a Mainland conference with Native American tribal chiefs and spiritual leaders, I wanted him to have the Hopi running clown kachina that I had purchased in Santa Fe. I told him that what had drawn me to the doll was that the persona of the running clown was true to cultural form, only wearing contemporary cutoff blue jeans rather than a traditional loincloth. He shared that one of the major subjects of the meeting was the protection and perpetuation of cultural practices. He said it was funny that many of the Native Americans were looking to him for answers while he was hoping to learn from them. He took the Hopi clown, set it on the ledge over his kitchen window, and chuckled that perhaps the next conference should include some artists.

🌲🌲🌲

On August 12, 1993, Fernanda, a category 4 hurricane, was bearing down on Hawaiʻi with the eastern coasts of Maui and the Big Island most likely to be hit. In the early-morning hours of August 14, the storm suddenly deflated when a wind shear inexplicably clipped off its top a few hundred miles east of Hilo. Other than some rain and high surf, the impact of the storm was minimal. The impact of a tragedy that happened that night, however, was monumental.

On Friday evening as the storm was approaching, Parley Kanakaʻole presided over an ʻawa ceremony on Puʻukoholā heiau on the Big Island. The event commemorated the healing rite that Parley had officiated on the heiau two years earlier. On that occasion, marking the two-hundredth anniversary of Kamehameha's sacrifice of rival chief Keōua, representatives of both families came together for a Hawaiian reconciliation and forgiveness ritual known as hoʻoponopono. The rite brought closure to lingering misgivings about the event that launched Kamehameha's ascent to power and the founding of the Kingdom of Hawaiʻi.

Later that evening while driving back to his sister's house, Parley suffered a massive heart attack and crashed into an oncoming car. I learned of his death early the next morning when Ron Hill called to say that something terrible had happened. He had heard the news on the radio but didn't have any details. I hung up the phone in disbelief. Parley was more than just a close friend; he was my teacher, mentor, and spiritual inspiration.

The night before Parley's memorial service I attended a family vigil at his house. There, Parley's wife, Ipo, introduced me to a quiet, unassuming man who was sitting on the floor next to Parley's casket. John Stokes was the founder and director of The Tracking Project, a New Mexico–based foundation dedicated to reconnecting individuals with the natural world, and was instrumental in getting Parley involved with the Native American tribal leaders. He also led the small contingent of Native Americans that participated in the Kahoʻolawe healing weekend. As we talked, we discovered that Parley had spoken to each of us about the other and had wanted us to meet. It was heartbreaking that it took his passing to make it happen.

The turnout for Parley's funeral was so large that it had to be held in the high school gymnasium. The massive room was filled with flowers and packed to the rafters with family, friends, acquaintances, and admirers from throughout the Islands and elsewhere. After the service the mile-long funeral procession snaked its way through Hāna town and out to Kīpahulu, where Parley was laid to rest. The burial site was on a bluff facing the ʻAlenuihāhā Channel toward Parley's birthplace on the Island of Hawaiʻi. While walking back to my car, I recognized Billy Richards, a stately Hawaiian man I knew through his work with the Oceanic Institute. Billy was there as a member of the elite honor guard that lined the corridor that led to the grave site. As I approached, Billy put aside his spear and gave me a warm embrace. We paused a moment, then asked each other the same question almost in unison: "What do we do now?"

That same question caromed throughout Parley's many circles of influence. His death left a void that no one person could ever fill. The best that any of us could do was to follow Parley's lead and continue with our respective aspects of his work. In time the pieces started to fall back in place, and though never the same, life moved on.

The timing of Parley's death and the breaking up of the hurricane did not go unnoticed. One local kapuna commented that it was like Fernanda's head was sheared off by a supernatural force.

First Harvest

A month after Parley's passing, a state-sponsored fishpond symposium took place in Hāna. The conference, held at the Hotel Hāna Maui, brought together representatives of government agencies, Hawaiian cultural practitioners and historians, fishpond owners and operators, and a scattering of other interested parties. Unlike the smaller hands-on fishpond workshops that I had attended on Molokaʻi and the island of Hawaiʻi, the Hāna conference dealt with the bigger issue of preserving and restoring Hawaiʻi's few remaining fishponds. Several ponds had been targeted for restoration, but those plans were stalled due to permit complications and a lack of funding. The purpose of the symposium was to establish the historical and cultural importance of fishponds and find ways to facilitate their restoration.

Of the eighty or so ponds still identifiable, only a dozen were in productive use. I knew most of the pond operators from the workshops, and we tended to gather as a group between sessions. During the predinner break I led my associates on a tour of loko Waihua, just a short walk down the road from the hotel. It was late afternoon and the fish were already agitating on the surface in anticipation of their evening meal. I tossed a handful of pellets into the water, and the surface boiled in a feeding frenzy. The Oceanic Institute representative, Buddy Keala, impressed with the size and quantity of the fish, commented that the awa looked ready to harvest. Walking back to the hotel we talked about the possibility of working a small harvest into the following day's agenda.

Over dinner that evening I sat next to Frenchy DeSoto of the Office of Hawaiian Affairs. Finding that she had also been close to Parley, I asked her advice about going ahead with a harvest now or waiting until spring as planned. She thought harvesting some fish during the conference was a great idea and suggested talking to the restaurant about adding the fish to the menu for tomorrow night's dinner. I knew it would be a special honor to offer fish from Ioko Waihua for the closing meal. Nonetheless, I was hesitant about harvesting the first crop from the stock that I had raised from fingerlings.

At breakfast the next morning I approached Danny Akaka about doing the blessing for the fish harvest. Danny was the kahunapule (keeper) of the fishponds at the Mauna Lani Hotel and a Hawaiian cultural authority and practitioner. I had met him a few months earlier at the Big Island workshop, when he gave us a tour of the hotel grounds. He said he would be glad to preside but asked for some time to put together the ceremony. I consulted with fellow Hāna pond operators Robert Malaiakini and Jackie Kahala and decided to set the harvest for one o'clock. Gary Chow, manager of the Ranch Restaurant, had agreed to put the awa on the dinner buffet and needed time to prepare the fish.

Like kids cutting class, Robert, Jackie, Buddy, Frenchy, Danny, and I, along with the rest of the pond operators, sneaked out at lunch break and headed over to loko Waihua for the makeshift harvest. Our goal was to net about twenty awa: a dozen for the restaurant, two as offerings, and the remainder to be given to Ipo Kanakaʻole as a tribute to Parley. Robert, the most skilled fisherman in our group, was given the honor of casting the net. My job was to toss pellets into the water to bring the fish to the surface.

Danny, wearing a red kihei (a cloth wrap tied over one shoulder), began the proceedings with a chant. Holding a wooden bowl of saltwater in one hand and a fist full of ti leaves in the other, he started sprinkling seawater in front of the cave while offering his pule. Danny then began a clockwise circle around the pond, all the while splashing it with water from his bowl. At that point I began chumming the water to bring up the awa. When Danny completed the circle, he gave Robert the signal to proceed. The fish, however, were slow to surface.

Seems the fish had their own internal feeding clocks and were still scattered about the pond. I began tossing heaps of pellets in the water and banging the feeding cup on the side of the bucket like ringing a dinner bell. Eventually, we were able to create enough commotion to attract their attention. As the fish clustered, Robert stared intently at the surface waiting for the right moment. Then, in an instant he flung his net into the pond. Jackie and I grabbed hold of the attached rope and helped haul the catch onto the bank. Buddy and one of the pond operators each picked up an awa, wrapped it in a ti leaf, and held it in place on the pondside heiau while Danny offered a prayer of gratitude to Kūʻula and his wife, Hina. The remaining awa were packed in a cooler and taken down to the bay for cleaning.

In the kitchen, Gary seasoned the catch and deep-fried the fish whole. He then cut them into bite-size pieces for sampling by the conferees attending dinner that evening. The awa were a hit. The serving tray had been picked clean by evening's end, and I was still receiving compliments about the flavorful fish at the closing session the next morning. As we adjourned, I invited Danny to come back to Hāna in March to preside over the harvest being planned for the taro festival. I told him to bring his family for the weekend. He accepted the invitation and said he felt something very special about the pond and cave and wanted to research stories and chants about the ʻaina. Buddy came by as he was leaving to say he would also be back for the taro festival. Then he chided me to fatten up the fish: "This time it was just appetizers for a party. Next time it will be feeding a festival."

Going to the Hukilau

December 4, 1993 – Tree House Cottage

For the last three weeks I have been assembling a photo history of Hale Mālamalama. Intention being to put the whole project into perspective and serve as a transition piece for the next owner. Finished writing captions and amazed at what an incredible journey this has been so far. Whatever happens next, the opportunity to contribute to the living history of this remarkable ʻaina has been a rare privilege indeed.

※ ※ ※

My resolve for the new year was to find a buyer for the property. After lingering on the market with only three showings and no offers, Carl, the real estate agent who was also a friend, agreed that the listing was getting stale and did not object to my decision to take property off the market while considering other options. I had long thought of the property as rightfully belonging to a foundation or institution; the Office of Hawaiian Affairs seemed to be a good place to start.

I contacted Frenchy DeSoto to test the waters. I told her how I had shared with Parley my desire that Hale Mālamalama could one day become an educational center for cultural practices and fishpond management. I added that I didn't know how much longer I could hold on to the property and asked if she had any ideas of how I might be able to steer it into the right hands. Frenchy agreed the ʻaina was an important cultural asset that should be kept in productive use but was not sure it was something in which OHA could become directly involved. She asked if I could send her some photos of the property with a summary of its history. She said she would talk to her associates and see if they could come up with some ideas.

The first public harvest of fish from loko Waihua was scheduled to take place during the second taro festival in late March. Maria Orr and I had been discussing the harvest for some time, and in January I formally presented a plan to the taro festival committee. I proposed that we open the festival with a fish harvest on Friday afternoon, then cook and sell the fish on-site at the festival the next day. All proceeds would be used to support the festival. The proposal was accepted, and I was invited to join the committee to help coordinate the events.

In early March I got a call from Frenchy to say that OHA chairman Clayton Hee was flying into Hāna the next afternoon and wanted to visit Hale Mālamalama while he was in town. She asked if I could pick him up at the airport and give him a tour of the property before his meeting at the hotel later that evening. I cringed at the short notice but told Frenchy that I looked forward to the chairman's visit and that the grounds would be ready for review by the time of his arrival.

Houseguest Jennifer, a Canadian bodyworker on an extended holiday, took charge of cleaning up my cottage while I grabbed a bathing suit and jumped into the pond to weed the walls. The biggest problem in maintaining the pond in the early days was keeping the walls cleared of vegetation—the roots if left unchecked would cause the rocks to destabilize and collapse. Sometimes the weeding process itself would bring on a break, and that is precisely what happened at the worst of all possible times. I was able to restack some of the rocks, but a complete repair would require more time and at least one additional set of helping hands. Having done what I could, I took leave of the pond to prepare myself for the arrival of my distinguished guest.

My nervousness at meeting Chairman Hee quickly vanished as soon as I picked him up at the airport. Soft spoken and amiable, Clayton seemed more like a friendly neighbor than a politician. After touring the property and feeding the fish, we went back to my cabin to talk story. Jennifer had set out some refreshments, and the three of us sat on the deck overlooking the pond and watched the fish gobble up the last of the pellets that were floating on the surface. Clayton's first comment was that he was relieved to see that we didn't use any cement to hold the walls in place. He noted the small collapse and recalled dealing with the same problem when working on ponds on Molokaʻi in his youth. He candidly said that Hawaiians believed that rocks needed to breathe and, when encased in cement, lose their mana. He complimented me in doing what was right even if it meant more maintenance.

We finished our conversation just as the sun was beginning to set. Clayton and I spoke briefly as I drove him the short distance down the road to the hotel. He said he was very impressed with the property and agreed that it could be an ideal learning center but, like Frenchy, was not sure that it fell within the jurisdiction of OHA. He said, however, that he would bring the issue before the board to see if they could come up with something. As we parted he cautioned me that bureaucratic wheels move slowly and suggested that I keep other irons in the fire while they evaluated the project.

I rented Hale Mālamalama out to myself for the taro festival. I put Danny Akaka and his family in the Royal Suite and Buddy Keala and his wife downstairs. Jennifer and I moved into the Tree House Cottage. She was traveling to Thailand in a few days, so the taro festival would be our last hurrah.

Robert Malaiakini and his cousin Moke came by Friday morning to prepare for the harvest. We were going to follow the protocol set during the symposium, with Danny blessing the pond and Robert casting his net to begin the harvest. Once the first two fish were wrapped in ti leaves and offered on the heiau, the plan called for Buddy and his assistants to zigzag a long net across the pond using a large inner tube as a float. When everything was in place, a dozen or so keiki would get to dive into the pond and chase the fish into the net. From there on it would be an old-fashioned hukilau, where everyone is invited to help pull in the catch.

An hour before the guests started gathering for the three o'clock event, television personality Emme Tomimbang and her crew came by to set up their equipment. They were in Hāna to cover the taro festival for a segment on *Emme's Island Moments*. While waiting for the ceremony to begin Emme interviewed me about the history of the pond and Danny about what fishponds mean to Hawaiian culture. As the crowd gathered at the appointed hour I thanked everyone for coming, gave a brief history of loko Waihua, and then turned the proceedings over to Danny.

Danny addressed the gathering with a chant, then started to circle the pond as I tossed pellets into the water to bring up the awa. I had been gradually feeding the fish earlier each day for a week, so by the time of the harvest they were cracking the surface as soon as the feed hit the water. The crowd cheered as Robert tossed his net and we pulled up the first fish. Soon the pond was alive with happy keiki jumping and splashing as they herded the fish into the net. With the help of several onlookers we pulled the net into the shallow end of the pond and dragged the bounty ashore. The meshing in the net was tight enough to entangle the mature fish but loose enough for the juveniles to slip through. When the net was strung out along the side of the pond, everyone joined in to pick out the catch.

After the fish were packed in coolers and the spectators thinned out, I returned to the Tree House to find that Jennifer had run a bath in the double-size Jacuzzi tub that sat regally perched behind the Balinese temple door. Dripping wet and covered in mud, I detoured first to the outdoor shower to scrub away the muck. By the time I returned to the cottage the bath had cooled and Jennifer was dressed and ready for a night on the town. Feeling dapper in a fresh pair of shorts and my favorite aloha shirt, Jennifer and I strolled down to the hotel to partake in an evening of local music and festivities. We topped off the night back at the cottage. Wrapped in a blanket in the love seat on the deck above the pond, we slept and snuggled until dawn.

By any measure the harvest was a success. Ninety fish averaging a pound and a half apiece were taken from the pond, and close to two hundred plates were sold, raising almost a thousand dollars for the festival. Things never worked out with OHA. It wasn't lack of interest, just not the right fit. By the next taro festival harvest, things would be different.

Jennifer enjoying a splash in the bamboo shower while Woody Woodpecker bears her clothes. Hāna, April 1994.

A guidebook made note of late afternoon fish feedings, and the event became a daily attraction. Hāna, April 1994.

Rebirth

May 7, 1994, marked the date that jurisdiction over the island of Kahoʻolawe was conveyed from the US government to the state of Hawaiʻi. The state, in turn, placed the conveyance in trust until the establishment of a sovereign Hawaiian entity to hold title to the island. Located eight miles off the southern coast of Maui, Kahoʻolawe had been used for military training and bombardment exercises since World War II. Protests against the use of Hawaiʻi's eighth-largest island as an active bombing target had been ongoing since the conclusion of the war. However, it wasn't until a small cadre of activists started clandestinely occupying the island in 1976, that the plight of Kahoʻolawe became a statewide issue. Concurrently the Hawaiʻi supreme court upheld an injunction to halt the bombing to allow for a through archaeological survey of the island. Upon completion of the review, the entire island of Kahoʻolawe was designated a national historic site and added to the register of historic places. The incongruity of a nationally sanctioned historic place also being an active bombing site was rectified in 1990 when the federal government put a halt to all bombing operations and set in motion procedures to return to Kahoʻolawe to the state of Hawaiʻi.

In the intervening years, the Navy mounted a massive cleanup effort, while volunteers under the direction of Hawaiian cultural practitioners began restoring the life of the land by building water catchments and planting trees. Above all else, it was the prevailing spirit of aloha and mālama ʻaina (caring for the land) that was nurturing the recovery.

Frenchy DeSoto called me late in the afternoon on May 6 to confirm that I was going to attend the ceremony the next day. She suggested that I arrive early and meet some of the participants that were instrumental in the recovery of the island. As she was hanging up to take another call, she hastily asked that I bring some awa for the ceremony. Initially I assumed that she meant to bring a couple of fish as an offering. Later I had second thoughts and questioned that maybe she meant the 'awa plant to be made into the ceremonial beverage kava. To be safe, I thought it best to bring both.

After feeding the fish, I took the long-handled net used to pull leaves and debris out of the pond and scooped up a couple of small awa that had strayed close to the bank. I wrapped them in ti leaves and stored them in a container with ice. Next, I called Tom, a friend who lives in Nahiku, a small community a few miles north of Hāna. Recalling that he had mentioned finding an 'awa plant growing wild in the jungle near his property, I asked if I could take some root to the ceremony. Tom told me to come by early in the morning on my way out of town. He said the plant was about a half hour hike from his house and advised bringing work clothes and boots.

The next morning, I packed my car with the sacrificial fish and a fresh set of clothes and left my cottage at daybreak. Tom and his wife greeted me with a steaming cup of coffee and a couple of slices of papaya from their garden. After the pleasantries, Tom handed me a machete and an empty backpack, and we were on our way. Nahiku is one of the wettest places on the island. Even on clear days the sun barely penetrates the thick canopy of trees and vines, leaving the ground in a near perpetual state of mud. Most of our trek was on a semblance of a trail, but we had to whack our way through some overgrowth before reaching our find. Tom was glad to see that the plant had grown and had not been discovered by unscrupulous parties. He walked around the large shrub and found a root outcropping that could be taken without hardship to the host. We took only what I thought to be a respectful offering, the rest left behind for another time.

Parking and catching the shuttle to La Perouse beach took longer than expected, and by the time I found Frenchy, the event was about to begin. She gratefully accepted the ti-leaf-wrapped 'awa root and awa fish and directed her assistant to place them on the shore with the rest of the offerings to be taken to Kahoʻolawe after the proceedings. She introduced me to several of her colleagues, including Danny's father, Senator Akaka, then took her place with the dignitaries.

I found a spot on the lawn and joined eight hundred or so others to watch as the undersecretary of the Navy and Governor Waihee of Hawaiʻi stepped up to a worn wooden table from the living room of Harry Mitchell, one of the founders of the movement. With the island of Kahoʻolawe looming on the horizon behind them, the governor and undersecretary exchanged signatures on the documents, written in Hawaiian, that returned authority over the constricted island back to the state of Hawaiʻi.

A week or so later I got a note from Frenchy. She had taken the awa fish and root with her when she sailed over to Kahoʻolawe after the formalities on the beach. The awa fish were offered to the akua Kanaloa on the heiau that had been built under Parley's direction two years earlier, and the ʻawa root was cut, pounded, and prepared for use in the circle that evening. She thanked me for the contributions and remarked that by way of the fish that were offered, loko Waihua was also represented in the ceremony. She concluded by saying that both are places of rebirth and hope

Close to the Edge

December 21, 1995 – Paniolo Bar, Hāna Hotel

High mark of the year was Hale Mālamalama coming into its own as a travel destination. Occupancy reached sustainable levels, and the inn gained notice in the media — featured in Condé Nast Traveler and National Geographic Traveler and coverage in most of the major travel guides. Most satisfying of all, HM is attracting an interesting mix of guests. Be they artists, academics, or just free spirits, I'm finding our guests to be (for the most part), good company.

Concurrently, the consequences of years of negative cash flow are coming home to roost. State's pushing hard for lagging business tax payments and legal proceedings have been initiated for delinquent child support. Only the near miracle of a local booking service forwarding a slew of reservations (with deposits) they couldn't accommodate held off foreclosure on the mortgage. Making matters worse, my folks' loan is overdue, and they are feeling the pinch. Something has to happen.

One of Hāna's best-kept little secrets, the annual New Year's Eve pyrotechnic extravaganza, was just what I needed to kick-start the new year. The tradition started when Carl Lindquist managed the Hotel Hāna Maui in the early 1980s, and it had become a New Year's Eve ritual for members and guests of the community to gather in front of the Hāna Hotel to collectively witness the fireworks and cheer in the new year. This year I started the evening dining with a couple who had been staying in the Tree House Cottage and a friend visiting from the other side of the island. After dinner we told stories and shared dreams and aspirations for the coming year. A half hour before midnight we packed a bottle of champagne and some plastic cups in a basket and walked down the road to catch the show.

By the time we arrived, most of the guests had evacuated the bar and dining room and migrated outside to mingle on the street with the gathering crowd of townsfolk. The air was already heavy with smoke from firecrackers and bottle rockets that had been fired randomly all evening like an unscripted opening act. As the bewitching hour drew near, we worked ourselves through the crowd and found a spot next to a small rock wall. There we popped the bottle and toasted the arrival of what we agreed was going to be a magnificently magical year for one and all. As we lifted our glasses upward, the sky suddenly exploded in rainbows of fiery embers and thunderous booms heralding the arrival of the new year. A breathtaking finale of a multitude of starbursts in strobe-like sequence was followed by a lone rocket whistling above our heads and exploding into a million tiny droplets of light that trickled to the ground like stardust. After a moment's pause, the crowd cheered and broke into rounds of hugs, kisses, and high-fives, then slowly started to disperse. Arm in arm, my guests and I high-stepped our way home. 1996 was going to be *the year*.

A Plan and a Plan B

I had put Hale Mālamalama back on the market in early 1995, listing with a real estate agent on the other side of the island who was also the president of an environmental protection, cultural rights, and sustainable growth nonprofit. Yet despite his connections both within and apart from the real estate community, showings were few and no offers were forthcoming. It seemed that, one way or another, I was going to have to become more directly involved in finding a buyer. My first priority was to prepare a business plan.

After gathering photos, files, and financial statements, I went to work constructing the document. In doing so I forged another relationship with the property, this time as a commodity or asset with the capacity to generate a profit. I had reluctantly come to realize that aesthetics, location, and history were not enough. The property had to be shown capable of being self-sustaining at least and have the potential for future growth. I had five years of operational statements that showed a steady increase in revenue that, apart from service to my sizable debt, could be marginally profitable. I envisioned the possibility of acquiring an adjacent property to expand the business. As the numbers came together, the plan made sense. To make the business succeed, it needed to grow. The buyer I was looking for would recognize the potential to build Hale Mālamalama into a truly exceptional mini-resort and have the means to make it happen. For the first time since deciding to sell the property I was getting a sense of the buyer.

Excitedly, I got in touch with Joann in Newport Beach and asked for her help in doing the layout and packaging of the plan. She had put her graphic design business aside to help run her inherited business, but graciously made an exception and offered to be of service. I provided her with text and charts as well as a historical overview of the land, a photo story of the taro festival fish harvest, and pictures and quotes from magazines and travel guides. Concluding the plan was a vision statement assessing the potential for expansion. After more than a month of phoning, faxing, and dial-up emailing, I flew to Los Angeles to help complete the job. We printed only six bound copies, one as a master for her files and five for discreet distribution. What started as a business plan ended up with the look and feel of a well-crafted prospectus. I didn't know if I wanted to buy or sell.

⁂

The opening event scheduled for the fourth annual East Maui Taro Festival was the Hōkūle'a sailing into Hāna Bay at daybreak Friday morning to open the festival. This was to be the first visit of the revered sailing canoe to Hāna, though its appearance had been anticipated for years. What made the visit especially eventful was that Hāna resident Sam Kalalau Jr. had been a crew member on the Hōkūle'a's historic voyage from Hawai'i to Tahiti in 1976. That voyage and the occupation of the island of Kaho'olawe at approximately the same time were benchmark events early on in the Hawaiian cultural renaissance.

The double-hull sailing canoe, built between 1973 and 1975 under the supervision of the Polynesian Voyaging Society, started as a vision by society founders Herb Kane, Ben Finney, and Tommy Holmes. The vessel was crafted to replicate the sailing canoes that traversed the islands of Polynesia in ancient times. Re-creating a seaworthy voyaging canoe was only part of the accomplishment. Rediscovery and mastery of the art of "wayfinding"—traditional navigation based on the reading of currents and wind, acute observation of stars, moon, sun, birds, fish, and ocean swells, and educated intuition—was another endeavor altogether. As the practice of wayfinding had been lost throughout Polynesia, the society had to recruit Mau Piailug of the tiny Island of Satawai in Micronesia to lead the Hōkūle'a to Tahiti. In the process Mau mentored Nainoa Thompson to become the first Polynesian navigator in the postmigration era.

The Hōkūle'a left Maui on May 1 and reached Papeete harbor on the island of Tahiti thirty-four days later. A jubilant crowd of over 17,000 well-wishers, said to be more than half the island's population, was on hand to greet its arrival. The reenactment of a feat that hadn't been performed in hundreds of years was a source of pride for all Polynesians. It not only confirmed the seafaring capabilities of their ancestors, it also brought a sense of unity among the island groups within the Polynesian triangle, an area more than twice the size of the continental United States.

The Hōkūle'a's arrival in Hāna was considered of such importance that representatives of multigenerational families from Kaupo to Ke'anae had been invited to participate in a formal 'awa ceremony to welcome the crew. Sam Ka'ai was set to officiate the most reverent public ceremony performed in Hāna in generations. Another related activity was the debut of the thatched-roof canoe hale at the Hāna Cultural Center located across the street from the bay. Hāna resident and cultural revivalist Francis Sinenci, the leading authority on traditional hale building, enlisted the service of several Hāna keiki for the intricate task of tying thousands of ti leaves (Francis now uses less-labor-intensive fan palm leaves) to the skeletal A-frame structure. As a reward, his crew got to fly over to Honolulu to sail back to Hāna on the Hōkūle'a.

Early Thursday morning I stopped by the Hāna Ranch Restaurant for breakfast and learned the disquieting news that the Hōkūle'a's visit to Hāna had been scrapped. Official word was that the cancellation was due to adverse weather conditions, but Francis felt there were other issues involved. In any case, it was out of his hands, and he was flying back to Hāna with his heartbroken crew. The Hōkūle'a's arrival had been announced in the press and printed on the posters; it was too late to reschedule another event. To some in the community the

Hōkūle'a's no-show was more than just an embarrassment—it was considered an insult.

It was fitting that the man with the coolest head in the clamor of disappointment and confusion was Sam Kalalau III, son of the regarded steersman on the Hōkūle'a's maiden voyage. While others were trying to figure things out, Sam III quietly rounded up a couple of Hāna Canoe Club members, went down to the bay, and got to work on plan B. The club at the time had only two dated racing canoes, too heavy to compete but sturdy and suitable to form an auwa'a 'a ho'apipi (two canoes hastily joined to form or use as a double-canoe). By early afternoon a dozen paddlers, myself included, convened at the bay and gave the double-canoe a trial run. Finding the craft maneuverable and seaworthy, we went ahead with the plan.

Before dawn the next morning, with Robert Malaiakini (draped in the ti-leaf cape of a high chief) seated on the deck that connected the canoes, we paddled out to a position behind the Hāna pier and awaited the call. As the sun broke over the bay, Sam Ka'ai blew his trumpet shell and beckoned us to come ashore. We paddled around the pier and saw a sizable crowd awaiting our arrival on the beach. Reaching the shore, we were greeted by Sam who led us to the reception line of family representatives assembled to welcome us to Hāna. Following the traditional greeting protocol of pressing noses to share ha, the breath of life, we took our places on the lauhala mats that had been carefully placed on the lawn behind the beach. After each of us had been served a cup of 'awa, we expressed gratitude to our hosts and appreciation to the more than a hundred visitors who had turned out to witness the event. Even though we were only a stand-in crew with a makeshift canoe, Hāna had overcome adversity with honor.

March 25, 1996 – Home

The surreal image of Comet Hyakutake arching over the Royal Palm reflected on the surface of the fishpond this evening was a sight not soon to be forgotten. Unlike Haley's Comet's anticipated but unspectacular return ten years ago, Comet H appeared without warning or fanfare, discovered by an amateur astronomer in Japan just a few months ago. A people's comet if there ever was one!

Could Comet H, like Haley's of old, be a harbinger of change and disruption? At this point I'm ready for anything.

Still awed by the ceremony on the beach last Friday. Felt like I was being initiated into the community. From disappointment came a rare privilege. Learning once again to trust in the greater scheme of things.

Turning Point

An automotive breakdown in the summer of 1995 set the stage for an event a year later that would turn my life around. My car at the time was a Geo Tracker (Suzuki Sidekick under the Chevrolet brand) that I had purchased from a rental car company in 1990. Though bigger than the discontinued Samurai, the Tracker was still a pleasure to drive across the Hāna Highway—that is, until the day the engine blew about two-thirds of the way into town. The car was still operational but the banging under the hood meant something was seriously wrong. Without means to call for a tow and figuring that the damage was already done, I managed to nurse the car to my mechanic's shop in Kahului.

Frank confirmed that the head gasket had blown and estimated the cost of repair would be around two thousand dollars. I was already at a loss as to how to pay a costly insurance premium that was about to come due—paying for the repair was out of the question. Frank, who did a bit of car trading on the side, offered to take the Tracker off my hands in return for a ten-year-old, well-worn Nissan and a thousand dollars cash. I drove the "Maui cruiser" home that afternoon and used the money to pay the insurance premium. Once again, a near calamity turned out to be a minor miracle.

In June 1996, Joann called to ask if she could reserve a room for her friend Patricia Steele. Trisha had recently lost her father, and Joann wanted to treat her and her visiting sister Anne to some healing time in Hāna. I owed Joann a favor and offered to accommodate the sisters for a couple of nights in the Royal Suite. After working out dates and details, Joann cautiously asked if I had gotten any response to the prospectus. I answered that three copies were sent to what I considered to be good prospects, but none had yet replied. She told me to keep the faith; finding a buyer was just a matter of time. A quantity that I was running short of, I reminded her.

I made my weekly supply run to Kahului on the day of Trisha's arrival. On the way home, I recognized her and another woman I assumed to be her sister photographing flowers at the rest stop about a half hour outside of Hāna. I stopped and was about to back up to say hello when the transmission locked up. I was stuck in drive and could only move forward. I called out to Trisha and told her what had happened and asked that they follow me home in case I needed a rescue. Limping down my driveway, I circled around the parking area and came to a stop pointing forward, figuring that I would at least be able to get back on the road without a tow.

Trisha parked next to me and, as we got out of our vehicles, introduced me to her sister Anne. While walking down the path to their suite, Anne asked what I was going to do about the car. I answered that I really didn't know. Surprisingly I felt more relieved than alarmed.

At Trisha's invitation I joined my guests for dinner at the hotel. Over the meal I learned that Trisha and Anne's father had founded and taken public a successful industrial machinery business. His real passion, however, was sailing, and the girls, particularly Trisha, knew the sea as a second home. As the conversation shifted to my story, I told them that my immediate priority was to find a buyer for my property. I explained that I felt my work on the land was complete and it was time for a new steward to take Hale Mālamalama to the next level. Additionally, I hinted that pressing financial obligations were forcing the issue, case in point replacing the crippled clunker at the bottom of my driveway.

Back at Hale Mālamalama, Anne asked if I had any material describing the property that they could take back to their room. I about tripped over a step leaping up the stairs to my cottage to pick up one of the two remaining copies of the prospectus that Joann and I had just prepared. As we said goodnight, Anne suggested we meet in the morning and continue our conversation.

Whereas I was under the impression that both sisters were interested in the property, it was Patricia alone who was considering the purchase. Over coffee and pastries on the deck overlooking the fishpond, she inquired if I was set on selling the property altogether or would I consider selling a half interest and stay on as managing partner? I thought about it for a minute and confided that I had grown weary living on the edge and thought it best to sell outright and start anew. Trisha said she would very much like to be involved with the property but not running the inn on her own. She asked what it would take for me to reconsider and carry on as manager. Without forethought, my response was that first and foremost I needed a decent place to live with indoor plumbing and a bed that was not in the cramped loft as well as a salary or commission that would provide a reasonable standard of living. I added, however, that I didn't think that would be possible without purchasing the adjacent property and expanding the business.

Rather than being put off, Trisha said everything sounded doable, yet she wished to become involved incrementally, saying she needed time before making a full commitment. I agreed with her reasoning and told her I would prepare a budget for the estimated costs of catching up with overdue maintenance and additions to my cottage.

Trisha accepted the budget and we sketched out a tentative accord that evening. To start things off she gave me a good-faith check that was enough to replace my car and send some financial relief to my family. The reality of what had just happened didn't sink in until the next morning when I set out to buy back my repaired and newly repainted Tracker from Frank in Kahului. Trisha and Ann followed me up the driveway and covered my back all the way across the long and winding road. When they finally turned off toward Makawao, I gave them a thumbs-up and continued into town. Only then did I dare consider that my fortunes were turning.

Home

In September I flew to Southern California to meet with Trisha and her accountant. Peter had already studied the business plan and was satisfied with the terms of the transaction. After the meeting, we had lunch at one of Trisha's favorite restaurants in Newport Beach, then spent the afternoon at her mother's house on Lido Isle. As a child growing up in Long Beach I had dreamt of one day living in Newport Harbor. Spending time with Trisha at her family home was a vicarious sampling of how life might have been had fate not led me north to Malibu.

Meanwhile, as we went ahead with plans to reroof the main house and renovate my cottage, I continued my involvement with the taro festival and started planning for the next harvest. This time the harvest was to be under the direction of Lyons Naone, a traditional healer and the founder of the Hāna men's warrior group Na Koa. Also known as a *lua,* the Na Koa consisted of forty Hawaiian men trained in traditional martial arts and versed in chants and exercises espousing might and intimidation.

One morning in mid-October Francis Sinenci approached me in Hasegawa's parking lot and asked if I was a member of the taro festival committee. When I answered affirmatively, he invited me to attend an 'awa ceremony with Nainoa Thompson at Coila's house later that morning. The nature of the event, I soon learned, was a ho'oponopono, a traditional reconciliation and forgiveness ceremony. Nainoa had heard the local grumblings about the Hōkūle'a not showing up for the previous taro festival and, even though he had nothing to do with the incident, had come to Hāna to clear the air. My job, I was told as I was led to my place on the mat in the meeting hale, was to speak on behalf of the taro festival and say how badly I was hurt when the Hōkūle'a failed to make an appearance.

When parties agree to participate in a ho'oponopono, they commit to finding a pono solution that is fair and just to all. It is further understood that when the session is over the underlying issues are cleared and negative feelings forgiven and forgotten. I counted eighteen participants representing Hāna, with Nainoa Thompson being the sole representative of the Hōkūle'a. Coila and I were the only non-Hawaiian participants. Among the Hawaiians were some of the most respected leaders in the community, including Sam Kalalau, Robert Malaiakini, and J. Kalani English. The ceremony began with each participant (with the exception of Coila, who sat in the outer circle) being served a cup of 'awa as his name was called. After everyone had been served, Lyons Naone, facilitator of the event, opened the session by announcing the reason for the ho'oponopono and recapping the events that led to calling for the ceremony. Everyone was told to speak only in turn and to clap once to be served another cup of 'awa anytime during the proceedings.

Nainoa was the first to speak, apologizing for the problems and embarrassment caused by the Hōkūle'a not sailing into Hāna as committed. He emphasized, however, that factors beyond the canoe were the problem and he asked that our anger be directed at him and not the canoe. One by one we voiced our frustrations and disappointments. All the while Thompson humbly listened to our grievances with his head bowed in submission. When my turn came I found it difficult to look a living legend in the eye and tell him how much he had hurt the taro festival and its reputation, yet I was there for a purpose and had to put personal feelings aside.

After everyone had spoken and vented their feelings, we moved on to finding a just remedy to the situation. Nainoa asked that we give the Hōkūle'a another chance and, speaking on behalf of the Polynesian Voyaging Society, offered to bring the canoe to the next taro festival at no cost to the committee. The remedy was deemed acceptable, but there was disagreement about the penalty to be imposed should the Hōkūleʻa again fail to show. When it was proposed that a twenty-year kapu be placed on the Hōkūleʻa, prohibiting it from visiting Hāna, some objected on the grounds that it would be shortchanging our keiki by taking away their rights to see the historic canoe. Others argued that we were in fact demonstrating to our keiki the importance of honor and respect. That argument won out, and the session ended with Nainoa promising to personally deliver the canoe to the next taro festival. Failure to do so for reasons other than bad weather would bring about a kapu that would prohibit the Hōkūleʻa from visiting Hāna for twenty years.

In early December I picked up the building permit to add a bedroom and bath to my cottage. I hired local carpenter and longtime friend Tony Wickey to do the carpentry. It was a relatively easy project, just an eleven-by-sixteen-foot box attached to the eastern side of my cottage. It was essentially finished by Valentine's Day, and I moved in the following weekend. The new quarters provided more room, running water, and a queen-size bed, but the location at the top of the stairway offered little relief from the prying eyes of guests as they trudged back and forth to the parking area. Still, it was a big improvement in my life, and I was grateful for the added space and functionality.

The addition of the Hōkūleʻa to the taro festival agenda was a bonus to what was becoming the most ambitious festival to date. The Na Koa, already scheduled to preside over the fish harvest, were also being readied to challenge the crew of the Hōkūleʻa as it sailed into shore Friday morning to open the festival. We decided to tie the two events together with the early-morning arrival ceremony leading to the afternoon fish harvest. The catch would then be prepared at the bay by local fishermen and later served to the Hōkūleʻa crew members and special guests. Friday's events also presented a perfect opportunity to bring Trisha into the picture. The harvest, in particular, would be a chance for her presence to be known as the new co-steward of the ʻaina.

The Hōkūleʻa arrived at Hāna Bay as scheduled at dawn on Friday morning. The Na Koa lined the beach and approached the canoe as it came to a stop a few yards offshore. The new arrivals were challenged to state who they were and the reason for the visit. After a short exchange became heated, Robert Malaiakini stepped forward and threw a spear in the direction of Francis Sinenci, who was leading the Hāna contingent on board the Hōkūleʻa. Francis quickly jumped aside and caught the spear in midflight and handed it to Nainoa Thompson for dispensation. Nainoa disembarked the canoe, waded to shore, and planted the spear deep in the sand, symbolizing that the Hōkūleʻa had come in peace. The rest of the crew followed Nainoa to the reception line and proceeded with the arrival ceremony that we had been stand-ins for the year before. The Na Koa brought a dimension to the ceremony that would have been missing had the Hōkūleʻa arrived as originally scheduled. Maybe that was the mysterious reason for the no-show. Hāna just wasn't quite ready.

The fish harvest took place midafternoon. A crowd much larger than that for the previous harvest had been gathering and staking out positions for some time before Lyons led his warriors onto the grounds and circled the pond. I made a brief announcement thanking everyone for attending and spoke about the recent history of the pond. I introduced Trisha and welcomed her into the ʻohāna, then turned the proceedings over to Naone. After his men went through a *haka* (war chant), I tossed pellets into the water to bring up the fish. Robert, who had thrown the perfect spear in the morning, cast a perfect net, catching exactly two large awa for offering and missing the decorative koi that were also swirling on the surface. Once the ti-wrapped awa were offered in prayer, Lyons gave the signal, and a half dozen of the young warriors jumped into the pond to set the net while the men on the bank went through another haka. Finally, everyone joined in to chase the fish into the net and drag the catch ashore. Handing the haul over to the waiting fishermen, Lyons reconvened his lua and led the men off the property to thunderous applause from the spectators.

Assisting Robert Malaiakini retrieve net with bountiful catch. Hāna, April 1997. (Photo by Anne McLennan)

Preparing first two fish for offering to Kū'ula and Hina. Hāna, April 1997. (Photo by Anne McLennan)

A month later I met Trisha in Wailuku to conclude the nine-month-long partnership transaction. We went to the state tax department and closed out my sole proprietor account and opened a new account for the partnership. After paying off my delinquencies with the county, we opened a new partnership account at the Bank of Hawai'i in Kahului, where we signed the closing documents. Most of my remaining debts were retired when escrow closed a couple of days later.

Trisha came out to Hāna in late May to talk over some business matters and to attend a reception in her honor. We had opened discussions with the owner of the adjacent property and wanted to work out the terms of a formal offer before I left for a two-week holiday in the South Pacific (at Trisha's request). We also discussed Laura, a naturopathic doctor whom we had just hired to head up our housekeeping. Laura was new to town and Trisha suggested we lease the cottage next door and offer it to her as employee housing and as a place to set up her practice. We decided to tie the lease to a purchase option that we could exercise anytime within the year. That settled, we started preparing for the party that evening.

With Patricia Steele after fish harvest. Hāna, April 1997.

The reception was warm and ripe with aloha. Trisha said she felt like a debutante at a ball. At the end of the evening after the last of the well-wishers had left, I took Trisha out to the lava wall that fronted the entrance to the house. There in a shrine-like, flat-bottomed lava tube stood the bronze statue of Shiva that I had brought with me from Malibu. I lit the two candles that flanked Lord Shiva and told Trisha how he represented the ever-changing cycle of creation and destruction. I recounted watching the deity dance on the New Year's Eve before moving to Hāna, and how three weeks later I was on an airplane heading to the Philippines to make a deal for the house. I suggested that we humbly ask the mighty deity to dance again and bring forth a new cycle of growth and prosperity. I felt we were about to create something extraordinary.

Around Thanksgiving I got a call from Carl telling me that he had just listed the neighboring beach cottage and, knowing that Trisha and I were planning to expand our operations, wanted to give us the first chance to look at it. I knew the property well; in fact, I had often fantasized about the tiny cottage being a dream beach house. It was located on the other side of the parcel that we were already considering and had a small fourteen-foot adjacency with Hale Mālamalama. Best of all, the oceanfront 'aina was listed for less than what we were preparing to pay on the lease option. I told Carl that we were definitely interested and that I'd get back to him after discussing it with Trisha, who was on the Mainland. A week later he called back to say that another offer was coming in and if we wanted the property we would have to move quickly. He suggested that I come by his office to write up an offer that afternoon. When I hesitated, saying that I first needed to reach Trisha to get a deposit, Carl pointed out that all we needed was a thousand-dollar check to attach to the offer while stressing again that time was of the essence. Realizing that I had more than enough funds in my account to cover the deposit, I told Carl to start writing up the offer and that I'd be by with a personal check in a few minutes. In that epiphanic moment I knew the struggle was over. I had made it home.

Hale Mālamalama as featured in *Sunset Magazine*, November 2001. (Photo by Douglass Merriam)

The Road to Eden Revisited

At a time of unprecedented threats to the survival of our species, our fate may well depend on relearning what we have forgotten. Adherence to an economic reality driven primarily by growth and profit has exploited the natural world and threatens that which sustains us. The problem is not economics alone; without a shift in consciousness that recognizes the interconnection between the health of humankind and the well-being of the planet, we remain alienated from the roots of our being.

Our early residency on this planet entailed adapting to indigenous environments and utilizing local resources for shelter and food. In time, cities arose, and trade developed, leading to the commodification of resources. As populations grew and as evolving technology enabled the extraction and distribution of resources on a planetary scale, our relationship to the natural world became estranged. Add to this the evolution of a global economic system based on supply and demand, and sustainability is often at odds with economic growth. In short, we have become trapped in an economy of our own creation that is out of sync with the well-being of the planet.

What drew me to Hāna was that it still holds an underlying presence of a culture that lived in balance with the mysteries of life. The Hawaiian people, prior to Western contact, knew everything in closeness to one another. The separation between humankind, the gods, and nature was one of distinction, not distance. And though the ancient worldview has been superseded with one of Western origin, Hāna still carries the essence of a way of life at one with the environment.

By contrast the culture from which I was born is one of separation and distance from life's mysteries. It is a cosmology based on the preeminence of humans and consolidates all that is outside scientific knowledge into a singular God. Estranged from our God by a disobedient act of free will at the time of our genesis, our primordial ancestors were expelled from the garden and given both dominion over all things of the earth and scriptural law for guidance, resulting in a worldview structured on dominance and hierarchical authority.

We have created a civilization of great magnitude, and our history is a testament to the scope and complexity of our culture's self-expression. Yet, disconnection from our bond with the natural world has led to an environmental crisis that is impacting the planetary ecosystem's ability to sustain human existence as we know it.

I must, however, also make this admission: Although Hawaiian culture has been my spiritual beacon, it too seems incomplete in the contemporary world. A more inclusive worldview is needed, where indigenous values of stewardship and preservation of the planet and its resources govern a technologically driven future. For this to come about, essential spiritual truths known to aboriginal cultures must be understood as universal. Further, the sovereign rights of aboriginal cultures must be recognized and accepted as equal, in every sense of the word, to ours. The problems we face are too complex for singular-perspective solutions, and only through productive engagement can we forge a sustainable future.

I have seen the best of both worlds and know that they are not mutually exclusive; rather, they are equally essential. For me, it is not a choice of one or the other, it is integration of the best of both.

Only now, with the ability to interplay thoughts and ideas among billions of minds, do we have the capacity to envision a future unconstrained by the past. A future imagined rather than projected, a history born anew, not repeated. By engaging ancient wisdom with progressive technology, we have the means to bring about a new Eden where we are at peace with the natural world and dare to dream about reaching the stars. It may seem an impossible dream, but I believe it to be our destiny.

John S. Romain
New Orleans, December 2018

(Photo by Jack Fisher)

Acknowledgments

The joy of writing a book such as this is the opportunity to reconnect with so many friends and associates accumulated over the years. In addition to comments from those included in the story, mahalo to Alexia Loehde, Robin Johnson, Carla Crow, Hillary Bedell and Sandra Napua for reading and critiquing earlier drafts. A special cheer to Lori, of Lori's Hair Shack, for listening to the story unfold year by year while patiently grooming my graying hair.

Mahalo to Sam Kaʻai for insights about Hawaiian history and storytelling, Arnie Kotler and Julia Steele for guidance and encouragement from the beginning, Dr. Ronald Williams Jr. for Hawaiian language editing, Karen Seriguchi for fine-tuning the final manuscript, Paula Carver for web design and technical support and Tim Gable, writing coach and editor, without whose help this book couldn't have been written.

And to Margot Ott, cover illustrator and art director, a special mahalo for once again being there as my right hand in making this book happen.

About the Author

(Photo by Suzie)

John Romain resides on the island of Maui with his dog, Snoop.

www.ingramcontent.com/pod-product-compliance
Lightning Source LLC
Chambersburg PA
CBHW071147070526
44584CB00019B/2688